Also by Jack Nelson

THE CENSORS AND THE SCHOOLS
(with Gene Roberts, Jr.)

THE ORANGEBURG MASSACRE
(with Jack Bass)

THE FBI AND THE BERRIGANS
(with Ronald J. Ostrow)

CAPTIVE VOICES: HIGH SCHOOL
JOURNALISM IN AMERICA

TERROR
in the
NIGHT

JACK NELSON

The

Klan's

Campaign

Against

the Jews

SIMON & SCHUSTER
NEW YORK LONDON TORONTO
SYDNEY TOKYO SINGAPORE

SIMON & SCHUSTER
SIMON & SCHUSTER BUILDING
ROCKEFELLER CENTER
1230 AVENUE OF THE AMERICAS
NEW YORK, NEW YORK 10020

DESIGNED BY SONGHEE KIM
MANUFACTURED IN THE UNITED STATES OF AMERICA

10 9 8 7 6 5 4 3 2 1

LIBRARY OF CONGRESS CATALOGING-IN-PUBLICATION DATA

NELSON, JACK, DATE.

TERROR IN THE NIGHT: THE KLAN'S CAMPAIGN AGAINST THE JEWS / JACK
NELSON.
P. CM.
INCLUDES BIBLIOGRAPHICAL REFERENCES AND INDEX.
1. ANTISEMITISM—MISSISSIPPI—MERIDIAN. 2. ANTISEMITISM—MISSISSIPPI—
JACKSON. 3. JEWS—MISSISSIPPI—MERIDIAN—HISTORY—20TH CENTURY. 4. JEWS—
MISSISSIPPI—JACKSON—HISTORY—20TH CENTURY. 5. KU KLUX KLAN (1915–   )
6. MISSISSIPPI—ETHNIC RELATIONS. I. TITLE.
DS146.U6N45 1993
305.892'4076251—DC20

92–29539
CIP

ISBN: 0-671-69223-2

TO MY WIFE,
BARBARA MATUSOW

CONTENTS

In Germany they came first for the Communists, and I didn't speak up because I wasn't a Communist. Then they came for the Jews, and I didn't speak up because I wasn't a Jew. Then they came for the trade unionists, and I didn't speak up because I wasn't a trade unionist. Then they came for the Catholics, and I didn't speak up because I was a Protesant. Then they came for me, and by that time no one was left to speak up.

-Martin Niemoeller
1892-1984

PROLOGUE

It happened more than twenty years ago. "Okay, Jack, get your pencil out," the booming voice commanded. "We've got a big one this time, a Goddamned big one. There's gonna be some wailing and gnashing of teeth."

It was two o'clock on Sunday morning, June 30, 1968. There was no mistaking the voice on the phone: Roy Gunn was the police chief of Meridian, Mississippi, a pivotal figure in the most savage outbreak of racial and religious terrorism in modern U.S. history.

As Atlanta bureau chief of the *Los Angeles Times* and one of the few reporters in the country assigned to cover civil rights in the South full-time, I went to Mississippi often. I had grown up in the state—my family moved to Biloxi when I was twelve—but the Mississippi I covered did not match my innocent memories. It had become a dark and fearful place, violently obsessed with race, a virtual police state. Civil rights advocates were hounded throughout the South, but only in Mississippi did the state government maintain a network of surveillance, coercion and control to preserve the status quo. Working together, the tax-supported Mississippi Sovereignty Commission and the private White Citizens Councils were able to crush even the most modest forms of dissent.

By the spring of 1964, however, the ruthless system was beginning to break down. Washington's mounting pressure on behalf of blacks and the hundreds of young civil rights volunteers who poured into Mississippi from the North pushed the tension level toward near-hysteria, and the White Knights of the Ku Klux Klan, headed by a fanatic named Sam Bowers, unleashed a campaign of terror. "The events which will occur in Mississippi this summer may well determine the fate of Christianity for centuries to come," Bowers declared.

The killing spree started that May when a twenty-year-old black civil rights activist named Charles Eddie Moore and a nineteen-year-old companion, Henry Hezekiah Dee, both of Meadville, Mississippi, disappeared. On July 12, a man fishing in the Mississippi River near Tallulah, Louisiana, found the lower half of a human body, its legs bound with rope. The next day another body, this one decapitated, was pulled from the river. They were the bodies of Moore and Dee. Eventually, two members of the White Knights—James Ford Seale and Charles Marcus Edwards—were arrested for the killings. Edwards gave the FBI a signed confession saying he and Seale had tied Moore and Dee to trees, beaten them into unconsciousness, then tied heavy weights to their bodies and dropped them into the river on the Louisiana side. The FBI gave the confession and other evidence to state prosecutors, but Seale and Edwards were never indicted or brought to trial.

Meanwhile, three civil rights workers—Michael Schwerner, James Chaney, and Andrew Goodman—vanished near Philadelphia, Mississippi. Chaney was a black teenager from Meridian, and Schwerner and Goodman were white New Yorkers; their disappearance created a national furor. After a massive investigation, the FBI discovered the three had been shot to death and their bodies buried beneath an earthen dam.

In addition to those killings, the Klan beat and terrorized scores of blacks and others. It bombed or set the torch to forty-four black churches during the summer of 1964 alone. The violence, almost all directed at blacks, continued unabated and virtually unpunished in Mississippi for three more years. So many black churches were bombed or burned in rural areas that the FBI had a hard time keeping track of them. Some law enforcement agencies were riddled with Klansmen and Klan sympathizers. Witnesses, when they existed, kept silent.

The White Knights committed at least three more murders during 1966 and 1967: Vernon Dahmer, an NAACP leader in Hattiesburg, was killed when the Klan firebombed his home in January 1966. In July, Ben Chester White, a black farmer and Korean War veteran, was picked at random and shot to death by a White Knights cell known as the Cottonmouth Moccasin Gang.

And Wharlest Jackson, treasurer of the Natchez NAACP, was killed seven months later by a bomb planted in his truck.

But Chief Gunn's telephone call had nothing to do with the crimes against blacks. He was calling about what happened when the White Knights turned on the Jews.

I lost no time getting to Mississippi, where I wrote a series of page-one stories. But my own involvement in the Meridian case did not begin to deepen until many months later. Thus, Book One is written in the third person. In Book Two I appear as a character when I begin to be drawn into the story in ways I could not have foreseen.

Long after I wrote these stories, the events in Meridian continued to gnaw at me. I had saved all my original notes, files, and tape-recorded interviews. Eventually, I decided only a book would do the story justice, and over the course of several years I amassed four large cartons of information about the case. Using the Freedom of Information Act, I gained access to FBI files and additional official records. Recently I went back to Jackson and Meridian, where I conducted extensive interviews with scores of witnesses, including policemen, former FBI agents, leaders of Mississippi's Jewish community and Klansmen. In an old safe at the Meridian Police Department I found more records.

Most of the participants are still living and all of them, including me, found their lives, and in some cases their beliefs, changed by what happened when the Klan came for the Jews.

BOOK ONE

1

It was evening, June 29, 1968. The sun was beginning to set, but the heat lingered under the trees and in the softened tar along the edges of the road. A dark green Buick Electra headed slowly along the south shore of the Ross Barnett Reservoir outside Jackson, Mississippi. Kathy Ainsworth sat quietly beside the driver. She was twenty-six years old, five feet four and buxom, with a pretty oval face and brown eyes that matched her thick brunet hair. If any of her friends had seen her, especially any of the teachers she worked with at the Lorena Duling Elementary School or the parents of her fifth-grade pupils there, they might have been surprised at the way she was dressed. Tight-fitting, high-cut shorts and a low-cut jersey top were unusual attire for a quiet young schoolteacher going out for dinner on a Saturday night. But then, as her friends were soon to learn, there had been a good deal about Kathryn Madlyn Ainsworth they did not know.

The driver, Thomas Albert Tarrants III, was twenty-one years old, but he had an air of confidence that set him apart. He was tall and trim—about six feet three and 170 pounds—with brown eyes and black hair combed straight back. Women were attracted to him. Kathy had met Tarrants in Mobile, Alabama, in 1966 when she was Kathy Capomacchia. She later married Ralph Ainsworth, a health club operator, but she was drawn to Tarrants because of the passionate views they shared, and perhaps because of his daring: Tarrants did what others only talked about. She had eventually become his partner in terrorism and their relationship had evolved into romance.

Tarrants pulled the Buick onto a dirt track that branched off from the shore road. Another car was waiting in the quiet evening and a muscular young man with close-cropped brown hair was standing beside it. Tarrants stopped beside the second car and nodded to the young man, Danny Joe Hawkins. Quickly, Hawkins put a brown cardboard Clorox carton into the trunk of the Buick and handed Tarrants a small, carefully wrapped package, which he gently placed on the front seat.

"Are you sure you don't want me to go along?" Hawkins asked. "You might need an extra gun."

"No," Tarrants replied. "It's an easy operation."

Tarrants swung the Buick back on the main road and drove at a leisurely pace toward a restaurant called the Captain's Table, which stood on the crest of a hill above a small inlet. At the restaurant, he and Kathy Ainsworth chose a table by a large window overlooking the water. The twenty-seven-mile-long reservoir, lying just north of the capital, was named for a man they both admired. As governor, Ross Barnett had made national headlines in 1962 by defying a federal court order to desegregate the University of Mississippi. His action helped precipitate a riot that left two people dead, more than one hundred U.S. marshals injured, and the university campus in shambles. Barnett had been a hero to Tarrants and Kathy ever since.

They ordered steak and seafood. Outside, the sun set, turning the reservoir into a dazzling sheet of silver and red. Tarrants and Kathy, absorbed in their plan, paid little attention. He reassured her that things would go smoothly—as smoothly as the last time they had worked together.

Their mission tonight would be in Meridian, a little more than eighty miles from Jackson. In the parlance of their master, Samuel Holloway Bowers, Jr., organizer and imperial wizard of the White Knights of the Ku Klux Klan, the mission was a "Number Four"— a murder.

In Meridian, Detective Luke Scarbrough was preparing to go back to work. "Vic, tonight's the night," he said to his wife, Lyda Victoria. He had made the same remark when his older brother Calvin had stopped by his house on the way home from an army reserve meeting. He had spoken the words without emotion. Vic and Calvin knew he was involved in undercover work that concerned a rash of church burnings and the bombing of the Meridian synagogue. They suspected something big was about to happen, but neither asked what he had meant. Vic thought it was better if she did not know, and Calvin knew his brother would clam up if he did ask.

Scarbrough was a devout Methodist who valued his privacy and was secretive about his police work. He liked nothing better than to work his thirty-acre patch of land outside town, where he kept a cow and raised a good portion of the food that sustained his family. But he also thrived on the long hours he worked as a detective. His fellow officers admired him for his dedication and his courage. All had heard the Korean War story of how he and other marines, although badly frostbitten, had fought their way out of the Chosin Reservoir after being cut off by North Korean troops. And they knew of harrowing experiences he had endured as a detective. But not many of them knew about tonight's assignment.

Meyer Davidson was being stubborn. His wife, Frances, was packing an overnight case as Meridian police officers and FBI agents in the living room and kitchen checked and rechecked their plans, but he would not budge. Davidson was hard to reason with once he had made up his mind. He and his brother Sammie had taken their father's junk business and built it into the Southern Pipe Company, one of the largest distributors of plumbing supplies in the South. Meyer was president of the company and the two brothers were among Meridian's most prominent citizens.

In a city that had risen to wealth and prominence with the coming of the railroads in the nineteenth century and faded when rail transportation went into eclipse, the brothers stood out for their entrepreneurial energy. All over town there were businesses that had been quietly backed with Davidson seed money. Those they had helped had repaid them for their faith and made them rich. In spite of that, Meyer clung to his old ways. Among other things, he had an unbending habit of personally paying the Southern Pipe Company's bills at the beginning of every month in order to get the discount for prompt payment. Seated at his desk in his pine-paneled den, a brown cardboard box of statements before him, he brushed aside his wife's entreaties and the urgent warnings of the police.

Finally, the police dispatched a car for Bill Ready. Ready and Davidson "were as close as two men could be without being homosexuals," as the hulking Irish lawyer once put it. He understood Davidson, a short, pudgy figure with a brusque manner. And he understood the rage Davidson had aroused among racial extremists. The previous September, when "the Jewish bombings" had begun with the synagogue in Jackson, Davidson had lashed out at the "cowards who go out at night and bomb a house of worship." Though it was not his temple, he saw the bombing as an assault on all Jews. And he was right—the White Knights, convinced that Jews were the driving force behind the civil rights movement, had shifted their attacks from blacks to Jews. It was widely known that Davidson had helped raise money to fight the White Knights.

Two nights earlier, the police had had a tip that Davidson's house would be attacked and Ready had insisted that Davidson and his wife evacuate. Davidson had reluctantly cooperated, but was furious when it turned out to be a false alarm.

This time Ready escorted Frances out of the large brick ranch house to a car waiting in the broad driveway. Then he waited until Davidson's attention was diverted, scooped up the box of bills, hustled it out to the car and told his friend, "You've got to go to the Holiday Inn. The police say they're on their way with a bomb this time. You've got to get out of here."

Davidson resisted. "They didn't come last time and you don't know what the hell you're doing. I've got work to do."

Ready countered that he had made a reservation at the Holiday Inn—not merely for a room but for a suite with a desk; Davidson could finish paying the monthly bills there.

Davidson finally agreed to go, but only if he could take his favorite chair. Ready loaded the chair into the car.

A short time later, four men with rifles, pistols and shotguns, all in black, fanned out behind the trees and bushes on an embankment across the street from the Davidsons' darkened house. Several more police cars and three cars carrying FBI agents and a team of demolition experts arrived. More heavily armed men took up posts. FBI agents Frank Watts and Jack Rucker stationed themselves in a house on top of the embankment that had been evacuated at the FBI's request.

Watts and Rucker, along with Detective Scarbrough, were key players in the police operation. Together they had persuaded the man most responsible for the operation—Chief Roy Gunn—to stay home. They respected Gunn as a tough, dedicated police officer, but considered him too emotional to have a direct hand in the night's action.

Gunn had wanted to be there. Klansmen had repeatedly threatened him and his family and he had vowed to "send them straight to hell where they belong." But the FBI knew of his uncontrollable temper and how it had flared one night a few weeks earlier after police arrested a Klansman apparently intent on firing a shotgun into Gunn's house. Clad in pajamas and a bathrobe, the chief had rushed to the police station and held a cocked pistol to the Klansman's head, declaring, "I'm gonna shoot you if you say you didn't do it and I'm gonna shoot you if you say you did do it." An FBI agent had stepped in and ordered, "Get him out of here before somebody gets killed," and the Klansman had been led away.

The big Buick, back on the highway again, cruised toward Meridian. Tarrants checked the box of dynamite several times—more out of habit than concern. He didn't really believe anything could go wrong. He was an expert in explosives, a marksman capable of hitting a plastic milk jug at one hundred yards with a machine gun and a man used to operating in secret, and alone. Ordinary Klansmen might need the high they got from blustering for each other at Klan rallies, but not Tarrants. He never wore a sheet, never went to a Klan rally. Mixing with the rank and file, he knew, could bring him into contact wth FBI infiltrators and informants.

He began working with Kathy Ainsworth because he knew her to be as well trained and dedicated as he was.

At her desk in the basement of the Meridian City Hall, Marie Knowles, the secretary of the detective bureau, was trying to follow the scraps of conversation on the police radio.

City Hall was a dignified marble building with a row of white columns in front, but police headquarters, located in the basement, was a series of windowless, poorly lighted, smoky rooms with low ceilings. In the bullpen, where Knowles and the detectives had their desks, the floor was covered with cigarette burns. Beyond the bullpen were two small interrogation rooms, an identification room and, off to the side, a vault. In the vault were hundreds of pages of reports and other records kept by Knowles, including reports on "Joyner's guerrillas" and "the blackshirts," which she shielded from officers whom Gunn did not trust. Gunn had set up two teams to harass the Klan, a small one under Sergeant Lester (Gigolo) Joyner and a larger one dressed in black shirts and trousers for its night operations.

Knowles knew just about everything there was to know about the Meridian Police Department. A pretty, vivacious twenty-seven-year-old brunette, she was better educated and more articulate than the officers she worked with. She was the only woman in the detective bureau and was a confidante of some. She sat at a desk between Charlie Powell, a heavy drinker who was the assistant chief in charge of the bureau, and Detective L. A. (Hooky) Willoughby, a fatherly man who shielded her from the detectives' raunchiest behavior.

She had come gradually to thrive on the excitement of police work, but the strain had risen dramatically since the business with the White Knights began. Department members hounded her constantly about the records of the blackshirts. Some hoped to pass on information to the Klan. Others resented the blackshirts' overtime pay and suspected that their real purpose was to spy for Gunn and to catch their colleagues in improper activities.

Tonight, glued to the police radio, Mrs. Knowles resented the interruption when a patrol officer brought in a man who had just killed another man with a wooden plank. There was nobody else available, so she had to inform the prisoner of his right to remain silent and to have a lawyer present. Then she took his statement confessing to the killing.

The calls from Alma Powell, the wife of Assistant Chief Charlie Powell, one of the officers assigned to the Davidson stakeout, were even more distracting. Alma was worried. "I know a lot more than you think I do about what's happening down there," she kept saying. "I want to know if my husband is safe."

Marie Knowles did not know the answer to Alma's question, but one thing she did know for certain: the nightriders were not supposed to leave alive.

2

One year before Tarrants' Meridian mission, in the summer of 1967, he had knocked at the door of the Sambo Amusement Company in Laurel, Mississippi, looking for Sam Bowers. The dirty, dilapidated building, badly in need of a coat of paint, was located across the road from the ugly sprawl of the Masonite Corporation plant. Little more than an oversize shotgun house, it served as home to Bowers, as an office for his coin-machine business, and as headquarters for the White Knights of the Ku Klux Klan.

Thomas Albert Tarrants III introduced himself. He had come to enlist in the imperial wizard's crusade. Bowers listened, but he was not the kind of man who welcomed anyone into his confidence quickly.

Tarrants explained that he was applying for a job at Masonite, a multimillion-dollar manufacturer of fiberboard and other building products. The Masonite plant's regular work force was on strike and the company was recruiting new workers—strikebreakers. But the real attraction of Laurel was the opportunity for working with Bowers in the White Knights. Tarrants considered the forty-three-year-old imperial wizard a highly intelligent strategic thinker. He was also drawn to Bowers because his Klan was known for its willingness to act, not just talk. Tarrants compared himself to Arab terrorists, so committed to their cause that they believed their chosen ends justified any means.

Suspicious as Bowers was, Tarrants began to strike a responsive chord. The young man was talking passionately about the Jews and their role as instigators of the civil rights agitation that had thrown Mississippi into turmoil. The same idea had come to dominate Bowers' own thinking that summer: it was not the blacks who threatened all he held dear but the Jews who were manipulating them.

And Tarrants had appeared at a time when Bowers was besieged and the White Knights were reeling. The previous February, Bowers and seventeen of his followers had been indicted on federal charges springing from the murders of the three civil rights workers in Philadelphia. In addition, he and thirteen other White Knights had been indicted on state and federal charges in the death of Vernon Dahmer, the Hattiesburg NAACP leader. And it had become clear that the FBI, under pressure to stop the violence, was using a network of informants that threatened to paralyze the Klan.

A less committed person might be reconsidering his course. Not Bowers. He was settling on new targets and groping for new means of attack. The tall, slim young man standing in front of him might be the instrument he was looking for—unless, of course, he had been sent by the FBI.

Tarrants could see Bowers was suspicious; he expected nothing less. But Tarrants had a way of winning people over, and he set out on a shrewd campaign to gain the Klan leader's confidence.

Tarrants had grown up in a middle-class neighborhood in Mobile, Alabama; his father was a used-car salesman who had a reputation as a hot-tempered segregationist. In his teens, the younger Tarrants became fascinated with guns and right-wing politics. At Murphy High School, he ranted about the threat of a Communist invasion of the United States.

In 1963, when Murphy High desegregated under federal court order, hundreds of the school's two thousand students, egged on by Tarrants, engaged in a violent demonstration. They ran wild, raced around police lines, tore down fences and wrecked the school grounds. While his father watched, Tarrants led the students in shouting "Two, four, six, eight! Hell no, we won't integrate!" He was one of fifty-four students arrested and charged with disorderly conduct.

In 1964, in his junior year, Tarrants dropped out to devote full time to working with right-wing groups that preached hatred of blacks and Jews. He came under the influence of Robert M. Smith, Mobile director of J. B. Stoner's National States Rights Party, and John Crommelin, a retired navy admiral with a long record as a virulent anti-Semite. Tarrants visited Smith frequently in his Mobile office and Crommelin at his large estate not far from Montgomery for long sessions on "the Communist/Jewish threat."

He began making threatening calls to civil rights leaders and to two rabbis and the head of the Anti-Defamation League in Mobile. With several other young right-wing radicals, he formed the Christian Military Defense League, a group that hatched bizarre schemes that Tarrants later said ranged from "distributing the dismembered body of a key black leader around the black community to setting out booby traps in the black communities of Mobile." None of the schemes was known to have been carried out, but beginning in August of 1964, Tarrants' fascination with guns and terrorism got him into a series of scrapes with the law.

Police in Prichard, Alabama, a small town north of Mobile, seized an automatic shotgun from him after he got into a fight with a black service-station operator, but no charges were pressed. The next time he was stopped by police, he and Robert Smith were driving through a black neighborhood in Mobile. Police seized a .38-caliber revolver and a sawed-off shotgun and charged Tarrants with possessing an illegal weapon.

He pleaded guilty to the weapons charge in federal court in Mobile and Judge Daniel Thomas let him off with a probated sentence. But the judge warned him about the "bad company" he had been keeping and declared, "If I ever hear of you with a gun again—even a shotgun going dove hunting—I will revoke your probation."

Tarrants saw himself as something far different from an ordinary Klansman; he had a theoretical framework—a belief in an all-embracing international Communist-Jewish conspiracy. In his own eyes at least, he had come to Laurel a professional radical, a terrorist prepared, even eager, to make personal sacrifices for his cause.

By the beginning of August 1967, Tarrants had a job as a maintenance worker at the Masonite plant and a nondescript place to live not far from Bowers. Tarrants stayed away from Bowers' house to avoid being linked with the Klan leader, but the two would meet by prearrangement in out-of-the-way places to talk.

Then, in September, Tarrants did something that banished any remaining doubts Bowers might have had. He suggested it would be a good idea for Bowers to have an alibi for himself on a certain evening a little later in the month, when Tarrants planned a major strike against the Jews in Jackson.

Afterward, Tarrants knew, Bowers would be confident that he was not an FBI plant.

Bowers, like Tarrants, liked to think of himself as an intellectual. A slim figure with high cheekbones, heavily lidded hazel eyes and long sandy hair combed to the sides, Bowers was thought odd even by his friends. He related to people almost solely on the basis of ideology. He was a bachelor who never had much use for women.

Before joining the Klan, Bowers had had only one run-in with the law, an arrest in 1955 for illegal possession of liquor. He pleaded guilty and was fined one hundred dollars. It was an odd charge for Bowers, who was never known to smoke or drink. "He always said he didn't want to be a slave to any habit," his mother said.

Instead, he became a slave to an idea—the idea of an international Communist conspiracy, masterminded by the Jews. He believed the Kremlin was merely a front for a cabal of Jews attempting to bring down Christians throughout the world. In the United States, their chosen vehicle was the civil rights movement. Using Communists as their agents, the Jews sought to destroy white Christian society by mongrelization.

In 1955, the year he was arrested for illegal possession of liquor, Bowers joined the Original Knights of the Ku Klux Klan of Louisiana after the group spread across the Mississippi River and established a klavern in Natchez. By the early 1960s, with the civil rights movement growing stronger and more insistent, Bowers concluded that the Original Knights were too passive. On February 15, 1964, at a meeting in Brookhaven, Mississippi, he convinced about two hundred members of the Original Knights to defect and join a highly secret Klan he was forming that would not hesitate to use "physical force."

An imperial wizard of the new Klan—the White Knights— Bowers adopted a code of strict secrecy and set out as its goal the preservation of white supremacy "regardless of the cost and with the use of force and violence when considered necessary."

A persuasive talker with an exceptional organizational ability, Bowers was an instant hit with the kind of people who made up

the rank and file of Klan organizations everywhere in the south—
school dropouts, unskilled and semiskilled laborers and other
lower-income whites who feared blacks and the civil rights movement for economic as well as social reasons. Bowers also recruited
scores of individuals from his preferred target groups—law enforcement officers, jackleg preachers, ragtag attorneys and other
professionals and semiprofessionals who enjoyed a measure of
respect in their communities. "He could get these people to do
damn near anything," said a state investigator who kept tabs on
him.

As he bent them to his purposes, Bowers considered himself
superior to his followers in almost every way. "The typical Mississippi redneck," he said, "doesn't have sense enough to know
what he is doing. I have to use him for my own cause and direct
his every action to fit my plan."

Bowers established his headquarters in Laurel, a small city of
twenty-seven thousand. In the mid-1960s, many of Laurel's
whites—who constituted about 65 percent of the population—
became enraged when Masonite, the town's largest employer,
began trying to implement the equal employment opportunity
rules required of government contractors. Laurel was fertile
ground for Bowers' message.

He sought to intimidate all who did not support him, and his
passion for secrecy added to the White Knights' frightening aura.
He scared the citizens of Laurel. They were leery of talking about
him or the Klan because, as a local businessman said, "We never
know who we might be talking to. You don't know who all the
members are."

The Laurel *Leader-Call* considered the Klan too dangerous to
write about. Even that was not good enough for Bowers; in 1964
the *Leader-Call* was bombed. Later, he sent word to the editor
that the bombing was "not for anything you did to us, but because
you didn't do anything for us."

By the end of 1965 the FBI estimated that the White Knights
had grown to a membership of between five thousand and six
thousand. True to Bowers' promise, it preferred covert action,
shunning the parades, rituals and other public displays that many
Klans promoted. His Klan, as Bowers wrote in one of his internal
memoranda, was "a nocturnal organization that works best at

night. We must remember that the Communists who are directing the agitators want us to engage in pitched battles in the streets so that they can declare martial law."

"As Christians," he wrote in an executive order, "we are disposed to kindness, generosity, affection and humility in our dealings with others. As militants we are disposed to use physical force against our enemies. How can we reconcile these two apparently contradictory philosophies? The answer, of course, is to purge malice, bitterness and vengeance from our hearts."

Only the imperial wizard could order a Number Four—a murder—but that, too, could be done in the name of Christianity: "If it is necessary to eliminate someone, it should be done with no malice, in complete silence and in the manner of a Christian act."

In 1964, with Freedom Summer looming, Bowers launched his organization on the equivalent of a holy war. In a chilling executive order, he called for "counterattacks against selected individuals."

Within a matter of months, Charles Eddie Moore, Henry Hezekiah Dee, Michael Schwerner, James Chaney and Andrew Goodman were dead. Then a year and a half later, the White Knights turned to Vernon Dahmer, who had drawn Bowers' rage by working successfully to help blacks register to vote.

On January 10, 1966, shortly after midnight, two carloads of Klansmen drove from Laurel to the Kelly Settlement, raked the front of Dahmer's brick-and-frame house and his nearby grocery store with shotgun fire and set the buildings ablaze with Molotov cocktails. Dahmer's wife and three of his seven children—four sons were away in the armed forces—were at home. Dahmer helped them escape through the rear of the house and remained behind to fend off the attackers, firing a shotgun through the wall of flames that engulfed the front of the house. Dahmer was terribly burned, his lungs seared by smoke and flames. He died in the Hattiesburg hospital several hours later.

It was Bowers who had ordered that Dahmer's house be burned and that he be killed "if any way possible," according to testimony by T. Webber Rogers, who quit the White Knights after the attack on Dahmer. Rogers testified that when the Klansmen seemed slow to carry out Bowers' orders, the imperial wizard would "pound on the table and say he was tired of fooling around, something has got to be done about that damn nigger down south."

If Bowers had silenced another voice in the civil rights movement, he would pay a high price. Vernon Dahmer's murder brought a massive response from the FBI.

When Roy Moore, the special agent in charge of the Jackson FBI office, heard a radio report that Dahmer had been fatally injured, he telephoned the FBI office in Hattiesburg. "Reserve me a dozen rooms at the Holiday Inn and get me some office space," he ordered. "We'll be setting up."

Every day and night for seventy-six straight days, except for three days when he visited his home in Jackson, Moore drove his men in Hattiesburg to exhaustion. "We're going to get the bastards who did this," he told them.

Finally, Moore obtained arrest warrants charging Bowers and thirteen other Klansmen with civil rights violations. All-white juries tried Bowers three times in the Dahmer case; hung juries resulted in mistrials twice in federal civil rights cases and once in a state murder case. But the FBI's tactics in relentlessly investigating the case, coming on top of the Philadelphia investigation and a massive campaign against the Klan all across Mississippi, was decimating the ranks of the White Knights.

It was at this juncture, with the Justice Department preparing to try Bowers and seventeen others in the Philadelphia case, that Tarrants had shown up in Laurel. The new Klan campaign of violence, Bowers and Tarrants agreed, would focus on the Jews. And what better way to signal the shift in strategy than to bomb the new synagogue in Jackson.

Tarrants felt exhilarated at the way things were going. He was gaining Bowers' confidence and he had paired up with Kathy Ainsworth. She was with him as he drove through the darkened streets of Jackson on September 18, 1967. Their mission that night would seal Tarrants' relationship with Bowers.

To Bowers, Tarrants and Ainsworth seemed the perfect instruments, and not only because they were prepared to take violent action—the White Knights had other members willing to do that. What made these two special was that they operated in such secrecy that the FBI and police knew almost nothing about them.

Ainsworth's link to Tarrants was not known by anyone outside Bowers' tight inner circle. In their personal backgrounds, in their right-wing radicalism and in their associates, Kathy and Tommy were a different species from the Klan members the FBI and local

police were focusing on. The lawmen's formidable network of
informants would be of little help.

In Ainsworth's case, even most of her friends had no inkling
of her extremist beliefs. In Miami, where she grew up, Adon Taft,
the highly respected religion editor of *The Miami Herald,* was so
close to her that she sometimes baby-sat for his two daughters.
To him she was "the personification of sweet, an ideal girl from
all we knew, the kind of girl we had long told our daughters we
would like them to grow up and be like."

Neither Taft nor Ainsworth's colleagues at Duling Elementary
School were aware of her activities with the Klan and the Americans for the Preservation of the White Race. It never occurred
to them that she kept stacks of hate propaganda in her bedroom
dresser—including a tract that warned about "the thousands of
white women and girls who have already been raped in their own
beds by invading Negroes" and "the thousands of women and
young girls who have been made dope addicts for the specific
purpose of moral debauchery and mongrelization to be their willing slaves for their sex orgies, lust and diseased filth."

And no one outside Bowers' inner circle knew that on makeshift
firing ranges in the woods outside Jackson she was becoming
proficient with a variety of weapons—including two kinds of submachine guns. Or that she had been learning to make bombs and
had teamed up with Tarrants.

It was after 10:00 P.M. on September 18, 1967, and there was
almost no traffic. Sheets of ground fog cloaked the lawns and trees
of the sleeping neighborhood as they approached their goal. The
great soaring roof of Jackson's Temple Beth Israel synagogue
loomed up. Tarrants pulled to a stop nearby and turned off the
headlights. They sat silently in the car for several minutes. All
was quiet. The device on the seat between them was simplicity
itself: sticks of dynamite bundled together with a blasting cap and
a fifteen-minute length of common fuse. It would leave no clues.

Tarrants took the bomb under his arm and moved quickly across
the lawn to the synagogue. He knelt for a moment beside a wall.
The cigarette lighter flared briefly. He hurried back to the car.
Kathy swung the door open and they drove slowly away. As they
reached the outskirts of Jackson they heard the bomb explode.

3

A little past 10:00 P.M. that night, the shock of an enormous explosion shook Al Binder's antebellum home in a fashionable section of Jackson, literally lifting him out of bed. Instantly the young lawyer was wide awake. Temple Beth Israel was only a half mile away and because of all the Klan threats against the Jewish community he immediately figured it had been bombed. He worried about Rabbi Perry Nussbaum, who often worked late in his office; he might be inside the synagogue. Binder pulled on his clothes and drove as fast as he could through the empty streets.

Joe Harris, a prominent building contractor, and his wife, Maxine, also were jarred awake. "Joe, something big blew up," she exclaimed. "You better get up and see what's going on." As he struggled to get his clothes on, she turned on the radio. At first there was music, but then a bulletin: Temple Beth Israel had been bombed.

"I knew it," Joe had said as he hurried out to his car. "The rabbi's gonna get us all killed."

Binder was the first to reach the scene. The night was dark, with a warm mist hanging in the air. The smell of dynamite stung his nose. He looked around, but saw no other cars in the parking lot and no lights shining in the synagogue. Maybe the rabbi had not worked late after all.

Police cars, ambulances and fire trucks arrived, sirens screaming. The spotlights of the emergency vehicles illuminated the building. The blast had ripped through the administrative offices and a conference room, torn a hole in the ceiling, blown out windows, ruptured a water pipe and buckled a wall. An octagonal

structure dominated by a massive roof, Temple Beth Israel had
been dedicated only seven months earlier. Now Binder could see
smoke coming from the windows.

Scores of neighborhood residents, some in their bathrobes,
were beginning to collect on the lawn. The night was so dark and
foggy that people in the crowd had difficulty recognizing one
another. Standing in groups of two and three, everyone spoke in
whispers, as though talking aloud would violate something already
defiled by what everyone assumed had been a bomb. Over and
over they asked one another, "Why would anybody do such a
thing?"

The crowd opened a path for Rabbi Nussbaum and his wife,
Arene. The Nussbaums too had been awakened by the blast and
were already dressing when FBI agent Jim Ingram, in charge of
civil rights enforcement in Mississippi, called to confirm their fear
that it had come from the temple. Now, nervously surveying piles
of shattered glass and plaster, Arene said, "Just think what would
have happened if someone had been inside there."

"This is a fear I've been living with," Nussbaum answered.
Turning to a local reporter, he added, "I had intended to do some
work in my study tonight, but changed my mind at the last minute
and stayed home."

Joe Harris was not the only Jew in Jackson who blamed the rabbi
for the bombing. Perry Nussbaum did not have many friends in
or outside the congregation. Although well educated and highly
principled, he was tactless, abrasive, outspoken and headstrong
in his views. A medium-sized man with thinning hair, a bristling
mustache and horn-rimmed glasses, he had a way of irritating
people from the moment he met them. He liked to fire verbal
darts, abrupt comments that he seemed to think were funny but
others found inappropriate or even rude.

Soon after arriving in Jackson from Pittsfield, Massachusetts,
in 1954, Nussbaum had sized up the modest, two-bedroom
"starter" house Al Binder lived in then and declared condescend-
ingly, "I guess you're good for the minimum"—meaning the
young lawyer could afford a five-dollar weekly contribution to the
synagogue. Arene, who tried to pass off the rabbi's remarks as
"just Perry's sense of humor," told Binder her husband was trying
to be funny. Binder did not find it funny.

The night Nussbaum first met Elaine Crystal, wife of business executive Emanuel Crystal, the rabbi provoked an argument by saying he was going to downgrade the role of Hadassah, the Jewish women's organization, in Temple Beth Israel's activities. Hadassah would have to hold its meetings someplace else. Elaine Crystal, an outspoken woman, told the rabbi the temple congregation was so small it needed all the support it could get from Hadassah and other Jewish organizations. When she got home she telephoned Nussbaum, gave him another piece of her mind and slammed down the receiver.

The rabbi could not seem to resist needling people. Joe and Maxine Harris had a son whose dark complexion became deeply tanned during the long Mississippi summers. Encountering the boy one day, Nussbaum remarked, "Son, I always knew your mother was a loose woman, but I never thought she'd go this far." Maxine was furious. "He managed to insult every member of the congregation at least once," Joe Harris recalled. "Everyone would cringe, waiting to see what he was going to say next. We had always revered rabbis and treated them with great respect. We didn't expect them to always be making wisecracks."

Nussbaum not only had a difficult personality, he was still—after more than a decade in Mississippi—seen as an outsider. The rabbi himself had grown fond of the state and its people—an affection that compounded his inner conflict as the civil rights struggle intensified. But he rejected the elaborate strategies that most Jews in the South had developed for dealing with their vulnerable situation. Members of his congregation felt that he did not really understand what it meant to be a Jew in the South.

Jews had lived in Mississippi since before it joined the Union in 1817. They had fought on its side when it tried to leave the Union in 1860; many were proud that a Jew, Judah Benjamin, had been an important figure in Jefferson Davis's Confederate government. Along with other whites, they had supported and prospered from "the peculiar institution" of slavery in its pure form before Emancipation and in its covert form afterward. Yet even when they tried to convince themselves of their acceptance by their fellow Southerners, deep down they always knew they were viewed as aliens in a land of uncompromising, militant, fundamentalist Protestantism. "Judaism may rank higher in the moral order of Bible Belt fundamentalist circles than, say, Black

Christianity or Roman Catholicism, but it remains nonetheless a
less-than-equal sect, an extraneous and foreign religion in an area
of xenophobes," Murray Polner wrote in *Rabbi: The American
Experience.*

To thrive, many Jews concluded, they had to assimilate into
the dominant culture in every way possible. Becoming "200 percent Southerners," they submerged their own religious and cultural heritage, partly out of a frankly acknowledged appetite for
the comfortable life and partly out of fear of the violence that
never seemed far below the surface in Mississippi.

Nussbaum's predecessor, Rabbi Meyer Lovitt, who had served
as spiritual leader of Jackson's Jews for twenty-five years, understood and supported this approach. He—like most of his gener-
ation of rabbis across the South—avoided controversial issues such
as civil rights. He downplayed the differences between Judaism
and Christianity and supported as much assimilation as circumstances would permit. Jewish holidays were observed inconspi-
cuously, and if Jewish families wished to join the rest of the
community in putting up Christmas trees, Lovitt made no objec-
tion. Maxine Harris remembered Lovitt being "just like a little
Santa Claus. He'd check the Jewish houses to see who had Christmas trees and say, 'That's a nice little Hanukkah bush.' There
never was any trouble with Rabbi Lovitt."

All over the South, Jews, especially the dominant, assimila-
tionist-minded German Jews, adopted Southern ways while not
completely abandoning their old-world rituals. They went to their
Reform temples on Friday nights, but they shunned Hebrew
chanting and did away with bar mitzvahs. Kosher kitchens survived almost exclusively in the homes of Jews with eastern Eu-
ropean roots, who arrived later. In *The Provincials,* Eli Evans
described a not untypical Sabbath celebration in a Reform household in Anniston, Alabama. "First, Mama blessed the lights. And
then, we always had our favorite Sabbath meal—oyster stew,
steak, ham, or fried chicken; Mama's homemade biscuits and corn
bread too; hoppin john and sweet potato pie for dessert."

Nussbaum had sought to change all that. He criticized those
who put up Christmas trees. He reinstituted bar mitzvahs and
other Jewish ceremonies. He embraced Zionism and Israel, both
of which Southern Jews had traditionally held at arm's length.
He insisted openly that Judaism was a distinct religion and not

just an earlier, Old Testament form of Christianity—"the Jewish church," as many people in Jackson often called it. Altogether, in large ways and small, he made the congregation more aware of its Jewishness and he made that Jewishness more conspicuous in the larger community—neither of which the members of Temple Beth Israel welcomed.

Nussbaum's personal manner and his approach to Judaism had only compounded what bothered the congregation most about him: the rabbi was just too liberal on the race issue, and much too close to the civil rights movement for all but a few members. Assigned to congregations in the northern United States for most of his career, Nussbaum right from the start had aroused concern among Beth Israel's leaders about where he stood on race. Although he had given them a reassuring pledge never to do anything that would cause problems for the congregation, over the years he had done a series of things that caused some members to worry. They feared his activities would put a spotlight on the Jewish community, antagonize the Jackson Establishment and disturb the uneasy peace that Jews throughout the South struggled to maintain with the Christians who dominated their society.

As it turned out, the worriers were right. With Perry Nussbaum, considering his life and his nature, it could hardly have turned out otherwise.

Nussbaum was born and raised in Canada but settled in the United States in 1926. He studied for the rabbinate at the Hebrew Union College in Cincinnati, later received a degree from the University of Cincinnati, and did graduate work at universities in Colorado, Ottawa and Melbourne, Australia.

As it turned out, he was better with books than people. Ordained in 1933, he embarked upon the nomadic life of a small-town rabbi, first accepting a post at a Reform congregation in Melbourne and then, before World War II, serving as a prison chaplain in Pueblo, Colorado. There he accompanied a teenage Jewish boy to the gas chamber at the prison in Canon City. Writing about it later, he said: "I have never forgotten that awful experience of the gas chamber, and particularly the crowd of sheriffs, deputies and lawmen who avidly peered through the glass watching him in the last throes, as well as hearing one of them say, 'Take that, you damn Jew.' "

After serving as an army chaplain in the Philippines during World War II, he accepted appointment as an associate rabbi in Trenton, New Jersey, a post several other prospective candidates had turned down. New Jersey was followed by stints in Texas, Kansas, Long Island, and Pittsfield, Massachusetts.

In June of 1954, Rabbi Nathan Perilman, chairman of the placement committee of the Central Conference of American Rabbis, suggested Nussbaum apply for the post in Jackson where Meyer Lovitt had just retired. As Polner described it in *Rabbi,* Perilman told Nussbaum: "It's a wonderful congregation. There they'll appreciate you. The South is known for its *derech eretz*—respect— for its rabbinical leaders. You can do as little or as much as you want to. Jackson is beautiful—wide streets, clean, a wonderful southern city. Perry, you'll like it. Take Arene and your daughter down there—and drink mint juleps the rest of your life."

Nussbaum flew to Jackson for an interview. Almost exactly a month before, on May 17, 1954, the Supreme Court had handed down its decision outlawing segregation in public schools. National Jewish organizations had hailed the ruling, but the reaction among the Temple Beth Israel congregation was less favorable to say the least. Landing at the Jackson Municipal Airport, Nussbaum was met by a small group of local Jews. The temperature was a staggering 103 degrees and humid. They had hardly finished exchanging pleasantries when a member of the delegation got down to business: "What is your position about school desegregation?"

With uncharacteristic restraint, Nussbaum finessed the question. After twenty years of bouncing from one anonymous post to another, he was eager for the job, which, he told friends, offered a unique challenge in the wake of the Supreme Court's desegregation decision. He did not exactly lie to the selection committee. He merely said he had never paid much attention to the issue, and that was the truth as far as it went. He told the committee he would have to follow his conscience, but would never do anything to cause problems for his congregation. That was at least half true, because he did intend to follow his conscience, and he was not indifferent to the feelings of the congregation.

In the beginning, Nussbaum kept his views on race relations pretty much to himself. His wife, Arene, a native of Texas, thought he did not understand Southern race relations and was naive about what he could and could not do about civil rights. But when the Freedom Riders began pouring into Jackson and all across the South in 1961, he could no longer finesse the issue—with his conscience or with his congregation.

The first Freedom Ride began in Washington, D.C., on May 4, when six whites and seven blacks set out on a Greyhound bus to challenge the segregation of travel facilities in Virginia, the Carolinas, Georgia, Alabama, Louisiana and Mississippi. The initial demonstrators, and the scores and hundreds who followed, were met almost everywhere by police harassment and violence. In Jackson, police routinely arrested the demonstrators and charged them with violating a section of the Code of Mississippi originally drafted in 1960 to prevent "wade-ins" by blacks trying to use Biloxi's whites-only public beaches. Violating the provision was a misdemeanor with maximum punishment of a two-hundred-dollar fine and four months in jail.

Eventually, the Jackson jail overflowed and civil rights demonstrators began to be transferred to Parchman state prison almost 150 miles away.

Once a week throughout the blistering hot summer of 1961 Nussbaum drove to Parchman alone to visit the demonstrators. The car was not air-conditioned and the temperatures often soared into the high nineties. The rabbi took personal items, soap and cigarettes and such, to the prisoners. He collected the names and addresses of relatives and other people close to them. After each visit, Nussbaum sent mimeographed letters of reassurance to other demonstrators' relatives and friends. He included in the envelopes any personal notes he had been given as well.

Even then, fearful of upsetting his congregation and perhaps antagonizing Jackson's political leadership, Nussbaum kept a relatively low profile. He never tried to conceal the visits, but he did not go out of his way to draw attention to them. Once, he needed authorization from the Hinds County sheriff to get inside Parchman and the sheriff asked, "Why would you want to go visit those nutty people?" Nussbaum, not wanting to jeopardize his chance of receiving the authorization, replied, "I'm not making any judgments about whether what they do is right or wrong, but they need some kind of contact with the clergy."

He was struggling to live up to his pledge to the selection

committee. He knew that, given the increasingly fevered climate in Mississippi, being more open about his views on racial justice could threaten not only his own safety and that of his family but the safety of his entire congregation. Yet he had an increasingly difficult time squaring that concern with his conscience and with what he saw as his failure to take more overt action on such a momentous moral issue.

Like everyone in the state, Nussbaum knew the penalties for failing to embrace segregation wholeheartedly. For her defiance of racists, Hazel Brannon Smith, publisher of the Lexington *Advertiser* north of Jackson, lost her advertising, her county printing contract and all her friends in town. Her insurance was canceled, her husband lost his job as a hospital administrator and a cross was burned on their lawn. Somehow, Smith managed to keep publishing, but most businesspeople were not so resilient. In McComb, after insurance executive Albert (Red) Heffner, Jr., wrote a letter asking the governor to make a statement supporting law and order following the burning of four black churches, segregationists harassed him with obscene telephone calls, threatened to bomb his house, then terminated his office lease and spread rumors that he had Communist connections. His insurance business withered and old friends shunned him. The Heffners packed up and moved.

Even voicing support for the public schools was dangerous after the legislature gave local officials the authority to close them to avoid desegregation. Every Friday morning a group of women met secretly in different homes to discuss ways to keep the schools open. One of them, Gloria Minor, the wife of Bill Minor, Jackson correspondent of the New Orleans *Times-Picayune,* bridled upon hearing Harry Reasoner in a CBS documentary ask why moderates were not speaking out in Mississippi. "I jumped up and said, 'You come down here and find out what happens to people when they do speak out.' And I thought to myself, This is the way it must have been in Germany in the thirties."

Despite the climate of fear, an occasional ludicrous incident relieved the tension. Winifred Green, a young Jackson housewife, was one of the founders, along with Patricia Derian, Elaine Crystal and Joan Geiger, of Mississippians for Public Education, the statewide organization that evolved from those emotionally

charged Friday morning coffee klatches. Traveling around encouraging people to organize on behalf of the public schools,
Green wound up receiving a wave of hate telephone calls. The
Jackson White Citizens Council, in a recorded message program
called "Dial the Truth," said, "If you want to know why your
child will be forced to go to school with niggers, call Mrs. Samuel
Falls"—Green's married name at the time—and gave her telephone number. Her husband fielded the calls, and one Sunday
morning, fed up with the stream of hate, he grabbed the telephone
and, without waiting for the caller to speak, shouted "You son
of a bitch! Stop bothering us and don't ever call here again!" Falls
was fair-skinned and his wife watched as the back of his neck
turned a deep red. Finally she heard him say, "Yes, Mother. We'd
be happy to come over for lunch after church."

The main instruments for preserving white supremacy, in addition to the Ku Klux Klan, were the private White Citizens
Councils and the state-supported Mississippi Sovereignty Commission. The councils were so effective that after the school desegregation decision, the Klan did not become a major factor in
Mississippi until Sam Bowers organized the White Knights in
1964. In their recruiting literature in 1960, the councils took credit
for the fact that in Mississippi, unlike other states, blacks had not
even attempted sit-ins.

The councils were a direct response to the Supreme Court's
1954 school desegregation decision. Shortly after it was issued, a
group of bankers, lawyers, planters and businessmen met secretly
in the Delta town of Indianola to discuss the impending danger.
The minutes of that Citizens Council meeting, reprinted in an
Anti-Defamation League (ADL) bulletin, contained the crux of
the approach the councils followed: "It is the thought of our group
that the solution of this problem of desegregation may become
easier if various agitators and the like could be removed from the
communities in which they now operate. We propose to accomplish this through the careful application of economic pressures."
Their goal was to drive out dissenters—black and white—by de-
stroying their livelihoods.

Within a year, there were approximately three hundred councils
and sixty-five thousand dues-paying members. Thousands of chapters sprang up in nine other Southern states, but none acted with
more ruthless efficiency than Mississippi's. Professors who did

not support segregation were blacklisted, companies that flouted
the rules were boycotted and the names of people who signed
petitions promoting desegregation were publicized.

In such a climate, everyone was fearful, no one more so than
Mississippi's comfortable but vulnerable Jewish population, which
in 1955 numbered about 3,250—roughly 1.5 percent of the state's
total population. Small wonder that Rabbi Nussbaum tried to hide
his true feelings as long as he did.

As word began to spread about his civil rights activities, Nussbaum became increasingly nervous. Writing during the early
1960s in the *Journal of the Central Conference of American Rabbis,* a Cincinnati-based publication unlikely to be read in Mississippi, he declared: "Sometimes you were sure your phone was
tapped. You wondered about some of the mail, delivered and
undelivered. Talk about the clergy and mental health! Some of
us were chapter and verse in the textbook of the paranoid. . . .
When we were reasonably sure of one another, we dared voice
what was treason (to the South) behind closed doors and admittedly foolhardy and impractical from the pulpit."

The other emotion he struggled with was guilt. In 1961, when
Nussbaum received reports that a group of Freedom Riders coming to Jackson would include several rabbis, he agonized over how
to keep them out. He admired their willingness to protest, but
felt their presence in Mississippi would expose the Jewish community to controversy and possible danger. One night he sought
out William Kunstler and Carl Rachlin, two young New York
lawyers who represented some of the demonstrators. Kunstler
was just beginning to make a national reputation as a civil rights
attorney (he later cited Jackson as the searing experience that
radicalized him) and Rachlin was general counsel for the Congress
of Racial Equality. Nussbaum thought they could help him stop
the rabbis.

Kunstler and Rachlin had been in a trial at the Hinds County
courthouse that had not adjourned until almost 11:00 P.M. and it
was close to midnight when they returned to the Sun 'n Sand
Motel. Dead tired, they were surprised to be approached in the
lobby by a man wearing a dark business suit and a worried expression. Nussbaum introduced himself and apologized for the late
hour but said he had an extremely important matter to discuss.

They went to Kunstler's room. Nussbaum sat on the edge of the bed. Rachlin and Kunstler sat down in upholstered chairs. The rabbi said Jackson was becoming a racial powder keg that might explode.

"I'm a Jew and you're Jews," Nussbaum began, "and you ought to help keep the rabbis from coming in here because they're going to cause severe problems for the Jewish community."

The lawyers were stunned. Kunstler thought Nussbaum looked terrified and could not understand why. As someone with no experience in the South, Kunstler had not the slightest idea of the conflicting pressures and fears of reprisal and violence that weighed on Nussbaum—the Jewish tradition of social consciousness, the sense of obligation as a leader of an oppressed minority, the keen awareness of his congregation's vulnerabilities, the hard-earned knowledge that in Mississippi it was often necessary to put realism before idealism. Kunstler did not know that for months, quietly and largely behind the scenes, Nussbaum had defied his congregation by ministering to imprisoned Freedom Riders.

Nussbaum tried to explain that the White Citizens Councils were imposing devastating economic sanctions on anyone even suspected of holding racially moderate views. Jews too were under pressure to conform, even to join the councils. In some cases in which whole Delta towns went Citizens Council, the few Jewish residents joined too—some out of fear and some because they were hard-rock segregationists. "I sympathize with what you're doing and think it's a just cause," Nussbaum told Kunstler, "but you have an obligation to your fellow Jews, too."

Kunstler believed a rabbi should be out in front on the issue of racial justice. Jews had a proud history of working for civil rights. Rabbi Stephen Wise was one of the incorporators of the National Association for the Advancement of Colored People in New York in 1909 and two Jews had served as presidents of the organization. Kunstler felt that after centuries of enduring discrimination, Jews should be the first to protest when others were victimized and rabbis should put into practice the principles of justice woven into their sermons.

"It's crazy to think we'll urge rabbis not to participate in the Freedom Rides," Kunstler told Nussbaum. "We have an obligation to do something about the injustices down here. Don't you

know that Dr. King has asked all sorts of clergymen to come here
and his own executive assistant [Reverend Wyatt Tee Walker] is
here?"

"That's different," Nussbaum replied. "Christian congregations don't have the same vulnerability that Jewish congregations
have. It's particularly different in the Deep South, where we're
a small minority. If the rabbis come in here, it'll just draw attention to the Jews and could cause a pogrom."

Kunstler found Nussbaum's comments depressing. Someone
had told him that the local rabbi was a liberal but here Nussbaum
was pleading for him to keep other rabbis from coming into Jackson. Yet Kunstler was intrigued by the entreaty, too, and he
listened to Nussbaum intently. They debated the issue until almost
three o'clock in the morning. The rabbi left confident he had done
his best to argue his case, but disappointed that Kunstler was
unswayed.

During this period, the ceaseless pull and tug of conflicting
obligations tried Nussbaum's spirit.

On October 6, 1964, he wrote to Rabbi Samuel S. Soskin of
Brooklyn, New York: "I have never shut my door or rebuffed my
colleagues. But some things are hard to take—like the young man
who was here for a total of 48 hours, told me how thrilled he was
over his insights and how thrilled he was for me that I am helping
to make history. I told him to make history in his own back-lashed
community."

On another occasion, he complained to Ken Dean, the young
Baptist minister he helped select to head the Mississippi Council
on Human Relations, of being "criticized from all sides."

"My people in the Jewish community think I expose them to
vulnerabilities they don't need and they're already a minority
group," he told Dean. "They say I'm bringing on the potential
for violence and criticism and they're already discriminated
against because of being Jewish. On the other hand, the Negroes
criticize me for being white and not doing enough. Even when I
offer a prayer at a civil rights meeting, I catch it from all sides.
Christians don't like it because I pray as a Jew."

Nussbaum told Dean that as poor as the Jackson Jews' record
on civil rights was, it was "better than the records of any Christian
group you can point to."

"Rabbi Nussbaum, you can't name but four people in your

congregation that really support civil rights for Negroes," Dean said.

"Well, you're right," Nussbaum replied, "and that's four out of a hundred forty families and that's twice what any other religious group in Jackson can point to."

Nussbaum did have a handful of soul mates in the congregation. Emanuel and Elaine Crystal supported the civil rights movement and defended Nussbaum. They also provided food for many of the Freedom Riders and served as contacts for parents in the North concerned about sons and daughters who had traveled to Jackson to demonstrate. Manny Crystal was chairman of the board of Crawler Parts, Inc., a large firm that imported parts for heavy equipment from Italy. He was relatively immune to the economic pressure that forced many to conform. Elaine Crystal was even more active and outspoken on racial matters than her husband, having been a founder of Mississippians for Public Education.

Privately, some other Jews supported the civil rights cause but were afraid to be identified, more out of fear of economic retaliation than out of any concern about physical danger. But the overwhelming majority of Jews in Jackson and elsewhere in Mississippi held views that were indistinguishable from those of their neighbors. For them, an unwelcome complication was that so many of the demonstrators were Northern Jews—roughly 50 percent of all the demonstrators and about 70 percent of the lawyers who represented them were Jewish. It made it much harder for Southern Jews to remain inconspicuous.

The way Joe Harris looked at it, "the outside agitators should have stayed home. Here we have all these people coming down here that are obviously Jewish—Schwerner, Goodman, the Goldbergs and the Levines and the Cohens and all these obvious Jewish names. We're all sitting here trying to make a living and trying to get along and trying to live in a superpredominant, very, very Christian society and all of a sudden here they are. And the way it's looked on down here is that all Jews think alike."

Harris was one of the Jewish community's most outspoken defenders of the Southern way of life. Once, during a visit to St. Louis, he encountered a young civil rights activist who was excited to learn that he was from Jackson. "I was down in Jackson," the young man said proudly. "I was a Freedom Rider down there."

"Yeah?" Harris replied acidly. "How did you like our jails?"

Against such sentiment, Nussbaum was hard-pressed to hang on to his job. He needed all the support he could get from defenders such as the Crystals and Sidney Geiger, the president of Delta Steel Corporation, a Jackson-based metal fabricating concern. Several times they helped squelch proposals to fire the rabbi that came within inches of succeeding.

Nussbaum, in the article in the Cincinnati rabbinical journal, portrayed himself as perhaps the last remaining liberal clergyman in Jackson, and described his feelings in Old Testament terms: "So this last survivor is running scared. Tell me, colleagues, how did Isaac feel when the knife was poised over his head?"

The summer of '64 marked a turning point for Nussbaum. Stepping out of the shadows, he took a leading role in organizing the Committee of Concern, a biracial, interdenominational group founded to raise money for rebulding black churches torched by the Klan. He was one of six clergymen who founded the committee, which subsequently grew to include scores of ministers throughout the state. Nussbaum, the only rabbi on its thirty-member executive committee, was a leader in helping raise about $750,000 to rebuild forty-four churches.

With everything else that was happening that summer, Nussbaum's efforts on behalf of the committee might have passed unnoticed. Hundreds of white volunteers were flooding into Jackson, Meridian, Hattiesburg and several other cities as part of Mississippi Freedom Summer. The state, from the highest public officials on down, considered itself under siege. The White Knights—formed only the previous February but already a force to be reckoned with—were engaged in a rampage of violence and destruction. And the combination of Nussbaum's efforts to help the black churches and the Freedom Riders was enough to set Sam Bowers off. He ranted against "the Communist-Jewish conspiracy" at Klan meetings.

In the end, a Klan informant reported to the FBI, Bowers concluded that Mississippi's Jews faced too many problems of their own to spend much time participating in civil rights activities and decided not to target them at that time. The informant might have added that Bowers' plate was too full just then to deal with Nussbaum: while the rabbi was raising money to restore burned-out black churches, Bowers and his fellow White Knights were busy planning and carrying out the kidnapping and killing of Schwerner, Chaney and Goodman.

Bowers did not forget about Nussbaum, however.

In March of 1967, the Beth Israel congregation had arrived at a momentous point in its 106-year history. A long-planned new temple had at last been completed and ambitious arrangements were being made for the dedication. The first Temple Beth Israel, built in 1861, had been burned by federal troops during the Civil War. A replacement temple, erected in 1867, also fell victim to fire. The third temple, a "beautiful gothic building" according to a news account of the day, was built in 1875 with solid walnut pews and an elegantly carved altar. Reflecting the times, it was architecturally indistinguishable from Jackson's Lutheran, Methodist, Episcopal and other Christian churches. A fourth temple also carried on this assimilationist tradition. Nussbaum changed that with a vengeance: the new temple was as unmistakably "Jewish" as he could make it, with its sprawling roof suggesting the tents occupied by the children of Israel during their forty years of wandering in the wilderness after the Exodus.

At the same time, when it came to the dedication, the rabbi went to great lengths to make it ecumenical. The site of the new Temple on Old Canton Road was close to two Protestant churches—Christ Methodist immediately to the east and St. Philip's Episcopal just across the road. Nussbaum called the area Holy Corners. The neighboring ministers, as well as other Christian church leaders, were invited to the ceremonies. Nussbaum also insisted that the ceremonies be interracial. White ministers, including a Catholic bishop and an Episcopal bishop, were joined by two black Protestant ministers in the procession carrying the Torah into the temple. Three of the five members of the building committee refused to participate in the ceremonies.

The broader issue of holding interracial gatherings in the synagogue created a raging controversy inside the Beth Israel congregation. A month after the dedication, Nussbaum endured what he conceded was "one of the roughest congregational meetings I've ever attended." He was stripped of his authority to approve non-Jewish meetings at the temple.

The controversy within the congregation received no outside

publicity, but the larger Jackson community was well aware that blacks had participated in the dedication of the new temple.

For almost everyone in Jackson, the spring and summer of 1967 were a period of mounting strain. The customs and values that had shaped life in Mississippi for more than two hundred years, the unwritten assumptions of white, Christian ascendancy, seemed under attack from almost every quarter.

The federal government was still pushing for voting rights, school desegregation and equal opportunities in the workplace. The FBI was no longer a passive observer as it had been in the early days of the civil rights movement: on March 7, the White Knights blew up the Blackwell Real Estate Company office in Jackson for selling houses to blacks in previously all-white neighborhoods; the bureau investigated so vigorously that one of the Klansmen confessed to participating in the bombing, identified Danny Joe Hawkins and another Klansman as accomplices and agreed to testify against them. An all-white jury acquitted Hawkins, but the intensity of the FBI's investigation was not lost on the Klan.

Blacks themselves also had become more assertive, for which they paid a heavy price. Only three years earlier, during the Freedom Summer of massive demonstrations, most Mississippi blacks had been so terrorized that persuading individuals to try to register to vote had been difficult. Now, they turned out en masse to protest on issue after issue. More than one thousand had marched outside the all-white state legislature in 1966. As 1967 dawned, students at predominantly black Jackson State College began protesting the activities of police on the campus. On May 10, students and nonstudents clashed with police, setting fire to barricades that had been set up to seal off the area. The next day, the State Police and National Guard were brought in. When protesters began throwing rocks and bricks at a line of police, some of the officers opened fire with shotguns. Some fired into the air but some apparently aimed at the crowd of protesters.

A young black truck driver named Benjamin Brown was hit. Though a former youth worker and civil rights activist, Brown had taken no part in the protest. Instead, he was on an errand— getting a sandwich for his wife, who was expecting their first child.

At the sound of the first gunshot, Brown began to run. He was struck in the back and the head by police buckshot.

Brown died the next day, on his twenty-second birthday. Police attributed his death to a "wild shot."

By now, Rabbi Nussbaum seemed at times to be courting controversy. After the Six-Day War ended in a smashing victory for Israel in June 1967, an evangelist named Anis Shorrosh, a Baptist minister and a native of Jordan, delivered a blistering attack on the Jewish state. In remarks reported by the Jackson *Clarion-Ledger,* Shorrosh accused Israel of dividing Palestine and taking "the best land." The American news media, he said, continued "to push the Jewish viewpoint even though 15,000 of my people in Jordan were slaughtered in three days last week."

Nussbaum, in a scathing rebuttal also printed in the *Clarion-Ledger,* accused the evangelist of a "blatantly malicious canard," adding, "People of all religious faiths, nationalities and races this side of the Iron Curtain have expressed their admiration for the courage of some two million Israelis daring the might of several times that number of Arabs encouraged by the USSR to make good their threat to drive them into the Mediterranean, and whose heroic efforts led to a military victory hardly anyone thought possible."

The exchange between Nussbaum and Shorrosh was a sensation in Jackson, which was not accustomed to having its religious leaders mix so openly into international politics.

In July of 1967, Nussbaum also played host to a meeting of the Jackson chapter of Ken Dean's Mississippi Council on Human Relations. The chapter had been inactive during the preceding year and a half but had revived with the increased tempo of civil rights activity. An FBI report on the meeting, compiled in September as part of the bureau's bombing investigation, quoted an informant as saying three earlier requests to use the synagogue for interracial meetings had been turned down before permission was granted for the July 27 meeting. It reported that, of the 130 people who attended, 40 percent were black, and pointedly noted that the meeting had been announced in advance on radio and in the newspaper.

One religious group that resisted any ecumenical attempts was the Baptists, largely because of opposition from Bob Hederman, the publisher of the *Clarion-Ledger*. He and his brother Tom, who was the editor of the paper, exerted enormous influence not just in the state capital but throughout Mississippi. They and other Baptists had decreed that no Jews could attend the powerful First Baptist Church, and they also kept blacks from joining the existing Jackson ministerial organization. Nussbaum took a leading role founding the Greater Jackson Clergy Alliance, a biracial organization that eventually included sixty ministers from ten denominations—a direct rebuke to the religious power structure of the city, the Baptists and the Hedermans. Nussbaum also served as secretary of the Clergy Alliance, which held meetings in black as well as white houses of worship.

Nussbaum's activities infuriated Sam Bowers, who continued to mastermind Klan violence despite his upcoming federal trial in connection with the slaying of the three civil rights workers at Philadelphia and state and federal trials in Vernon Dahmer's death. Bowers was determined to show authorities that the White Knights remained a potent force.

A new campaign of terror was planned, aimed at selected white and black leaders. Jews would be the prime targets. Aware of constant FBI surveillance, Bowers and his lieutenants usually met in remote wooded areas and changed meeting places frequently. On the rare occasions when they met in buildings, they were so fearful of FBI listening devices that they scribbled messages to each other on notebook paper instead of talking. Once, after a meeting in his Laurel office to discuss targeting the Jackson Jewish community, Bowers was so concerned about security that he burned the messages, ground the ashes, placed them in a bucket of water, then flushed the contents down the commode.

Much of this was known to the FBI, which had infiltrated the White Knights with a substantial number of paid informants. But there were no informants within the tiny cell of Klansmen that Bowers talked to about specific plans for attacking the Jews. And almost no one except Bowers, Danny Joe Hawkins and Kathy Ainsworth knew that Thomas Albert Tarrants III had joined the cell.

•   •   •

In early September, it was Temple Beth Israel's time to host the annual meeting of the Mississippi Religious Conference, another interracial and interreligious organization Nussbaum had helped found. Emanuel Crystal, the congregation president, realized that the synagogue board, dominated by those who either were outright segregationists or did not want the temple involved in controversy, would not approve a meeting that included blacks.

So, shortly before leaving with his wife for a long-scheduled business trip to Italy, he decided to bypass the board and assume personal responsibility for approving the meeting. It bothered Crystal that other members of the congregation might think he had approved the session knowing he would not be present to catch the heat. He should not have worried. One thing other members of the congregation knew was that the Crystals were firm in their support of racial justice and never hesitated to confront the issue directly.

A number of blacks traveled to Jackson for the conference and several stopped at service stations and food markets in the vicinity to get directions to the temple. Word spread quickly that an integrated meeting was being held at the synagogue. Reports that blacks attended the meeting appeared in the Jackson *Clarion-Ledger* and *Daily News*.

The meeting and the publicity did indeed touch off a firestorm of protest within the Beth Israel congregation. At a subsequent meeting, several older members accused Nussbaum of endangering the Jewish community and demanded that he resign. Nussbaum, whose long-term contract had five years to run, made it clear he had no intention of quitting. In fact, he was so incensed by the suggestion that he paced up and down in front of the congregation denouncing his accusers and declaring they opposed his policies simply because they wanted to keep blacks out of the synagogue.

The attack on Nussbaum was led by John Hart Lewis, a wealthy home builder whose grandfather had settled in Jackson in 1848. A man of strong opinions, Lewis had taken a dislike to Nussbaum when the rabbi, shortly after arriving in Jackson, refused to confirm Lewis' two sons because their mother was not Jewish—a decision that accorded with Jewish law but not with the customs of many Mississippi congregations. Now, Lewis warned Nussbaum that if his policy of integrated meetings continued, the rabbi probably would find himself the target of a bomb.

In the end, however, a substantial majority of the congregation, led by Manny Crystal, Sid Geiger and Al Binder, lined up in support of the rabbi.

Emboldened, Nussbaum declared, "I've been in the Jackson, Mississippi, area for fourteen years and I haven't been bombed yet."

"Rabbi," Lewis replied, "I hope you make it through fifteen years."

Smoke still drifted up from the wreckage of the synagogue, mixing with the strong smell of insecticide—the city had been spraying for mosquitoes earlier that night. Scores of police officers and FBI agents swarmed over the damaged building and the grounds around it in search of clues. Tarrants had jimmied open several doors and had planted a box of dynamite near a small bathroom adjacent to Nussbaum's study. The explosion wrecked the study and would clearly have killed the rabbi if he had been there.

Jim Ingram, the FBI agent in charge of civil rights enforcement in Mississippi, arrived at the scene. He was shocked that the Klan had decided to target the Jewish community because in his view it had done "nothing to incite the wrath of the Klan."

The blast had also awakened Ken Dean at his house four blocks away. He called Ingram to confirm his apprehension about what had happened, then had hurried to the scene. Dean had also telephoned A. I. (Bee) Botnick, regional director of the Anti-Defamation League, at his house in New Orleans. Botnick had promised to set out for Jackson immediately by car.

A *Clarion-Ledger* reporter asked Nussbaum if his work with the Committee of Concern and new reports of integrated meetings at the synagogue might have been a factor in the bombing. Nussbaum thought for a moment before answering. Finally, he chose a response that was politic, if not entirely true.

"Ridiculous," the rabbi declared. "My work with the Committee of Concern had nothing to do with it. My congregation believes in the prophetic utterance 'My house shall be a house of prayer for all people.' And we have never—repeat, never!—turned away anyone from our doors. The sad fact is that there was a lot of bigotry during the recent [state Democratic] primaries. And distribution of anti-Semitic literature didn't help the situation."

Then the rabbi's eyes focused on a huge pile of books that lay jumbled on the floor of his ruined study. Over the years, he had carefully accumulated more than three thousand volumes of Jewish history and literature, including what he considered the best reference collection on the Old Testament in Jackson. Hundreds of the irreplaceable volumes were soaked with water pouring from the ruptured pipe.

"It's heartbreaking," Nussbaum said, picking up one of the water-soaked volumes. "What they did was an expression of bestiality."

A policeman searching for evidence remarked that he could not understand anyone bombing a house of worship. The rabbi found the comment mind-boggling. Black churches had been destroyed by the dozens all around Jackson, and in the previous decade explosions had rocked synagogues and other Jewish institutions in Nashville, Miami, Jacksonville, Birmingham, Atlanta and Gadsden, Alabama.

"This is not the first synagogue that has been bombed," Nussbaum told the policeman.

While police and FBI agents roped off the synagogue and scoured the area for evidence, the Nussbaums drove back to their house. There the rabbi sat down and, in the early morning hours, wrote in his diary:

A few hours ago our synagogue was bombed. I have given up trying to get sleep, or to read. It is nightmarish, this reaction to what for years I have accepted as inevitable. How can a rabbi sleep, when the forces of evil attack his cherished House?

I sit here now and wait for the daylight "I told you so's," [the] "I warned you that the Temple would be bombed." And I wonder! Not afraid! Wonder! How will the majority of my membership react now? Long ago I have been helplessly reconciled to those who reject my concepts of Judaism and the role of the synagogue in Jackson. I have been unable to stop their pursuit of the multitudes for that evil which has afflicted this lovely city and state.

Last night a policeman said to me, "I can't understand how anybody would want to destroy a church!" My own trauma was too much upon me to remind this well-intentioned sympathizer that over 40 Christian churches have already been destroyed in Mississippi. . . . I sit in the middle of the night and pray for the light which will maintain Beth Israel in its Fifth House a symbol of brotherhood and Love for all people, whoever they are, whatever they are.

4

In the wake of the bombing, the FBI turned to its formidable network of sources and informants. While the Nussbaums, Binder and others in the Beth Israel congregation were still picking through the wreckage, FBI agents descended on the homes of Klansmen on the bureau's standing roster of suspects in racial bombings. Agents Sam Jennings and Ron Johnson hurried to the residence of Joe Denver Hawkins, the father of Danny Joe Hawkins.

When they rang the doorbell, Johnnie Mae Hawkins, Joe Denver's wife, opened the door almost immediately, although it was about 1:30 A.M. A close friend of Kathy Ainsworth's, she was one of the toughest, roughest-talking Klan women in Mississippi, a woman who agent Tom Webb said was "always talking about getting the niggers and outsiders."

She greeted the agents belligerently. "What do you want? Don't you know it's after midnight?"

The agents asked where they could find Joe Denver Hawkins. She said her husband was asleep and could not be awakened until 6:00 A.M. Jennings and Johnson were skeptical. Lacking authority to search the house, they left, but they decided to cruise the area on the chance that Hawkins might be nearby. Before long their diligence was rewarded: on a side street not far from his house, they spotted Hawkins, his son Danny Joe, and J. L. Harper all parked along the curb in separate cars.

As the agents approached, Harper sped away, careening down the street with his lights out. The agents followed. Suddenly, behind them, both Joe Denver and Danny Joe pulled out and began to pursue the bureau car. Jennings and Hawkins radioed their location and called for backup. Harper swerved into a parking lot. So did the other three cars, but Joe Denver and Danny Joe suddenly pulled around the bureau car and forced it to an abrupt stop. The agents jumped out.

"FBI!" Johnson shouted. "We're with the FBI!" He found himself staring at a snub-nosed pistol held by Danny Joe. Joe Denver and Harper joined the confrontation.

At that moment, several Jackson police cars converged on the scene. Danny Joe dropped his gun. He and the other two Klansmen, now heavily outnumbered, gave up and were arrested. All three refused to say where they had been that night, and there was no immediate evidence linking them with the synagogue bombing. Still, the FBI considered them prime suspects.

The response of the FBI and other police agencies in Mississippi to the Beth Israel bombing was extraordinary. The destruction of black churches and the terrorizing of civil rights activists had been commonplace since the summer of 1964. With few exceptions—the Vernon Dahmer case, the slaying of Goodman, Schwerner and Chaney in Neshoba County—there had been little response from law enforcement agencies. And except for the ministers who made up the Committee of Concern, there had been little or no public outcry against the violence.

But the Beth Israel bombing was different. Within hours, Roy Moore of the Jackson FBI office ordered an around-the-clock investigation by his agents and FBI director J. Edgar Hoover dispatched a team of demolition experts to Jackson. Other agencies also moved swiftly. Mississippi and Jackson police joined in a massive investigation, helping the FBI check the whereabouts of all known members of the White Knights.

Publicly, the FBI tried to convey the impression that local and state authorities had primary responsibility for the investigation. The opposite was true. Fully aware of how politically sensitive the matter was, Moore assigned his own men to check every possible lead. An internal FBI report to Moore a week after the bombing said: "All homes within a one-half mile radius of the Synagogue have been contacted by Bureau Agents. Numerous residents along the logical escape routes from the Synagogue have also been contacted by Bureau agents. This radius includes the following streets: Hialeah, Farnsworth, Kaywood, Briarfield, Balmoral,

Red Fox, Runnymede, Charter Oak, Westbrook, Meadow Oaks Park, Woodcrest, Reddock, Canton Heights, Banyon, Rollingswood, Kaywood Circle, and the applicable blocks of Old Canton Road."

In addition, Moore was told that agents had contacted numerous residents along the logical escape routes from the synagogue, including Old Canton Road, Colonial Circle, South Park Drive, and Adkins Boulevard. The report concluded that the investigation had met with negative results.

The dynamiting of the synagogue rattled every one of the 140 Jewish households in Jackson. It shook their long-cherished faith that their relationships with the Christian community, built at an enormous price to themselves, would keep them safe. Manny Crystal, the young president of the congregation, called a meeting of Jewish leaders to discuss a response to the bombing and ways to protect themselves from further violence. The ADL's Bee Botnick was invited, and Ken Dean sat in.

Some forty men from the congregation gathered in a second-floor conference room of the Sun 'n Sand Motel on September 19, the day after the bombing. The motel, near the state capital in downtown Jackson, was owned by M. A. Lewis, Jr., a lawyer and former FBI agent and the brother of John Hart Lewis. The meeting was tumultuous.

Many of the younger men, among them Joe Harris, wanted immediate action. After years of distancing themselves from confrontation, they suddenly came to see things differently. Joe Harris put it succinctly: "The blacks had problems with these people, but that was solely their problem until the temple was bombed and it became our problem, too."

His wife, Maxine, described her attitude with equal candor: "We never wanted to get involved. We just wanted to go along like almost everyone else and whatever is happening, let it happen. We didn't want our four children being pounced on. They were all in school. We just wanted to be Americans, to be citizens. We just wanted to be left alone. Until it affected us. And then it affected us and it was our problem."

Several men, including Harris and Binder—another latecomer to the cause—were ready for immediate action. Some suggested forming a vigilante group to protect the Jewish community.

The older men strenuously opposed any action that might lead to more violence. They had never dreamed the Klan would attack the Jewish community, and now they seemed almost paralyzed. Any conspicuous action could backfire, they warned, and calling attention to themselves could only hurt the Jews. After all, the Klan's wrath already had been incurred by the outspoken rabbi and the Crystals and a few others.

When the meeting broke up after two hours, there was no agreement on a strategy.

The next day, Binder went to the Jackson office of the FBI and asked Roy Moore for advice on how to proceed. Moore told him that bombings were among the most difficult of all crimes to solve because they usually left little or no evidence.

It was a subject Moore knew more than a little about. He had made his reputation in the FBI with a groundbreaking investigation of a famous case in which an airliner with forty-four persons aboard had been blown up over Colorado. Moore's success in that case had caused J. Edgar Hoover to turn to him in 1964, when the bureau came under pressure to solve the disappearance of the three civil rights workers in Philadelphia.

Scientific investigation had helped Moore crack the airliner case, but the best way to catch terrorists, he told Binder, would be to pay informants. To solve any crime, he said, you needed one of three factors: a confession, a witness or physical evidence. And a Klan bombing, he added, usually left you with none of the three—unless you put up money for informants.

The FBI had been paying Klan informants for some time. Such payments are a staple of police work everywhere, and they had been pivotal to the bureau's success against the Klan in the Philadelphia slayings and the attack on Vernon Dahmer.

Thus far, the bureau had operated with its own funds. In this case, Moore took a different tack. He told Binder the bureau did not have the money needed for an operation of this sensitivity. Moore was acting partly out of concern for a limited bureau budget; buying information was expensive and it was hard to know how much money might be needed. And the members of the Beth Israel congregation, unlike the poor blacks in Hattiesburg and Neshoba County—or the emotionally devastated families and friends of Schwerner and Goodman—might reasonably be expected to pay their own way. But according to Jim Ingram, Moore probably sensed that he was stepping into uncharted territory and concluded that it might be useful to operate off the books. As Ingram said, "We didn't want anything in writing."

Nothing came immediately of Binder's discussions with Moore, but a seed was planted.

A few days later, another meeting was called in what amounted to the center of Jackson's power structure—the conference room of the First National Bank. Almost every important business, professional and religious leader in the city attended. Binder and several of the other young Jews made it clear that what they wanted from the Christian community was not money or sympathy but clear expressions of outrage.

"We want you to say the bombing is wrong and we want you to come out in the newspaper and tell your people and the congregations of these preachers here that it is wrong," Binder declared. "And we want these preachers to get off the pulpit and go out into their flock and tell them this is wrong."

The capital's movers and shakers, clearly unhappy at being upbraided, tried to take a soothing approach. No one challenged Binder openly. As the meeting ended, however, Ed Brunini, a senior partner in one of Jackson's largest law firms and brother of Jackson's Catholic bishop, Joseph Brunini, put his arm around Binder and said, "Son, you're just too sensitive. You know we all love you. Why, you're the mayor's best friend. But you're just judging us too harshly."

Binder said nothing at first but did a slow burn as Brunini's patronizing remark sank in. Turning to Monsignor Bernard Law, Binder remarked, "Don't you know when they get through with us, you're next? They hate the Catholics worse than they hate the Jews. They always have in Mississippi." With that, he turned and left the meeting.

Binder was exaggerating. The Klan was hostile to Catholics, but its animus toward Jews had always been much more overt and intense. Nonetheless, Binder felt his comments might at least prod the Catholics into speaking out.

Gratifying expressions of support did come in from other quarters, including the Diocesan Council of Catholic Women, which deplored the "cowardly acts of violence." Mayor Allen Thompson, who had remained silent about the black churches, now expressed "shock" that anyone would bomb a house of worship.

"Some of our best people are members of the Jewish faith," Thompson declared in a prepared press statement. "Many of these are descendants of people who helped build this city that we all love and are ready to defend from any and every form of bigotry and violence."

Just as outspoken was Governor Paul Johnson, who also had not spoken out about antiblack terrorism: "It is almost unthinkable that this kind of cowardly assault on a house of worship could be carried out in this civilized state among our civilized people," he said.

The *Clarion-Ledger* ran a letter from Mrs. Robert Levy under the headline "Temple Blast Could Be a Bell That Tolls for All of Jackson." Mrs. Levy, who had taught twenty children in the temple the night before the bombing and whose own two children had been in other classrooms that evening, wrote that the bombing had shocked her Christian friends, and that while it was not the first time they had heard of a synagogue being desecrated, "possibly it is the first time that they really know a Jewish family who worships there.

"They will take this violence more personally," Mrs. Levy wrote. "But the message will not get through. My Christian friends will not see that when my Temple was destroyed, their churches suffered the same fate. And when my children's lives are in danger, so are the lives of their children."

In a more significant departure, the *Clarion-Ledger* printed, in A. B. Albritton's "Magnolia Mirror" column, an attack on the "coward who had terrorized blacks and finally resorted to violence against Jews." Addressing the night riders, Albritton unabashedly underscored the difference in the Mississippi Establishment's response to terrorism when it was directed against whites rather than blacks: "Every now and then you kill a Negro just to show you 'mean business,' but this time you've destroyed a beautiful place of worship where people who share a common belief come together to worship. You've bombed churches before, but never one where white people worship. This is Mississippi and we've had enough. We'll get you and all the rest of your gutless friends."

Scores of Mississippi's Christian ministers, silent while blacks were terrorized, now came forward to express their outrage and, in some cases, their guilt. In an editorial, the *Methodist Advocate* said:

> We are guilty of having allowed a climate to be created about us which lends itself to the propagation of prejudice, a climate based upon opposition to and the open flouting of federal law, and have thus created disrespect for law at all levels. We have been silent in the face of obvious injustice and murderers walk the streets of our state because no jury had the courage to convict them. We have been afraid to get involved in anything that might be the least bit disturbing to the established power structure. Just as long as good men of all faiths remain silent and inert, so long will this violence continue. Just as long as one house of worship is unsafe, so long will all houses of worship be the next target.

Four days after the bombing, Reverend Thomas Tiller, an Episcopalian who served as president of the Jackson Clergy Alliance, which Nussbaum had helped found two months earlier, led a "walk of penance" to the temple by about forty ministers, including three blacks. Armed police officers guarded the marchers, but there were no counterdemonstrators or incidents. The Jackson community had closed ranks around the Jewish congregation and the more vocal segregationists apparently decided to keep their distance.

A new day of understanding and courage had not arrived for all the Jackson clergy, however. Several conscience-stricken ministers who sympathized with Nussbaum and his congregation did some heavy soul-searching but concluded nevertheless that they could not afford to join in the walk of penance. The First Christian Church's minister, Reverend William Harold Edds, and associate minister William E. McKnight wrote Nussbaum a personal letter saying they regretted they could not participate. "Had we chosen to be a part of the walk we would probably need to prepare to leave as the ministers of First Christian Church. Our congregation has . . . grown we believe in the right direction, but the members as well as their pastors have a long way to go. Like other clergymen we too share the agony of frustration in such a time as this."

The two ministers wrote, "Especially are our hearts heavy when we are forced to realize the horrible disease that has afflicted so

many in our State, and in many ways we confess that we share it.
May God have mercy on us!"

And leaders of the largest, most powerful denomination in the
state, the Baptists, were conspicuous by their absence.

Nussbaum was worried about his own safety and that of his wife.
Even the discovery that a flowerpot in his yard had been knocked
over unnerved the rabbi. The FBI reported in a memo that he
"noticed that a small flower pot usually in his garden had been
turned over in the center of his sidewalk. He said he has no pets
around his house and can not imagine how the flower pot had
been turned over. He said he was fearful of picking up the flower
pot and replacing it in the garden. Rabbi Nussbaum was advised
to call the local police and advise them on the possible prowler
and of the flower pot situation and he said he would immediately
do so."

Mrs. Nussbaum later advised the FBI that the Jackson police
had come out to their residence and replaced the flowerpot in the
garden without incident. At Nussbaum's request, the Jackson
Police Department put his house under protective surveillance
during the nighttime. Two officers kept watch over the house every
night of the week, usually parking in the Nussbaums' driveway to
make their presence obvious. Occasionally, coordinating their efforts with the Nussbaums, they would park their patrol car some
distance away, then walk to the house and keep watch from inside.

Ten days after the bombing, J. Edgar Hoover responded to pressure from his good friend Senator James Eastland by ordering
the Jackson field office to step up its investigation and write a
specific report on what was being done to solve the bombing.

Roy Moore sent Hoover a memo outlining how three special
groups of agents were conducting a "vigorous, hard-hitting, im-
aginative" investigation, contacting all known Klansmen and using
"any technique that will bring results." The report discussed giving "concentrated investigative attention" to all suspects, which
meant putting them under tight surveillance and interviewing
them at their homes and businesses with the goal of harassing
and unnerving them enough to force someone to cooperate with
the investigation.

The Jackson FBI report noted that cases previously assigned to agents working on the bombing were being reassigned so the agents could "devote all of their time to the solution of the bombing of Beth Israel Synagogue." More manpower would be "made available as needed," Moore told Hoover.

Now the FBI also secretly began to employ the kind of domestic counterintelligence program, or COINTELPRO, that it had used in its investigation of the 1964 killing of the three civil rights workers in Philadelphia. First used by the Eisenhower administration against the Communist Party in the United States, COINTELPRO often employed extralegal or even illegal methods to disrupt targeted groups and sow discord among them. Although using pressure tactics in criminal cases was not uncommon for law enforcement agencies, COINTELPRO tactics often went further and crippled targeted individuals and organizations without following legal procedures.

"Our program at the moment," the Jackson FBI office said in a message to Hoover, "encompasses exploitation of the date furnished by our sources, especially the provoking of internal dissension among key people in the bombing suspect group. Particular attention is being devoted to provoking a feeling of insecurity among our principal suspects in the fidelity of their associates."

FBI agent Jim Ingram considered many of the Klansmen the bureau was stalking "animals, murderers," and he ordered his men to "just go out and pound on them until you get some results." Agents were ordered to keep suspects on edge by interrogating them frequently, to step up efforts to recruit informants and, wherever possible, to create suspicion among Klansmen that other Klansmen were informing on them.

Three weeks after the synagogue bombing, on the night of October 6, a bomb exploded at the home of Dr. William T. Bush on the campus of predominantly black Tougaloo College near Jackson. Bush, a dean at the college, was white, and the Klan believed he was living with a black woman. Tougaloo was a well-known gathering place for civil rights demonstrators; segregationists considered it a hotbed of Communism.

Although no one was injured, the incident got wide publicity and immediate action from the FBI and other investigative agencies because they assumed it was linked to the synagogue bombing.

They were correct. It was the work of the White Knights. But the agents who immediately swarmed into the field in search of the suspects on their list were pursuing Klansmen who had little or no knowledge of the terror campaign Bowers was conducting. The Tougaloo bomb had been planted by Tarrants.

Three days later, and more than three years after the murders in Philadelphia, Mississippi, eighteen men went on trial on charges of conspiring to violate the civil rights of Chaney, Goodman, and Schwerner. At the center of the conspiracy was Sam Bowers. The FBI had been dogging his steps for years, but Bowers seldom made the kinds of mistakes that tripped up so many of his followers.

He was not like them in temperament or background. Born in 1924 in New Orleans, he grew up in an educated, affluent household. His father, Sam Bowers, Sr., was a salesman from Gulfport. His mother, the former Evangeline Peyton, was the daughter of a well-to-do planter. Young Sam's grandfather, Eaton J. Bowers, a lawyer who served four terms in Congress, from 1903 to 1911, "read and talked constantly to Sam and he used to say he had the most brilliant mind of any child he had ever seen," young Sam's doting mother said.

At Fortier High School in New Orleans—then the city's top public high school—he got excellent grades in science, math and history and developed a passion for the Civil War and its battles that remained with him into adult life.

After the Japanese bombed Pearl Harbor, Sam, then seventeen, joined the navy against the wishes of his mother, who worried that he was "fanatically patriotic." Honorably discharged four years later, he passed a high school equivalency test and enrolled at Tulane University. A year later, he transferred to the University of Southern California, where he studied engineering for almost a year before dropping out. He moved to Laurel and went into the vending and pinball machine business.

An oddball with fixed routines, Bowers ate three meals a day, seven days a week at the Admiral Ben Bow Snack Bar, an all-night coffee shop in Laurel. It was a favorite Klan hangout and, according to a former employee, Bowers would sit at the counter and "make all kinds of scowls and terrible expressions while watching himself in the mirror."

Former associates said Bowers sometimes wore swastika emblems on his arm. On occasion, he was known to click his heels in front of his old dog and throw stiff Nazi salutes, exclaiming, "Heil Hitler!" He was obsessed with guns and explosives and talked for hours about how to make bombs.

When he got mad, he would stalk up and down, raising his voice and clenching his fist. But when President Kennedy was assassinated in 1963, Bowers danced around and, as one of his fellow Klansmen said, "he just thought it was wonderful. He went into happy, crazy acting."

The FBI agents who kept him under surveillance joked that he was "an unasylumed lunatic." But Bowers saw himself as a moral and intellectual descendant of the Founding Fathers, one of a long line of Southern aristocrats who had risen to defend their society's most basic legal and religious values. In a 1965 letter to J. Edgar Hoover, with copies to members of Mississippi's congressional delegation, Bowers complained that a man with his background should not be subjected to "harassment" and "belligerent" treatment by federal authorities: "The first president of the first constituted legislative assembly on this continent, the Virginia House of Burgesses, was my direct lineal ancestor. It was my own privilege to serve as a volunteer in the USN from 1941–45. My grandfather, E.J. Bowers, a former U. S. Congressman at whose knee I received a goodly portion of my education, was freely acknowledged by his contemporaries at the bar to be without peer in his grasp of the basic theory of the purpose of our law."

Bowers exhibited the same boastful, defiant streak when he went on trial in the Philadelphia case. Held in Meridian's massive granite federal courthouse, the trial played to a packed gallery of reporters and spectators for almost two weeks. U.S. District Court judge Harold Cox was no friend to civil rights—he had been known to call blacks "niggers" and "chimpanzees" in his courtroom—but he had made it clear from the outset that he intended to conduct a dignified proceeding.

The prosecutor was enough to sober the defendants too. He was John Doar, chief of the Civil Rights Division of the Justice Department and one of the heroes of the civil rights struggle in the South. The government had amassed an enormous amount of circumstantial evidence buttressed by testimony from Klansmen who had direct knowledge of the events leading up to the Philadelphia murders.

Sitting in the press section, reporters had a good view of Bowers and his fellow defendants, including Lawrence Rainey, the sheriff of Neshoba County, of which Philadelphia was the county seat; Cecil Ray Price, his chief deputy; and Alton Wayne Roberts, the hulking Meridian Klansman who was believed to have personally fired the pistol shots that killed Schwerner and Goodman.

As the jury began its deliberations, the defendants milled around in the corridors, laughing and joking loudly. At one point, Bowers suggested that the bodies that had been recovered from an earthen dam were not really the remains of the three civil rights workers.

"The federal government can get all the bodies it wants from the penitentiary," Bowers said.

"Most likely they're in New Jersey drinking vodka cocktails, or probably in Russia," said Roberts, with a loud guffaw.

While Roberts and his codefendants blustered in the hallway outside the courtroom, the jurors were concluding that they were hopelessly deadlocked. Instead of discharging the panel and declaring a mistrial as he could have done, however, Judge Cox delivered what lawyers call "the dynamite charge"—a stern order to the jury to try harder to reach a verdict.

In the corridor, Roberts mocked the judge: "We've got some dynamite ourselves—for him."

On October 20, 1967, after three days of deliberations, the jury did indeed return with a verdict. It acquitted Sheriff Rainey and seven other defendants, and it reported itself irreconcilably divided on three other Klansmen. But it found seven of the eighteen defendants guilty as charged, including Roberts, Bowers and Price. Judge Cox, saying he "very heartily" endorsed the jury's verdicts, denied bond to Roberts because of the dynamite remark. Glaring at him, the judge declared, "I'm not going to let any wild man loose on civilized society and I want you locked up."

The judge gave him and Bowers the maximum ten-year prison terms. It was the first time a Mississippi jury had convicted members of the Klan—and a white law enforcement officer as well— for crimes committed against civil rights workers. Noting the trial's significance, *The New York Times* praised the verdicts as a "measure of the quiet revolution that is taking place in Southern attitudes—a slow, still faltering, but inexorable conversion to the concept that a single standard of justice must cover whites and Negroes alike."

The convictions brought cheer to the FBI, leading the bureau to hope that it had finally crushed the White Knights. Although the imperial wizard and some of his most violent followers were now under prison sentences, they remained free on appeal bonds. Largely because of the convictions, as well as informants, membership in the White Knights declined dramatically.

On November 1, Rabbi Nussbaum, perhaps believing the days of Klan violence were over, requested that the Jackson police discontinue their protective stakeout on his house.

In Laurel, however, Sam Bowers was far from neutralized. He was busy planning more violence. And the FBI was still looking in the wrong places for those who had bombed the synagogue, unaware that Bowers had drastically altered his method of operation.

Instead of a gang of Klansmen, Bowers was using only one or two people to carry out the new series of attacks he had launched. Planning was confined to the same tiny cell. And two of the key individuals—Tarrants and Ainsworth—either were not known to the police as White Knights or were living underground in distant "safe houses" beyond the reach of FBI pressure in Jackson.

One of the new attacks came shortly after midnight on November 15, 1967, in Laurel. An explosion ripped through the brick ranch-style parsonage of Reverend Allen Johnson, a black Methodist minister and NAACP leader long active in civil rights. The parsonage was located next door to St. Paul's Church, the home church of Metropolitan Opera star Leontyne Price, who had sung there several times. It was not far from the home of Sam Bowers.

The night before the attack, Tarrants had driven to the Johnson house with Bowers accompanying him as guide. With the target identified, Tarrants drove Bowers back to his house on Fourth Avenue. The leader of the White Knights would have a solid alibi when the police came calling. Then Tarrants returned to the Johnson house, crept up through the covering darkness and planted his bundle of dynamite in the carport beside the front of the house.

Just after midnight, he touched off the fuse with a cigarette lighter, tiptoed away and drove slowly off. Ten minutes later, when the fuse burned down to the detonator cap, he was well clear of the neighborhood.

Johnson, his wife and their four children had gone to bed at about 11:30 P.M., so they escaped serious injury. The blast destroyed Johnson's car and carport, hurled a heavy piano across the living room, and made a shambles of much of the house. "Except for the mercy of God," Johnson said, surveying the debris, "I don't see how it was possible for us to keep from getting hurt. And if this had happened an hour earlier, it would have gotten my whole family. My babies were playing the piano about eleven o'clock."

Four nights later, Tarrants struck again, this time accompanied by Kathy Ainsworth.

A layman engaged in religious work with poor people in Jackson, Robert Kochtitzky was active in civil rights. He had worked with Nussbaum and Reverend Johnson on the Committee of Concern. He had urged his minister, Reverend Warren Hamby of the Galloway Memorial Methodist Church, to speak out against racial violence. And he had been credited in news accounts with originating the idea of the "walk of penance" after the Temple Beth Israel bombing. His wife, Kay, worked with Ken Dean at the Council on Human Relations. The Kochtitzkys had occasionally had blacks as houseguests. There had also been a report, unfounded but widely disseminated in a White Citizens Council publication, that the Kochtitzky house on Poplar Street had been the site of a meeting between Stokely Carmichael, the civil rights leader, and Robert Kennedy when Kennedy was attorney general of the United States.

In hindsight, Kochtitzky also concluded that because of his name the Klan may have concluded, mistakenly, that he was Jewish.

On the night of November 19, Kochtitzky and Reverend John Adams, a Methodist minister from Washington who was staying with him, returned home after a meeting and sat in the living room talking until about 11:00 P.M. Mrs. Kochtitzky and her six-month-old son were also in the house.

Minutes after the two men went to bed, a powerful bomb exploded on the front porch of the two-story house. It tore away the porch, ripped through the front wall, shredded the couch on which they had been sitting. The blast shattered windows in the baby's room, showering his crib with shards of glass; miraculously, the child was unhurt, as were the three adults.

When police responded to the blast, a neighbor reported overhearing one of them say, "The son of a bitch got what he deserved. What did he expect?"

Early the next morning, a Sunday, Kochtitzky's pastor, Reverend Hamby, came by. A distraught Kochtitzky had telephoned at midnight to tell him of the bombing and to demand to know what the minister was going to do. Surveying the damage and recognizing how close his parishioner and his family had come to death or serious injury, Hamby regretted failing to speak out against the earlier violence. The Methodist minister in fact had done more for the civil rights cause than most Mississippi clergymen. He too had served on the Committee of Concern. His church had hosted weekly interracial, interfaith breakfast meetings for the committee, and Kochtitzky, as well as Reverend Johnson and Rabbi Nussbaum, had attended the sessions regularly.

Returning home, Hamby quickly wrote out a statement to read from his pulpit at church services later in the morning. He told his congregation he was offering his statement in an awareness of the truth once spoken by Abraham Lincoln: "To sin by silence when they should protest makes cowards of men."

"I speak with the full awareness that many of you will perhaps be disturbed that I elect to do so," he said. "I speak because of the greater disturbance of my own conscience should I fail to do so."

The bombing, he said, was committed by "paranoic cowards who would by their dastardly deeds of violence keep alive the fear that has spawned their breed and offered them not only silence and sanctuary for their deeds but a mandate to continue them under the illusion of public approbation.

"Let us not, however, draw a small circle of guilt, for we are all indicted," Hamby declared.

> The so-called decent and responsible people of our city, state and section are the Sauls at whose feet lie the clothes of the whole affair (along with numerous repetitions of it in recent

weeks). Upon our consciences the whole matter must rest. Justice Brandeis once said: "The greatest menace to freedom is an inert people."

Who is to blame? Every pulpit where justice and mercy and goodwill have not been enough proclaimed; every alleged Christian who has thought more of his or her prejudices than of seeking the will of God and the spirit of Jesus Christ in attitude and behavior; every newspaper that has defended indefensible positions and voiced its own prejudices; the responsible elected officials of city and state who have been more concerned with expedience than integrity—here, my friends, is the accumulated and collective guilt that is ours.

Soon after the Kochtitzky bombing, an FBI agent let Binder listen to a tape-recorded conversation involving two Klansmen that was so chilling it gave Binder a new sense of urgency.

Listening to the tape in an FBI car, the lawyer heard one of the Klansmen propose planting a firebomb in the temple's air-conditioning system, attached to a timing device that would set off the firebomb at 8:30 P.M. when the synagogue would be filled with worshipers. The result would be a mass Number Four. Everyone in the congregation would be suffocated, the Klansman said.

The prospect repelled the other Klansman. The explosion would kill children, he said.

"The hell with that," the first Klansman declared. "Little Jew bastards grow up to be big Jew devils. Kill 'em while they're young."

Binder thought of his own three small children. He vowed to do whatever it took to catch those who were responsible. From that moment on, he and Joe Harris and some of the other young men of the congregation who were meeting periodically to discuss ways to catch the terrorists began carrying pistols to services. Even when sitting on the bema next to the rabbi, Binder was armed.

"If the Kluckers come to the temple again," he told friends, "we'll shoot first and talk about it later."

5

Two days before Thanksgiving, Arene Nussbaum returned to Jackson from visiting the Nussbaums' daughter, Leslie Rubenstein, in New York. The rabbi met her at the airport and on the way home they stopped at Morrison's Cafeteria in North Jackson for a leisurely dinner. Nussbaum listened distractedly to the news from their daughter.

A little after eight o'clock, they returned to their ranch-style house. He watched television and Arene wrote letters until about 10:45 P.M., when they retired. He was soon asleep in his bedroom at the northeast corner of the house. His wife, whose bedroom was directly behind his, was reading in bed.

A car with its headlights doused pulled slowly up to the curb in front of their house at about eleven o'clock. The driver, a tall, slim figure, got out and walked about forty yards across the lawn to a spot near the front entrance. He placed a box under an air-conditioning unit jutting out from the dining room, then quickly returned to the car. A woman on the passenger side leaned over and opened the door for him. He slipped behind the wheel. The car moved off down the street slowly.

Forty minutes later, a powerful explosion ripped through the Nussbaum home, transforming the kitchen into a sea of glass and turning the dining room air conditioner into a mass of twisted metal that went hurtling through the dining room and into the living room. The force of the blast collapsed the ceilings of the Nussbaum's bedrooms, raining down glass and other debris. The Nussbaums staggered into the hallway.

By the time Nussbaum got to a telephone, the lines were already busy. Within minutes, the air was filled with the scream of sirens as ambulances, fire engines and police cars sped to the scene.

Al Binder was at his home about three miles away when he heard the explosion. Figuring immediately that it had to be the Nussbaums' house, he jumped in his car and drove at breakneck speed. He arrived to see the Nussbaums stumbling out a back door in their bathrobes. They were picking splinters of glass from their faces and hair, and Arene Nussbaum was crying hysterically.

Ken Dean had been about to go to bed when he heard the explosion. Before he could reach his telephone, it was ringing. Jim Ingram was calling to ask if he knew the source of the blast. Dean, who lived only four blocks from Nussbaum, said he was not sure, but it could not have been far from where he lived. Ingram hung up. Dean began to dress, planning to follow the sirens that were now flooding the neighborhood, when the telephone rang again. It was Ingram saying the Jackson police had just informed him it was the rabbi's house. Dean dashed for his car.

Police officers and FBI agents were already swarming over the house and yard when Dean jumped out of his car and rushed to comfort the Nussbaums. The rabbi, he thought, appeared to be in a state of shock but was aware of what had happened. Nussbaum kept saying over and over that it was the work of the Ku Klux Klan, that the atmosphere for violence had been created by religious leaders and others who had done nothing to stop it. Nussbaum asked Dean to contact Reverend Douglas Hudgins, pastor of Jackson's all-powerful First Baptist Church, and urge him to issue a statement denouncing the bombing.

Reporters, television cameramen and neighbors were arriving. As the Jackson police began to rope off the area to preserve evidence, two white teenage boys were seen running down a nearby street. Two officers chased after them. The youths, it turned out, had been peering through a neighbor's bedroom window two blocks away when they heard the explosion and had come to see what had happened. Frightened by the police and ambulance sirens, they had tried to run away.

With radio and television carrying the news of the explosion throughout the city, word spread among those at the scene that Governor Paul Johnson and some of Jackson's most prominent religious and political leaders planned to visit the rabbi. Nussbaum, feeling poorly dressed for the occasion, made his way through the debris to his shattered bedroom, where he changed into a sport shirt and trousers.

In the morning, Dean telephoned Hudgins and passed on Nussbaum's request. Hudgins' response so startled Dean that he never forgot it. "He told me that he resented my call," Dean said, "and that he could take care of his own business—never to call him again. I told him that the rabbi had suggested I call, and that he was the most influential pastor in town, thus having a responsibility in the matter. He slammed the phone down as I awaited his reply."

A half hour later, Dean returned to the Nussbaum residence and found the rabbi standing on what remained of his back porch rebuking the Baptist minister in person.

Lean, with wavy salt-and-pepper hair, the sixty-one-year-old Hudgins was an imposing figure, highly respected in Jackson and throughout Southern Baptist circles. He was an Establishment preacher and an unshakable conservative on social and theological matters who once said, "While some people are very vocal in their belief we must be activists, there's very little of this in Mississippi."

Nussbaum had never liked Hudgins. Now he shook with anger as Hudgins started to say how sorry he was about the bombing. Standing beside Hudgins were Governor Johnson and Lucian Harvey, Jr., a businessman and president of the Jackson Rotary Club. Dean, Binder, Ingram and Joe Harris were looking on and Charles Quinn of NBC was filming the scene. Nussbaum began wagging his finger under Hudgins' nose: "If you had spoken out from your pulpit after the synagogue was bombed and told your people it was wrong to have done that, this wouldn't have happened! Don't tell me now how sorry you are. Those son-of-a-guns attacked me and my family! They've attacked my house! I don't want to hear how sorry you are!"

Some of the witnesses were shocked at the vehemence of Nussbaum's attack. They looked at each other in disbelief that a rabbi—one who had promoted closer contacts and cooperation among different religions—could deliver such an attack on Mississippi's most prominent religious figure. Finally, Nussbaum told

Hudgins: "Doug, if you're really sorry about this, get on the pulpit Sunday and tell your people this is wrong. Talk to all those segregationists that fill up your church."

With that, the rabbi abruptly wheeled around, pointed his finger at Dean and declared: "You're a white Christian—a Baptist, the worst kind for Jews. You've got a responsibility for what happened too. It's the Sunday-school lessons from the New Testament in Baptist churches that lead people to commit such terrible acts."

Finishing with Dean, Nussbaum turned to Ingram. "When is the FBI going to put a stop to this?" Ingram would remember Nussbaum as "totally devastated that night and never quite the same afterwards."

FBI agents, fearing for the Nussbaums' safety, took them to a motel hideaway where they could stay temporarily with Jackson police providing protection. The FBI arranged transportation. Plainclothes officers drove unmarked cars. Not even leaders of his congregation knew where the rabbi was staying.

"Rabbi Nussbaum presently residing in local Jackson motel under fictitious name," an FBI report noted. "Will remain in this guise until at least 12/1/67."

Once again, FBI agents descended in force on the White Knights.

For more than three years, in a pattern that had been established with the Philadelphia murders and the Dahmer case and continued through numerous incidents that followed, the FBI had been waging a war of nerves against all known members of the Klan. After each episode of suspected Klan violence, Moore subjected leaders of the organization to lengthy interrogations designed not only to pry information from the Klansmen but to unsettle and frighten them. The unstated message was that the FBI was watching, looking for an opportunity to arrest them.

As Moore remarked, "Klan members were sick and tired of being visited all the time. Every time there was an incident, our job was to go out there and make each Klan leader account for his people."

One of Bowers' lieutenants was standing in his bathroom when Moore arrived. "Roy," he said in a weary voice, "when you gonna cut this stuff out?"

The next day was Thanksgiving Eve and Nussbaum sat amid the rubble at his house telling reporters that he was thankful to be alive but that Jackson officials should increase the twenty-five-thousand-dollar reward they were offering for the arrest and conviction of those responsible for the bombings to one hundred thousand dollars. He complained bitterly that no one had been arrested in any of the previous bombings and declared that the Ku Klux Klan and the Americans for Preservation of the White Race either were guilty of the terrorism or at least had provided the stimulus for it.

Nussbaum's anger did not stop with the Klan and the APWR. The bombing seemed to crack open a reservoir of bitter feelings about his own flock: the years of strain their moral equivocation had caused him; the unmistakable personal animosity of many; the paucity of close friends; the gulf that had never closed between the prickly Canadian who had seen so much of life's harshness and the accommodating Southern Jews who clung so tightly to their comfort.

Some of his neighbors made it clear they would prefer that he leave the neighborhood. He told the FBI that one congregant who lived in the immediate area had urged him to move, but "seemed scared and concerned with his own welfare."

Nussbaum was right about the anxiety of his neighbors. But the great majority of his congregation rallied behind their rabbi—even people such as Joe Harris who did not care for him or agree with him. "The bombing made people so doggone mad," Harris said, "that a lot of people—even though we didn't particularly like Nussbaum—weren't going to let 'em do it to us as a group."

On November 22, a day after the bombing, about fifty business and professional leaders of the Jewish community met at the Sun 'n Sand Motel. The discussion was intense. At one point, Joe Harris jumped up and shouted, "Let's go kill the sons of bitches! We know who they are!"

"No, no!" several people shouted.

Harris' father-in-law, Sam Millstein, told Harris that violence was no answer. Manny Crystal, who had called the meeting, agreed.

"Why not?" demanded Harris. "They tried to kill the rabbi. He was in the house. His wife was in the house. They planted a bomb in front of his house. Why the hell can't we go kill them? We know who they are. It's Danny Joe Hawkins and his daddy."

"We just can't do that," Crystal declared. "That's not the way we do things."

"That may not be the way you do things," Harris said, "but until something like that is done, you're gonna get nowhere. I say let's go kill 'em."

Eventually, it was decided that Crystal and Rabbi Nussbaum would go to see Mayor Thompson and press him to rally the Jackson community behind greater cooperation with the FBI in its efforts to catch the terrorists. When Crystal called to request an appointment, Thompson agreed to see them the next day. Their expectations were not high as they drove to City Hall, however. They had dealt with Thompson before. Politically and personally, he had little stomach for taking on the Klan.

Thompson's office was on the first floor of the four-story white-columned colonial-style City Hall, which had been built with slave labor in 1846–47. Yankee forces had torched Jackson three different times during the Civil War but the City Hall had been spared, perhaps because, as a large plaque at the front of the building proclaims, it was "used as a hospital for both Union and Confederate Soldiers during the War Between the States."

The mayor greeted Crystal and Nussbaum as they entered his spacious office, then sat facing them at his desk, flanked by a large American flag and a Mississippi flag, which incorporates the stars and bars of the old Confederate banner. Before the three of them got much beyond pleasantries, Thompson let them know he didn't think the rabbi's house would have been bombed in the first place if the rabbi hadn't been involved in civil rights activity. Besides, Thompson said, the city already was pressing a full-scale investigation by its police department and was offering a twenty-five-thousand-dollar reward for information leading to the arrest and conviction of the bombers.

If the Jews wanted more community support, the mayor advised, then they should "participate more in community activities." He suggested they become more involved in the Chamber of Commerce. The tenor of Thompson's remarks did not surprise

Crystal and Nussbaum, but the suggestion about the Chamber was particularly galling. The Chamber had opened its membership to Jews, but as Crystal knew from long years as a businessman in Jackson, it had never permitted a Jew to serve as an officer.

"Your Honor, we belong to the Chamber," Crystal declared, "but as long as we have belonged we have never had the opportunity of being elected to the Chamber's board of directors. You put out a list of potential members every year, and sometimes we're on the list, but we've never been elected."

Thompson insisted this was because the Jews had not participated enough in Chamber activities. When Crystal disputed his contention, the mayor, in a condescending ploy that Crystal had been subjected to several times in the past, said, "Manny, we need men like you in our community. I'm going to work things out. I want you to be part of what's going on in Jackson."

The report of the meeting that Crystal and Nussbaum brought back to their colleagues convinced the Jews that they would have to look to themselves—with the help of the FBI, not Jackson police or city officials. Binder told Roy Moore, "We're going to defend the temple. We're going to guard it at night and we're going to protect the rabbi. We're committed to defending our homes and we're going to find out who the people are that are attacking our homes, and if anything happens to us we expect the Jewish people to support our families."

"I understand," Moore told them, "and you can expect the full cooperation of the FBI."

Crystal called another meeting of men from the congregation at the Sun 'n Sand Motel. Binder urged that they add to the city's twenty-five-thousand-dollar reward. Again a raucous debate erupted. Several of the younger members suggested forming a vigilante group. Harris, in a comment recorded by the FBI, declared that for only a thousand dollars he "could get the Mafia to come to Jackson, Mississippi, to break some arms and legs." Once more, cooler heads prevailed. About forty of the men pledged to add a total of twenty-five thousand dollars to the city's reward fund. But they insisted on remaining anonymous.

The clutch of fear was everywhere, especially among the Jews. Adults routinely checked under the hoods of their cars in the morning to be sure bombs had not been planted during the night.

Frightened children asked their parents if it was safe to attend classes at the synagogue or if the temple would be bombed again.

On Friday evening, three days after the bombing, Nussbaum was delivering a sermon at Temple Beth Israel when he was passed a note from Binder. "I don't know where you are staying or where they're hiding you," it said, "but you're welcome to stay in my house."

Later that evening, after the service, Nussbaum telephoned Binder and said, "I can't tell you where I am, but did you mean what you said in your note?"

"Hell yes, I meant it, can I come get you?" Binder said.

"No, they'll bring me to you," said Nussbaum, and a short while later the Nussbaums arrived in an FBI car. The agents left after providing the rabbi with a car without a license plate.

The Nussbaums stayed with the Binders for the next week. As Binder later recalled, "The rabbi couldn't sleep at night, so we would stay up while he would rave and rant about what we could do or couldn't do in trying to protect ourselves from violence. We realized we could not depend on the police department; it was riddled with Kluckers. We couldn't depend on our local friends and we couldn't depend on the influence we had or thought we had in the community.

"And I told him we were going to have to help ourselves. I was a second-generation [Mississippi] Jew. I wasn't about to leave this state. I had always loved it here—I had my friends here and I came from a small town where I knew as much about the New Testament as I did the Old."

On Sunday morning, Binder and Nussbaum made sure they turned on the radio in time to hear the regular broadcast of services from the First Baptist Church. They wanted to see if Reverend Hudgins would speak out against the terrorists. The sermon was a curious blend of response and evasion. Hudgins talked about what a terrible thing the bombing had been and how it was wrong for anyone to bomb another's house.

Nussbaum noted wryly that he "didn't even mention it was a rabbi's house that got bombed." And the Baptist minister concluded with the extraordinary comment "The Lord works in mysterious ways." Binder and Nussbaum found the remark more than fatuous. It seemed to suggest the violence was part of a divine plan. They were more convinced than ever that the Jews could expect little help from the larger community.

A week later, Nussbaum traveled to Lexington, Mississippi, which had no resident rabbi, to conduct services. The Mississippi State Highway Patrol provided an escort. The situation was still considered so dangerous for Nussbaum that his whereabouts were known to few outside the FBI and some police officials. The rabbi later notified the FBI that he and Mrs. Nussbaum would be moving into an apartment while their house was being repaired.

An FBI report noted that he would live there under an assumed name and that his telephone would be unlisted. Only the bureau— not even his family and friends—would have his address.

FBI agents questioned almost every member of the Temple Beth Israel congregation. They turned up little hard evidence, but a lot of concern that the rabbi's continuing presence posed a threat to himself and to the community. One member told the FBI that the rabbi should resign "for his own welfare" because he did not want to see "anything happen to him or his family."

Nussbaum, according to an FBI report, told agents that there was only one member of his congregation who might be behind the bombing of his residence. The suspect's name was censored from a copy of the report the FBI released under the Freedom of Information Act, but the Bureau's subsequent questioning of John Hart Lewis, the wealthy home builder who despised Nussbaum and warned him that he might be the target of a bombing, left no doubt he was the one Nussbaum suspected.

Two agents questioned Lewis at length at his residence—a two-story, twenty-two-hundred-square-foot redbrick house on a tiny V-shaped lot that bordered an area of ramshackle houses occupied by blacks. The house, surrounded by a large metal fence and a towering brick wall, with watchdogs roaming the yard, was known to Jacksonians as "the fort" or "the battleship."

From the agents' questioning, Lewis concluded that he was suspected of being implicated in the bombing, or at least of knowing something about it.

"Do you think I did it?" he asked.

"Well you might not have done it, but did you have somebody else do it?"

"No," replied Lewis. He explained that he had warned Nussbaum he might be bombed simply because he realized that, given
the rabbi's civil rights activities and the Klan's pattern of violence,
it was a distinct possibility.

Lewis made no attempt to conceal his dislike for Nussbaum.
An FBI report quoted him as saying he disliked the rabbi not
for personal reasons "but because of the rabbi's civil rights
ideas, his arrogance, his orneriness, his impetuousness and his
outspokenness on civil rights matters, while acting as spokesman for the synagogue thus endangering the synagogue and its
members."

Lewis told the FBI he emphatically opposed Nussbaum's policy
of permitting non-Jewish organizations to use the synagogue as a
meeting area and felt it would cause hate organizations to attack
the Jewish community. His first cousin, John Hart Asher, had
opposed the policy at a synagogue meeting, Lewis said, but the
rabbi became "highly upset and ranted before the congregation"
that they opposed the policy to keep blacks out of the synagogue.
Lewis said he warned Nussbaum that if "the present policy at the
synagogue was continued, the rabbi was going to find himself
bombed."

"Then, to emphasize his point," the FBI report noted, "Lewis
pointed out to the interviewing agents that his prediction had
come to pass."

Lewis declared he would be delighted to see Nussbaum leave
the Jackson area, but had been advised by the synagogue's board
of trustees that the rabbi was under a contract that had five years
to run. In that case, Lewis advised "that as long as the rabbi was
affiliated with the synagogue, he felt there was going to be trouble
in the Jackson area for the Jewish community."

A few weeks later, Binder and Robert Berman, who was president
of the Beth Israel congregation at the time, invited Roy Moore
to address the Men's Club at the temple. Moore brought pictures
of some of the Klansmen he suspected of violent acts. Berman
took a stack of the three-by-five-inch head shots home and put
them on top of a dresser. Several days later he arrived home from
work to find his housekeeper shaking with fear. That day's Jackson
Clarion-Ledger had carried the photographs of two Klansmen

being sought in a shoot-out with Jackson police, and she had recognized them as two men who had been painting the inside of his house.

"You better lock your door and car tonight," the housekeeper told Berman. "Your housepainters' pictures are in the paper."

"What in the world are you talking about?" Berman asked.

She showed him the pictures in the *Clarion-Ledger*. "Oh, my God," he said, and rushed to his dresser to see if the photos and information supplied by the FBI matched those in the newspaper. Both the photos and the dossiers were gone.

Berman contacted Moore, told him what had happened and asked if Moore thought he or his family might be in any danger. Moore told him to stay alert and keep in touch with the FBI, but said that "seeing the pictures at your house probably was the best thing that could have happened because now they'll know you know who they are and will worry that many other people have photos of them."

On December 20, 1967, the FBI got what could have been a major break. Cruising the streets of tiny Collins, Mississippi, on a cold, rainy evening, Buster Lott, the night marshal, became curious about a car with Alabama license plates that had pulled into a closed filling station. Lott stopped to investigate. The driver, who produced an Alabama driver's license, had no satisfactory explanation for what he was doing so far from home in such an unlikely place. And Lott seemed to recognize the name on the driver's license of the other man in the car: Samuel H. Bowers.

Lott took the two into custody. On the front seat of their car, hidden beneath a sweater, he found a .45-caliber machine gun. The FBI and state police were called in. Thomas Albert Tarrants III was charged with illegal possession of a machine gun—a federal violation.

Tarrants' cover was blown. He and Bowers were publicly linked.

They had come to Collins to machine-gun the home of a black man whose civil rights efforts had drawn their attention, but the authorities were unaware of that. For the moment, though, the FBI made no connection between Tarrants and the bombings and he was released on bond.

Moore and his agents were still looking in all the wrong places.

The FBI believed Bowers was relying on the sort of Klansmen who had always done his dirty work.

As pressure on the FBI to solve the bombings mounted, the bureau turned up the heat on all known Klan suspects, not least among them the volatile Danny Joe Hawkins. On one occasion, Danny Joe and his mother, Johnnie Mae, reacted so belligerently when agents appeared at their house that the agents called for reinforcements.

FBI memos described Danny Joe as cursing and "yelling incoherently" and reported that, accompanied by his mother and his wife, Kathy, a beautician, he advanced toward the agents "in a fit of rage" and shouted: "You God damn son of a bitches. Set one foot on my property and I'll kill you."

His mother pushed agent Sam Jennings, shouting angrily, "You dirty sons of bitches, you'd better leave here." When the backup car arrived, the Hawkinses retired into the house.

The bureau considered the Hawkins family one of the meanest and most violent families it had encountered anywhere in Mississippi. Danny Joe (baptized Joe Daniel) was twenty-four years old in 1967 and was ranked among Bowers' most trusted night riders. One FBI memo referred to him as "a key man in the hit squad." The memo also noted that Bowers had been in contact with Robert Bolivar DePugh, leader of the Minuteman, a violent, paramilitary group and one of the FBI's most wanted fugitives— and warned that Bowers, Hawkins and DePugh were "all considered armed and dangerous."

FBI agents and Jackson police often made spot checks of Danny Joe's residence three or four times a night during their bombing investigations. Bureau bulletins reminded agents on several occasions that both Danny Joe and his father, Joe Denver Hawkins, forty-four, a construction worker, were known to carry firearms and explosives.

Employed on the loading dock of a trucking terminal, Danny Joe Hawkins weighed a solid 170 pounds and stood five feet ten inches tall. He had thick, dark brown hair and eyebrows and was Hollywood handsome. Tattooed on his left upper arm was "KAT," for his wife, Kathy. They had a six-year-old son named Jefferson Davis.

When Danny Joe was growing up, his father worked for many years with the Shelby Construction Company, a nationwide building firm that Danny Joe called "a big Jew outfit." The family moved frequently. As a teenager, Danny Joe was often in trouble and was picked up once for petty theft. He quit school in the ninth grade at the age of sixteen. Two years later he participated in the violent protest at Ole Miss, and a week after that he got his first visit from FBI agents. An article in the *White Patriot,* a publication of the Americans for the Preservation of the White Race, contended that the FBI threatened and intimidated Hawkins. He denied being intimidated, but he said—and FBI sources confirmed—that the agents did offer him money and told him he could be driving a Cadillac if he would testify against the leaders of the Ole Miss riot. He refused.

Later, sensing his connection to the Mississippi bombings, the bureau kept constant pressure on Danny Joe and his wife, following them and interviewing them frequently where they worked. On one occasion, the hot-tempered Hawkins responded by telephoning Moore and telling him, "You better tell your damn goons to leave my wife alone."

"I'll escort you up the courthouse steps one day," Moore answered.

"I'll see you in hell," Hawkins shot back.

Hawkins' nerves might fray, but the FBI did not crack him, and his toughness was to prove costly for the bureau and for Mississippi's Jews. Danny Joe, more than anyone on the FBI's target list, could have provided the elusive link between the White Knights and Tarrants.

No wonder Moore was frustrated. What with the unsolved bombings and now a fresh series of cross burnings that were spreading renewed terror, the FBI agent was in a foul mood when Ken Fairley, a Jackson *Clarion-Ledger* reporter, stopped by his office.

Moore was "really upset," said Fairley, and "said, 'I'm not going to have this kind of violence in this town.' And knowing Roy, I know he meant it."

Fairley, who later would go into police work himself, recognized Moore's irritability as part of a wider frustration that extended to state law enforcement officers. The authorities in Mississippi might not sympathize with the civil rights movement and those who supported it, but the Klan's brazen flouting of the law was giving both the state and its police a bad name.

"The best thing we could do is booby-trap a church and let 'em set it on fire and blow 'em up," one of the state investigators told Fairley, "and nobody would say anything about it."

"That wouldn't exactly have met due process standards," Fairley said, "but that's how they felt."

It was an idea whose time was drawing nearer.

6

The way Al Binder saw it, the Jews of Jackson were virtually friendless. They could not look to the city fathers or the religious leaders—or to the police force, which was riddled with Klan sympathizers. The Jews' only reliable allies, he concluded, were Roy Moore and the FBI. Although they made an unlikely team, Binder and Moore inevitably were drawn together.

Binder was political, gregarious and socially ambitious, a short, stocky, cigar-smoking spellbinder on his way to wealth and a certain fame as a criminal defense lawyer. He had never taken his religion very seriously. He was a latecomer to Temple Beth Israel, though his views on handling the White Knights had quietly prevailed.

Moore, solidly built and of medium height, was the personification of the FBI's straight-arrow legend. From the tips of his regulation black wing-tipped shoes to the top of his close-cropped hair, he was a no-nonsense pursuer of criminals. He had no time for storytelling, social climbing or politics—except the Kremlinesque survival politics of the bureau, which he played skillfully. Moore talked in clipped sentences laced with law enforcement jargon. He drove his men to exhaustion but commanded total loyalty because he worked as hard as they did. He was the ultimate disciple of J. Edgar Hoover, though he was prepared to bend the director's idiosyncratic rules when the need arose.

For all their differences, Binder and Moore would prove to be an effective team—two utterly pragmatic men who shared a preference for action over talk and a determination to lift the scourge of Klan violence.

Roy Moore grew up in Harrisburg, Illinois, a small town on the
Ohio River in the heart of the coalfields. His father ran the hard-
ware store, and Moore attributed his early knowledge of bombs
to the fact that the store supplied dynamite for the mines.

After graduating from high school, he joined the marines and
quickly took to the disciplined life of the corps. Promoted to
corporal, he was sent to the Quantico marine base near Washington, where he taught marksmanship to recruits at the FBI
training school. There he was so impressed by the young college-
bred agents that he resolved to join the bureau when his three-
year enlistment was over. Knowing the FBI preferred men with
college degrees, he studied accounting, got a degree and, in 1940,
became a special agent.

He specialized in investigating sabotage during World War II
and established a record as a painstaking investigator. He was an
innovator and a risk taker. Other agents were so fearful of Hoover
and the possibility of exile to Butte, Montana—the bureau's
equivalent of Siberia—that they went strictly by the book. But if
Moore saw an unconventional way to make progress on an investigation, or to assert jurisdiction over a case he thought deserved
FBI attention, he would try it.

In 1955, while assigned to the Denver field office, he directed
the investigation of a United Airlines plane crash that made his
name in the bureau and set a precedent that the FBI follows to
this day. The plane, bound from Denver to Portland, Oregon,
exploded and crashed eleven minutes after takeoff; thirty-nine
passengers and five crew members were killed. The local sheriff
asked Moore for help.

The FBI had never before investigated the cause of a plane
crash and had no apparent jurisdiction, but Moore ordered agents
to the crash scene. To cover himself, he located a wartime sabotage
statute giving the FBI peacetime authority to investigate inter-
ference with communications, transportation or anything else that
could be vital to prosecuting a war. It was enough to hold his
superiors at bay while he pressed his inquiry.

Resourceful as always, Moore borrowed two hundred enlisted
men from a nearby army outfit and put them shoulder to shoulder
to search for evidence. He commandeered two air force trucks
and outfitted them with electromagnets, which picked up thou-

sands of pieces of the plane and six remnants of the bomb. Thirty-five years later he could recall the smallest details of the crime scene: "It was two miles long and a mile wide and we had to get [the evidence] out within twenty-four hours because we had a snowstorm coming over the Rockies. We brought it back into Denver and laid it out in a hangar and started manufacturing the baggage compartment of the plane. We found the hole in the Denver baggage compartment."

Studying the passenger list, Moore turned up only one person from Denver, a woman named Daisy King, whose son Jack had been in trouble with the law. Digging into his background, Moore discovered that he had studied electrical wiring and that recently he had taken out an insurance policy on his mother's life. After intensive interrogation by Moore, King broke down and confessed.

Nine years later, Moore's thoroughness broke new ground for the FBI again, this time in combating Klan terrorism. The pressure to produce had come straight from the top. President Lyndon B. Johnson, faced with rising national concern over the three missing civil rights workers, knew he would have to institute major changes in federal policy. Johnson, like John F. Kennedy, had recognized that vigorous federal support for the civil rights movement would threaten Democratic political support in the South. Like Kennedy, he had sought to win a measure of Southern cooperation through conciliation and negotiation.

But the tactics of restraint had met with only limited success. Uncompromising resistance to equal rights for blacks remained the policy of the great majority of public officials below the Mason-Dixon line, and the disappearance and apparent murder of Schwerner, Chaney and Goodman suggested that, where civil rights activity was concerned, even the most basic guarantees of human safety would not be provided. Johnson sent Allen Dulles, the retired director of the Central Intelligence Agency, on a fact-finding mission to Jackson.

After two days of conferring with state and local officials, civil rights workers and business leaders, Dulles returned to Washington and recommended that FBI forces in Mississippi be increased and instructed to "control and prosecute terroristic activity" by the Klan and the Americans for the Preservation of the White

Race. At the same time, Dulles called on the National Council of Churches and other groups sponsoring the Mississippi Freedom Summer program to warn students that if they entered Mississippi they would be in "very, very grave danger."

The FBI had maintained a full-fledged field office in the Mississippi capital during World War II, but after the war the office was closed and Jackson was served only by resident agents. Now Johnson quickly embraced the idea of an expanded FBI presence in Mississippi, hoping to head off demands for even stronger federal intervention.

With civil rights volunteers pouring into the state and elected officials across the South breathing defiance of the law, the pressure on Washington to act had become irresistible. A nationwide Harris poll found that an overwhelming majority of Americans favored sending federal troops to Mississippi if the violence escalated further.

By late June, Hoover had more than one hundred FBI agents in Mississippi, but the massive ground search for the three civil rights workers, coupled with a growing flood of civil rights complaints, overwhelmed them. Hoover decided the only answer was to reopen a field office in Jackson and staff it with as many agents as it took to get the job done.

Moore, at fifty, was eligible for early retirement and was weighing an offer from the Hilton Hotels Corporation to head its security operations worldwide when Hoover called him on July 1. The director wanted him to go to Jackson. Moore would have ten days to obtain space, equipment and personnel sufficient for an official opening—to be attended by Hoover himself. Moore never gave early retirement another thought.

In Jackson, he rented the seventh and eighth floors of the Unifirst Savings and Loan Bank Building, then directed an almost around-the-clock push that somehow had the office ready on time for the dedication ceremonies. On July 10, Hoover and a covey of aides arrived for the official dedication aboard *Air Force One*—specially assigned for the occasion by President Johnson to underline the importance of the office.

Before making such trips, the director, always sensitive to criticism, insisted on thorough briefings on "friends and enemies" he might encounter. The confidential briefing book he carried with him to Jackson left no doubt that the bureau was prepared to embrace some of the state's staunchest segregationists so long as they were supportive of the FBI. The book called Jackson mayor Allen Thompson "adamant" in opposing integration, but "a firm believer in law and order." Joe Patterson, the Mississippi attorney general, "although critical of Supreme Court decision and the Department of Justice, has always expressed admiration for Mr. Hoover and the FBI." The FBI's relationship with the arch-segregationists who ran the Jackson papers—Robert Hederman and his brother Thomas—had been "very favorable," and Hoover had corresponded with them about their "favorable articles" on the FBI.

Hoover was advised to be wary of Robert A. Hauberg, the U.S. attorney in Jackson, because during a conference with Attorney General Robert F. Kennedy on civil rights cases, Hauberg had "contradicted Mr. Hoover on several occasions which placed the Director and Bureau in embarrassing situations several times."

To prepare Hoover for a press conference, the briefing book included a list of possible questions and recommended answers. Some of the answers underscored the FBI's contention that the South was no different from the rest of the country when it came to violence and that Communism was a driving force behind the civil rights movement:

> Question—Is there any Communist Party activity among the civil rights workers in the South?
>
> Answer—I testified before Congress (the House Subcommittee on Appropriations), earlier this year that the communists in this country had organized very intensively a drive to infiltrate into the racial discord and discontent in the country. The Party is not honestly interested in improving the status of the Negro. It seeks to present itself as the protector of the minority group, but in actual fact it is interested only in trying to advance the communist cause.

At the formal opening of the new FBI office, Hoover stuck to his prepared script in answering questions, including one about whether the FBI would protect civil rights workers: "We most certainly do not and will not give protection to civil rights workers. In the first place, the FBI is not a police organization, it's purely

an investigative organization, and the protection of individual citizens, either natives of this state or coming into this state, is a
matter for local authorities."

But Hoover made it plain that the FBI planned to pull out all
stops in going after the Klan. He took the occasion to order that
fifty more agents be assigned to the Jackson office.

If much of what Hoover did in public smacked of image polishing,
he was also quietly transforming the FBI in the South from a
passive observer of the civil rights struggle to an aggressive enemy
of the Ku Klux Klan. He was doing it under pressure, of course,
and he still had no use for Martin Luther King or the civil rights
movement and would continue to try to discredit and undermine
King. But now he began to redefine the FBI's mission dramatically. He increased its resources and transferred scores of agents
from around the country who had personal roots or work experience in the South.

Civil rights leaders worried about the sympathies of the new
Southern agents. Many of the agents stationed in the South in
earlier periods had developed close ties to the local officials they
worked with and often shared their views. Martin Luther King,
in a *New York Times* interview in 1962, had complained that FBI
agents in the South were mostly white Southerners who identified
with the values of the communities they served. He said they were
friendly with "local police and people who are promoting segregation," and added that every time he saw agents in Albany,
Georgia, they were with the local police force.

Critics pointed out that King was wrong about Albany, that
four of the five agents based there were Northern-born, even
though they worked under a Southerner, Marion Cheek.

However, complaints about the FBI—regardless of where the
agents were from—often were valid even after the FBI declared
war on the Klan in 1964. In one egregious case—the so-called
Orangeburg Massacre on February 8, 1968—FBI agents were on
hand as South Carolina state patrolmen opened fire on protesting
black students, killing three and injuring twenty-seven others.
Many of the students were running away when hit in the back.
The agents told Justice Department investigators that they were
not present at the shooting because they did not want to be called
to testify against the patrolmen.

On balance, though, the "Southern" FBI proved to be a powerful new tool against the Klan. Familiar with the region and its mores, able to speak its dialect and often helped by family ties and contacts, the Southern agents frequently were more effective than Northerners in interviewing witnesses, developing informants and working with local law enforcement officers. Like Southern-bred reporters covering the civil rights movement, the agents "walked the walk and talked the talk" of the South.

Frank Watts, who was a native of Hattiesburg, Mississippi, found recruiting Klansmen as informants more difficult than his previous assignment, penetrating the KGB. Most of the Klansmen were Christian zealots who believed passionately in white supremacy and hated the FBI. But Watts' mother was a schoolteacher who had grown up in Jones County, home of Sam Bowers and the White Knights, and she helped her son identify a number of people in the Klan who turned out to be relatives or people he grew up with. "I would go see these people and could gain entrance to their houses because I would say, 'Hello from Annie Mae, my mother,' just using the good-ole-boy routine. And that would get my foot in the door. And once you convinced one of them to cooperate, they would become stronger than any support person you ever imagined."

Before long, the Jackson FBI office had a strength of 250 agents and Moore—along with Jim Ingram, who became his chief assistant—was pushing his men at a killing pace. The caseload was running two thousand to twenty-five hundred cases a month, one fifth of them involving the Klan. Moore divided the office into five segments, giving Ingram the civil rights matters and keeping the Klan on his own desk.

Most of the time they worked seven days a week, with a half day off on Sunday. "From six in the morning, July tenth, when we opened the office, through the end of the year, there were no days off—half a day on Sunday to go to the church," Moore remembered—"six A.M. to midnight. I think back and wonder how we did it."

"We were working at night on the bombings and burnings of the churches," Ingram recalled, "but during the day we had to— at the instruction of the Justice Department—follow all the demonstrations, with thousands of protesters, and photograph every incident, such as arrests, to make sure there was no brutality."

Ingram, a big, outgoing Oklahoman—six feet three inches tall and 230 pounds—looked like a professional football player. Outwardly amiable, he knew how to intimidate a Klansman. During the investigation of the Vernon Dahmer killing, he heard that a suspect had publicly boasted, "Any FBI man steps on my property, I'm gonna shoot him." When Ingram and another agent, Jim Awe, showed up at the man's house outside Laurel, he confronted them with a double-barreled shotgun and a threat: "I'm gonna shoot both of you men if you don't turn and run."

Ingram, moving crablike to his left toward the shelter of a tree, motioned for Awe to move to the right, then shouted: "We won't turn our back on you and all we want is to talk with you about your whereabouts on the night Vernon Dahmer was killed."

"I'm gonna tell you one more time to get off my property or I'm gonna open fire."

"If you raise the barrel of that shotgun, we're armed and you can't kill us both. One of us will have to kill you."

The Klansman began to shake and then to cry. "I don't want any problems, but I have my orders not to be interviewed." His wife and three little boys were standing silently, watching as the Klansman sobbed and begged the agents to leave him alone.

"If you'll lay down your shotgun we can talk peacefully and get this over with," Ingram said.

Just then the suspect's brother drove up in a pickup truck. "Let me talk with him just a minute," the brother said. The two men walked into the house.

A few minutes later, the Klansman's brother came out. "I'm surprised my brother didn't shoot you because he's probably the meanest of the Jones County bunch," he told the agents. "But I'll bring him to a place where you can talk to both of us. I'd appreciate it if you would leave because Sam Bowers says Klansmen don't have to be interviewed on their property."

The agents later interviewed the Klansman at his brother's house and concluded he was not involved in Dahmer's murder. But that confrontation, and the way it was resolved, set a precedent: many members of the White Knights who were not involved in violent acts concluded the agents could not be intimidated and decided they would be better off agreeing to be interviewed.

The breakthrough on interviews made it easier for Moore's agents to recruit Klansmen as informers—the core of the FBI's campaign against the Klan. It was a difficult, often risky game played by the no-holds-barred rules of an alley fight. As Ingram said, "The informants themselves were rabid Klan followers. Many of them were the ones who started the klaverns. And the agents, through Roy's direction, would just start pounding on them, working on them."

It sounded mild enough the way Moore explained it: "Our program was to identify a Klansman, do a background on him, enough that you knew enough about him, then interview him. Out of every hundred interviews, we came up with an informant." What motivated Klan informants? "One, we explained the facts of life. Two, money might be involved. Three might be a threat against them that they didn't know about within the Klan group itself."

Translated, "explaining the facts of life" meant threatening and frightening the prospective informant in every possible way. Klansmen were warned that the FBI was combing their personal and business affairs for any vulnerability, no matter how small. Agents, who often used information about Klansmen's private lives against them, turned friend against friend, husband against wife and wife against husband. "Make sure you know everything you can about every Klansman," Moore instructed his men. "Go back again and again if necessary to try to recruit somebody you think would make a good informant. If you learn he's involved in something and you can use it against him, then use it."

The agents would try to win them over, but as Moore said, "As a last resort we would hold something over them. Fear had a lot to do with it."

Klansmen were notorious for "beating hell out of their wives," and the wives would complain to the FBI and request that their husbands be arrested. Instead the agents would inform the Klansmen of their wives' complaints, generating pressure within the families that the FBI could exploit.

Extramarital affairs were rampant among the Klansmen—another area of vulnerability. "They were always getting out of bed with their black paramour and then coming to talk with us—that's what bothered me," Moore said. As Tom Webb put it in his Mississippi drawl, "A lot of Klansmen used the Klan as an excuse to go off and screw some woman and their wife wouldn't know where they were."

Webb leaned heavily on his own Southern background in recruiting informants. "I'm a native Mississippian," he would tell them, "and I was brought up just like you were, not to mix with the nigras. We didn't eat together, we didn't socialize together. I can understand just how you feel, but if you don't want to give the Justice Department reason to force changes even faster down here, you better leave the civil rights protesters alone and cooperate with me. What the Klan is doing is just bringing on more integration faster than if you ignored the civil rights movement."

Sometimes if a Klansman were in financial trouble or somebody in his family was sick and he needed something, the FBI would offer a helping hand. Often the agents provided money, and they found that more persuasive than anything else.

Ministers were among the best informants. They believed segregation was part of Christianity and they preached it from the pulpit. "They would use the Bible to show they were correct," said Ingram. "We attended many rallies where they burned crosses and listened to the same messages over and over. And no doubt about it, they were spellbinders. They could incite a group. Ministers were looked up to."

In their quest for informants, agents sometimes took hair-raising chances.

Moore arranged for Frank Ford, an army veteran who had specialized in infiltrating the Chicago underworld, to be transferred to the Jackson office to infiltrate the White Knights. Pointing out the head of a local klavern, Moore told Ford, "I want you to get this guy in your pocket."

About a month later, Ford called Moore and said, "We're meeting tonight in the Homochitto Forest, both of us stripped to the waist."

"Have you got any coverage?"

"I don't want any coverage. How in hell can you cover in Homochitto National Forest?"

"I'm not instructing you to do it. If you think you can do it and get away with it, you have my permission."

Ford and the Klansman drove to the forest crossroads in separate cars, stripped to the waist so that each could see the other was not armed. They talked for half an hour.

The next morning Ford, his new informant in his pocket, met

with Moore at the King Edward Hotel in Jackson. Moore put the Klan leader on the FBI payroll.

"Working with an informant is like milking venom from a rattlesnake," Ford said. "You just have to be sure you don't turn the head loose."

The FBI's campaign to penetrate the Klan was so intense that throughout the South Klan leaders complained about informants. In Tuscaloosa, Alabama, Imperial Wizard Robert Shelton of the United Klans of America became so jittery that he proposed using lie detectors and truth drugs to ferret out any informants.

In Baton Rouge, Louisiana, Jack Helms, imperial wizard of the Universal Klans of America, raged bitterly about informers after appearing before a parish (county) grand jury investigating the bombing of the home of Victor Bussie, president of the Louisiana AFL-CIO. Helms denied an informant's testimony that he had ordered Bussie's home bombed and told reporters: "I'm just tired of these informers. I don't know how many may be in my organization. I can't even do my work."

Developing informants and riding suspects hard was standard police work, but the FBI went a significant step further in its campaign when Hoover authorized a counterintelligence program. A September 2, 1964, COINTELPRO memo that he sent to FBI offices throughout the country emphasized the secret nature of the program and expressed concern that public exposure of it would be embarrassing:

> The purpose of this program is to expose, disrupt and otherwise neutralize the activities of the various klans and hate organizations, their leadership and adherents. The devious maneuvers and duplicity of these groups must be exposed to public scrutiny through the cooperation of reliable news media, both locally and at the Seat of Government. In every instance, consideration should be given to disrupting the organized activity of these groups and no opportunity should be missed to capitalize upon organizational and personal conflicts in their leadership.
>
> The Bureau considers it vital that we expose the identities and activities of such groups and where possible disrupt their efforts. No counterintelligence action may be initiated by the

field without specific Bureau authorization. You are cautioned that the nature of this new endeavor is such that under no circumstances should the existence of the programs be made known outside the Bureau and appropriate within-office security should be afforded this sensitive operation. This new counterintelligence effort will take advantage of our experience with a variety of sophisticated techniques successfully applied against the Communist Party, USA, and related organizations since 1956.

The FBI offices were instructed to develop "compromise-type data [on] immorality, dishonesty and devious tactics" relating to Sam Bowers and other Klan leaders. "Mature experienced agents should be utilized and any investigation conducted should be done in a most discreet manner in order to AVOID ANY POSSIBILITY OF EMBARRASSMENT TO THE BUREAU."

Some elements of the COINTELPRO were entirely legal, if unorthodox, such as providing information on the Klan to reporters for use in stories in order to show the Klansmen how much the bureau knew about their supposedly secret activities. But some of the COINTELPRO tactics skirted the edge of the law, and others were illegal.

Agents frequently gathered compromising information through wiretaps, financial statements and tax records. Sometimes the information was used to compel or blackmail Klansmen into cooperating with FBI investigations. Often, it was used merely to sow mistrust and bad feelings among Klan units.

An FBI memo targeting Bowers and other Klan leaders, dated May 15, 1965, declared, "We are endeavoring, as a counterintelligence technique, to develop information discrediting or embarrassing to them and the ku klux klan. Through analysis of their income tax returns, we may be able to determine whether or not sources of their income or depositories used by them for their respective klan organizations are legitimate."

COINTELPRO got almost instant results. A year after it was initiated, Assistant Director A. H. Belmont, head of the FBI's Domestic Intelligence Division, secretly notified the Johnson administration that the program had been instrumental in solving five Klan murders—the killings of Schwerner, Goodman and Cheney at Philadelphia; the slaying of Viola Liuzzo, who was killed in the aftermath of the Selma-to-Montgomery voting rights march in March, 1965; and the shotgun death of Colonel Lemuel Penn in July, 1964, near Madison, Georgia.

Belmont wrote that the FBI was "seizing every opportunity to disrupt the activities of klan organizations" and that "nearly two thousand of our informants and sources are being operated to obtain up to date intelligence regarding racial matters . . . of those, 774 have been developed in the past year."

The next day Attorney General Nicholas Katzenbach wrote a letter to Hoover congratulating the FBI on its progress in solving civil rights cases and recognizing the need to keep a lid on its COINTELPRO tactics. "It is unfortunate," Katzenbach wrote, "that the value of these activities would in most cases be lost if too extensive publicity were given to them; however, perhaps at some point it may be possible to place these achievements on the public record, so that the Bureau can receive due credit."

While Moore presided over an institutional transformation of the FBI in Mississippi, Alvin Binder underwent a profound personal transformation.

Shortly after the Korean War, when Binder moved to Jackson with his first wife, he was a struggling young lawyer eager to rise and prepared to do whatever it took to win approval. He was a Jew. He was also a segregationist. And he was so deeply immersed in Mississippi's assimilation-minded Jewish community that two decades passed before the anomaly of his position occurred to him.

Living in an overwhelmingly Christian, predominantly Baptist society, Binder did his best not to look at himself as a Jew at all. Articulate, ego-driven, fast on his feet in a courtroom, willing to take on tough political tasks in order to get ahead, he considered himself first and foremost a Mississippian. He firmly defended the state's values and traditions, including its system of racial segregation and white supremacy. Mississippi's rulers in the 1950s and 1960s expected nothing less, but Binder embraced segregation willingly. He liked to point out that a Jew—Judah P. Benjamin—was the secretary of war in the Confederate cabinet, that 158 Jewish soldiers served with Confederate units in Mississippi, and that Jews fought against one another just as Christians fought against one another in what Binder, like most Southerners, called the War Between the States.

Religion had never been important to Binder when he was growing up. He knew he was a Jew and most of the people he was acquainted with knew he was. That was enough Jewish identity for him. When he attended Gulf Coast Military Academy, a high school in Gulfport, there was no synagogue in the area. He often attended services at a Baptist Bible school. Sometimes he went to Catholic masses; his best friend was a Catholic.

He experienced very little anti-Semitism until he attended Tulane University in New Orleans. There he was invited to pledge Phi Delta Theta, but the invitation was withdrawn when officers of the fraternity learned he was Jewish. It hurt, he recalled later, but he took comfort in knowing he had never been called a "dirty Jew" to his face or subjected to other anti-Semitic insults of the kind he had read about. At the University of Mississippi, where he went to law school, he blended in with the majority.

Binder's ambition when he settled in Jackson was to make enough money to build a spacious antebellum home and live like a Southern squire. By 1962 he had accomplished it. He and his novelist wife, Paige Mitchell, an attractive brunette, moved into a two-story, five-bedroom brick colonial with columns made of California redwood. With four thousand square feet of living space, it had a forty-seven-foot living room and a den to match. Standing on a corner lot in a tree-shaded, upper-middle-income area, it was a neighborhood showplace. In addition, Binder bought the two adjoining wooded lots to provide privacy and a magnificent setting for the home he intended to occupy for the rest of his life.

Neither Binder nor other Jews could belong to the Jackson Country Club even though Isadore Dreyfus, one of the most prominent Jews in Jackson, had donated the land for the club many years earlier when Jews were still welcome. Jews were also excluded from the Junior League and certain other civic organizations. But those were minor annoyances. Jews were excluded from private clubs throughout the country, not just in Mississippi. And if a Jew had the money and the will, he could find a way around some of the obstacles. After Binder's daughter Lisa was blackballed from a Girl Scout troop in 1962, he paid to have another Girl Scout unit formed that would accept her as a member.

The 140 or so Jewish families in Jackson in the 1960s were otherwise so well assimilated in the community that there was considerable social mingling with gentiles. The Binders were considered part of the Jewish community's social elite because of his success in the courtroom and Paige Mitchell's reputation as a writer. Upon publication of her well-received novel *A Wilderness of Monkeys*, the Hinds County Lawyers' Wives sent out "subpoenas" as invitations to a luncheon at which she was honored.

Binder moved up in the political world, too. He became an adviser and speech writer for Mayor Allen Thompson, undisturbed by His Honor's combatively segregationist views. In dealing with civil rights demonstrators, the Jackson police used a specially equipped armored car commonly known as the Thompson Tank. It had portals for machine guns and space enough for twelve armed men.

During the Freedom Rides in 1961, Jackson authorities hired Binder to prosecute the demonstrators who were arrested on charges of violating local "breach of peace" ordinances. He undertook the assignment with enthusiasm. And he accepted an invitation that year from Governor Johnson to make prosegregation speeches in the North on behalf of the Mississippi Sovereignty Commission, whose covert operations were a down-home version of COINTELPRO.

The Mississippi legislature had created the Sovereignty Commission in 1956—two years after *Brown* v. *Board of Education*—to preserve segregation in the face of court-ordered school desegregation. With funds appropriated by the legislature, the commission hired spies—blacks and whites—to infiltrate civil rights organizations and report on their activities and any "subversive" connections. Practically all of the commission's activities were aimed at blacks and civil rights activists. It investigated and compiled dossiers on hundreds of people, including teachers, ministers and students, and it brought pressure that cost some people their jobs.

On one occasion a commission investigator even spied on three hundred Jewish teenagers attending a five-state B'nai B'rith youth meeting at the Sun 'n Sand Motel in Biloxi. A commission memo, not unearthed until many years later, disclosed that the investigator came up empty-handed: "These youths sang songs and a general party atmosphere prevailed. We observed them and listened to them, but we could observe nothing or hear nothing that indicated that they were advocating subversion, integration or anything of a communistic nature."

On the whole, the Sovereignty Commission ignored Mississippi's Jewish community because it was relatively small and correctly considered to be as segregationist as the rest of the white population. That perception was reinforced by Binder's decision to speak on behalf of the commission.

He spoke in several Northern cities on the virtues of "the Southern way of life," accusing the press of distorting Mississippi's image. Certainly there were racial problems in Mississippi, just as there were in other states, Binder told Exchange Clubs, Rotary Clubs and other civic organizations, but Mississippians would solve their own problems if "outside agitators" would stay away. The outsiders were only complicating a complex social problem. Binder contended Mississippi had made so much progress in eliminating discrimination that any disadvantages Negroes faced resulted from past policies.

Speaking for the commission at a joint meeting of the Rotary, Lions and Kiwanis clubs in Wilkes-Barre, Pennsylvania, Binder insisted that "Mississippi assesses Negroes as individuals, not as a race, and is doing all within its power to overcome the culture lag resulting from sinning by whites in the past."

On one occasion, accompanied by Mike Martinson, a public-relations staffer for the commission, Binder was in St. Louis to address a prosegregation rally at a Masonic lodge. They were picked up at the airport by a driver who shocked them by declaring, "We've gotta do something about the niggers and the Jews and Catholics." Binder and Martinson, a Catholic, thought they had better find out what kind of organization had invited Binder. They contacted an editor at the *St. Louis Post-Dispatch* and got another shock. They were scheduled to attend a Ku Klux Klan rally.

"Oh, my God," Binder said. "They don't like Jews either. And they don't like Catholics. But I can't believe the Sovereignty Commission would schedule me to speak at a Klan rally." He and

Martinson prudently arrived at the Masonic temple before the rally was scheduled to begin so that they could scout out the situation. Standing on the sidewalk outside the temple and handing out pamphlets as their taxi pulled up was a man dressed in a white robe and hood. Binder instructed their cabdriver to take them back to the hotel.

They returned to Jackson on the first flight they could arrange. A chastened Binder told the Sovereignty Commission he would not be making any more speeches under its sponsorship. He never made another one.

The St. Louis trip was the first of a series of experiences that made him begin to reexamine the nature of Mississippi society and his place in it.

For a time, while divorcing himself from the extremism of the Sovereignty Commission, he continued to support segregation. Two encounters in the early 1960s called even that support into question. Both grew out of the Freedom Riders campaign to desegregate interstate travel, which had made the Mississippi capital a focal point.

Binder had befriended William Kunstler while the civil rights lawyer was in Jackson. Accounts of Kunstler's defense of Freedom Riders in the Jackson *Clarion-Ledger* and *Jackson Daily News* had stirred such hostility among whites that Kunstler was afraid to leave his room at the Sun 'n Sand Motel to eat dinner, and Binder had taken food to the lawyer's room. Later, the two sat together on a flight from Jackson to New Orleans. Kunstler asked Binder if he knew much about the work of Martin Luther King. When Binder said he did not, Kunstler gave him several pamphlets describing King's tactics and their roots in Gandhi's principles of nonviolence.

"Martin Luther King is one of the few Negroes who believes in nonviolence and you better pray nothing happens to him," Kunstler said.

Binder said nothing, but began thumbing through the pamphlets. Finally Kunstler broke the silence: "Someday you ought to get off your damn knees and stand up like a man and do something, Al Binder. You're not doing a damn thing. People like you are doing nothing about the racial injustices down here."

Binder flinched as though he had been slapped in the face.
Then he yelled at Kunstler, startling the other passengers: "You're
only saying these things to me because I'm Jewish!"

Kunstler would not say those things to a Christian, Binder
thought. Why was it okay to say something like that to a member
of a minority, to demand that he stand up and do something?

Binder had an even more unsettling encounter with King himself.

In the period from December 12 to December 16, 1961, a total
of 737 blacks, including King, were arrested and jailed in Albany,
Georgia, as a result of massive demonstrations supporting nine
Freedom Riders who were on trial there for sitting in the white
waiting room of the city's Central of Georgia Railroad station.
The city had tried to squelch the demonstrations with mass arrests, but the tactic threatened to backfire. King refused to be
released on bond after his arrest and said he would stay in jail
during Christmas as a symbol of protest. Albany mayor Asa Kelley was desperate to keep his city from becoming a major civil
rights battleground, especially over the holidays. He telephoned
Mayor Thompson in Jackson and asked for help, knowing Thompson had a great deal of experience dealing with demonstrations.
Could he send someone to advise the city on how to handle the
situation?

Mayor Thompson asked Binder to go to Albany. Binder wondered why he was being called on, but agreed to go. In Albany,
Mayor Kelley gave him carte blanche to negotiate. At the jail,
Binder found King, clad in the blue denims he usually wore in
protest marches, sitting on the floor of his small cell. The civil
rights leader was alone. Binder introduced himself and King stood
up and shook hands.

"I've come to help you get out of here," Binder said. "I've got
the power to walk out there and tell them to let you go. All you've
got to do is agree to leave town and go back to Atlanta."

The sudden offer startled King. He hesitated, but then said
firmly, "I'm here to stay."

Binder asked why.

"Because this is part of my passive resistance to unfair and
unconstitutional actions that have been devastating to my people."
King spoke in a pleasant voice, but refused to budge from his
position. They discussed the matter for about twenty minutes.

Finally, King shook Binder's hand and thanked him for coming by.

Binder was moved by the experience. It occurred to him that the South would be facing both civil rights protests and King's influence for a long time, and so far it had not found an honorable way of confronting them. The thought made him uneasy about continuing to participate in the system even though he had been raised within it, had defended it and believed in it. He was starting to think that, as a young lawyer, he should find a way to distance himself from segregation, but he was not sure how to do it.

Not long after his return from Albany, Binder was called upon to prosecute a group of protesters. He did it, but with little enthusiasm and less pride in the guilty verdict he won. Minutes after the trial, he saw three of the jurors walking out of Mayor Thompson's office. He knew instinctively that the verdict had been preordained, the conviction improper. The jurors had gone to the mayor's office to report the verdict and be congratulated.

Binder resigned from the prosecutor's office that afternoon.

That experience was part of what drove him to become active in the Temple Beth Israel congregation. He even became friendly with Rabbi Nussbaum, though he still considered him too liberal for Jackson and too involved in ministering to the civil rights protesters. Even so, when Nussbaum wanted to visit several young Episcopal ministers who had been arrested in the demonstrations, Binder arranged for him to slip into the Jackson jail through a back door at night so that his visits would not create problems for him or his congregation.

Binder said later that his visits with King and Kunstler, along with his experiences as a speaker for the Sovereignty Commission and as a prosecutor of Freedom Riders, were important elements in the change that occurred in his attitude on race and civil rights.

"I began to see the South was going to have this problem with us for a good period of time. I felt that as a young person I could not continue to be involved with this Southern conservative view, even though I had been born and raised with those prejudices. I had not looked at myself as a Jew until then. I had looked at myself as an up-and-coming young lawyer anxious to be approved by the Establishment and ego-oriented around the fact the Establishment was using my articulateness to participate in things that I had not really looked into too well."

•   •   •

The transformation of Al Binder, like the reshaping of the FBI
in the South, was a gradual process. By the fall of 1967, with the
bombing of the Jackson synagogue and Rabbi Nussbaum's house,
Binder's reformation and Moore's rebuilding of the Jackson field
office had gone far enough to permit the two men to enter into
a potent alliance.

The scene of the action was about to shift away from Jackson.
A host of new players would surge onto the stage.

7

Early in 1968, the FBI office in Meridian began to receive intelligence reports that the White Knights were altering their strategy. Feeling the heat after terrorizing Jackson's Jewish community, the Klan was now planning to shift its campaign to Meridian, more than eighty miles to the east.

In a secret meeting with an informant, agent Frank Watts learned the Klan had drawn up a Meridian hit list. The informant pulled a slip of paper out of his pocket and handed it to Watts. On the paper was a column of names scrawled in pencil. Meridian's police chief, Roy Gunn, headed the list, followed by businessmen Meyer Davidson, I. A. Rosenbaum, Al Rose and several other prominent Meridian Jews. Then Watts saw a name that jumped off the page at him. It was his own.

Watts blamed Gunn. The chief had gone around town boasting that he was working with Frank Watts and the FBI and that they were not going to let the Klan "get away with any of this violence crap." It was that kind of blabbing by the police chief, Watts told his fellow agents, that no doubt landed them both on the hit list.

Watts, who was a resident agent in Meridian but reported to Moore and Ingram of the Jackson field office, did not take the list lightly. He had a wife and three boys. Given the way the Klan operated, his family was in at least as much danger as he was. He wasted no time calling his partner, Jack Rucker.

"The Klan's putting out a list," he told Rucker, "and would you believe it, I'm on it. We've got to get busy and do a better job of infiltrating this bunch of thugs. And if we're going to get anywhere, it looks like we've just got to fight fire with fire. They play tough, we'll play tough."

They decided to contact Tom Hendricks, the former FBI agent who represented Alton Wayne Roberts and his brother Raymond, both notorious Klansmen.

The FBI had turned a corner in the war against the Klan.

Meridian seemed made to order for Sam Bowers. The town and surrounding piney woods area were already fertile recruiting ground for the White Knights. The FBI's Meridian office was skeletal compared to the Jackson field office. More important, Meridian itself had a raw side. Once the commercial and cultural hub of the state, it had become a city in which violence simmered so close to the surface that a surprising number of people carried guns, including such unlikely candidates as Reverend R. S. Porter, pastor of the all-black First Union Baptist Church; Lucille Rosenbaum, the diminutive but outspoken school board president; and Tom Bordeaux, the courtly, soft-spoken lawyer who headed one of the town's oldest families.

After prospering during the golden age of rail transportation—the late 1800s and early 1900s—Meridian declined along with the railroads in the years just before and after World War II. At its zenith a bustling rail junction, retail center and marketing hub for cotton and lumber, downtown Meridian by the 1960s was parched and down at the heels. The streets were nearly devoid of trees. Weeds poked through cracks in the sidewalks. Widemann's, the town's best-known restaurant and a favorite of out-of-town reporters covering the civil rights story, was busy with locals during the day, but at night it was as empty as the downtown streets. The once-elegant hotels, which had accommodated hundreds of travelers at night and boasted of their sumptuous dining rooms, now were vacant and sad. And the opera house was boarded up—the opera house built by Jewish merchants as a public service and graced by Caruso and Galli-Curci and Sarah Bernhardt in a flowering of high culture unmatched anywhere in the South except New Orleans.

Tucked out of sight were some attractive residential neighborhoods and a great deal of money, but the once-proud "Queen City" of Mississippi contrasted poorly with the capital city of Jackson, with its busy offices and grand, well-tended parks.

Along with the blacks and native Protestants, Meridian had a large Irish Catholic population and a deep-rooted Jewish com-

munity. The Irish built the railroads and operated the maintenance shops, the icehouses and the cotton compressors. And, as
they did in many American cities, they stayed to dominate its
politics.

"My family always had a joke," said Bill Ready, the bluff Irish-
man who represented Meyer Davidson and persuaded him and
his wife to evacuate their residence the night of the bombing
threat. "Meridian was a weird place because it was populated by
Baptists and other illiterates, financed and owned by the Jewish
community, but the government was always run by the Catholics.
The only people excluded were the blacks."

Meridian's prosperous Jewish citizens were integrated into the
larger community in a way that Jackson Jews could only dream
of. In 1882, Meridian's city directory listed fifty telephone exchanges, and although Jews were only a small percentage of the
population, nine of those exchanges belonged to Jewish firms.
According to Leo and Evelyn Turitz's *Jews in Early Mississippi*,
Meridian's Jews went into business with gentiles, sat on the boards
of banks and brokerages and were treated like the leading citizens
they were.

Along Meridian's main thoroughfares, many of the buildings
still bear the names of their Jewish merchant-owners: the Rosenbaum Building, the Arky Building, the Winner and Meyer Building. The tallest structure in town, the seventeen-story Threefoot
Building, was named after one of the oldest Jewish families in
Meridian, the Threefoots, whose name translates from the German Dreifus. During Meridian's heyday, the Marks-Rothenberg
family, three brothers and a half brother, opened what soon became a thriving department store. Isaac Marks and his brothers
built the opera house next to their store and operated it for years
on a nonprofit basis. Israel Marks donated land to Highland Park;
a statue of him still stands there. Two brothers from another
prominent family, Joseph and Samuel Meyer, built the city's first
skyscraper, the eleven-story Lamar Hotel, famous for its excellent
cuisine.

All were German Jews whose fathers, mostly small-town shop-
keepers and traders, had fled their native Bohemia to escape the
anti-Jewish riots that broke out after the failed rebellion against
Hapsburg rule in 1848.

The German Jews were assimilationist by nature and more

secular than the later waves of poorly educated but pious Jews who would pour into America from eastern Europe in the late 1800s. Growing up as Southerners, as Eli Evans wrote in *The Provincials,* German Jews "would absorb the regional defiance and unrestrained pride, the memories of rising to sing 'Dixie' in grammar school assemblies and, in history class, the surging poignance on reading Lee's farewell to his troops."

Anti-Semitism was virtually unheard of in Meridian. This remained true even in the wake of the Leo Frank lynching in 1915, which brought the latent feelings against Jews much closer to the surface elsewhere in the South.

As the city fought against decline, the children of its Jewish families tended to drift away. They preferred practicing law or medicine to tending their fathers' retail stores. They moved to Jackson or Atlanta, or even the North. The few who remained lived unpretentious lives of quiet comfort despite their wealth. It was these rich, still-prominent Jews living in the same town with top foot soldiers of the White Knights that made Sam Bowers focus his sights on Meridian.

At the beginning of 1968, the Klan's activities in Meridian aroused little reaction from local Jews or the white community in general. For the most part, the attacks were directed against black churches housing Head Start centers and individuals who had offended the Klan in specific ways.

Two church bombings in January and one in early February were not mentioned by the Meridian *Star*—the usual practice of newspapers in Mississippi when it came to crimes against blacks. Then, on February 20, Klansmen burned a grocery operated by onetime Meridian police sergeant Wallace Miller. Miller was not considered one of Meridian's brightest policemen; Chief Gunn liked to say that "you could take a five-acre field, get a bucket of manure and dig a hole and put the manure in it and cover it up, and Wallace would find it and step in it." But Miller was a former member of the White Knights who had become an FBI informant and a key witness in the Philadelphia case. He had implicated Bowers in the killing of Schwerner, Chaney and Goodman and had given crucial testimony about the details.

A few days later, according to FBI records, White Knights put the torch to New Hope Baptist Church, site of a Head Start program and civil rights activities. The next night, night riders fired a shotgun into the home of J. R. Moore, a black school bus driver for a Head Start program, and set fire to the parsonage of the Newell Chapel Methodist Church, another Head Start site.

The only incident directed against blacks that got prominent play in the paper was an attack on the house of Dr. Hobert Kornegay, a well-known dentist and one of two blacks included in the official history of Lauderdale County. Kornegay, his wife, Ernestine, a schoolteacher, and their two daughters were all at home around nine o'clock one night when a shotgun blast ripped through the house. One of the daughters, in her room doing homework, screamed that she had been shot; it turned out that she had been hit by flying glass.

Chief Gunn, upset by the increasing tempo of violence, warned that he had given his officers orders to "shoot to kill" where terrorism was involved. "We intend to stop it," he said, "and we will go to all legal lengths, use any number of men and any degree of reasonable force necessary. Anyone who will burn a church or a home or shoot into somebody's home is so lowdown that I can't really describe it in acceptable words. We are dealing with animals, criminals, persons who are lower than anything that flies through the air or crawls on the ground."

For Meridian's beleaguered blacks, Gunn's concern was too little too late, and in any case they did not trust him or his men. Even Dr. Kornegay, who got along well with Gunn and acted as his informal liaison to the black community, did not bother to call the police after the shooting incident. "I was afraid that some of them were involved," he said later. "Besides, I had my Enfield rifle."

The culture of Meridian's blacks was as distinctive as the cultures of its Irish and Jewish communities. Partly it was a matter of education. Until the late 1940s, Meridian was the only city in east Mississippi where a black student could go to a four-year high school. In fact, it had two black four-year high schools, making it a magnet for students from outside the area. This distinction could also be traced to the Jews; the Wechsler School, dating from 1888, was the first brick public school for black children in the state, and was named for the rabbi who led the drive to get it built. And from 1937 until it was desegregated in 1969, T. J. Harris Senior High was the pride of the black community.

Academically inferior, perhaps, by white standards, many of its
graduates nonetheless went on to become teachers, doctors, businessmen and skilled craftsmen. Blacks seldom found opportunities in Meridian's limping economy, though, and quite a few went
North in search of a better life. Many who left maintained ties
with their old hometown. In 1967, a group of Meridian expatriates
living in Detroit got tired of bumping into each other only at
funerals and formed a social club. The idea spread, growing into
the National Council of Meridianites, which grew to some three
thousand members with twenty chapters across the country.

Meridian's black community had strong local leadership in men
such as Reverend R. S. Porter, pastor of the First Union Baptist
Church; Reverend Charles Johnson, pastor of Newell Chapel
Methodist Church; and businessman Charles Young, who later
was elected a state representative and whose father, E. F. Young,
had founded one of the country's first cosmetics lines for blacks.
In 1967, it was hard to find sites for Head Start programs. At
First Union, the leading black church in town with 250 members,
parishioner Omera Austin said nearly half the congregation opposed using the church for that purpose. "They were afraid of
the church being bombed. Mostly it was older people, but some
of the younger parishioners protested too. Eight or ten members
left, but Reverend Porter was a strong pastor. He pushed us in
the right direction."

When civil rights leaders such as Martin Luther King and Andrew Young came to town, Porter was always ready to put them
up. First Union hosted most of the civil rights meetings in town.
It was the site of the funeral for James Chaney, the black youth
murdered in Philadelphia.

Charles Johnson was equally fearless. Small, wiry and dark,
Johnson may have been the only person in town who had the
nerve to stand up to Chief Gunn. "Gunn couldn't stand the sight
of him," recalled Johnson's friend Charles Young. "When we had
a meeting of some kind, Gunn would usually come. He would
glare at Johnson and say, 'What are you doing here?' Reverend
Johnson would say, 'What are you doing here?' They couldn't
stand to be in the same room together."

When the attacks on the churches began in 1964, Reverend
Porter organized a mutual protection society. Porter is remembered as a tough man who "liked his rifle." Aside from the Dea-

cons for Defense and Justice, a black self-protection group that operated in Louisiana in the 1960s, Porter's group in Meridian was one of the few known organizations formed by local blacks to defend themselves against Klan violence. For blacks, taking up arms was generally considered suicidal. The Meridian group was so informal it did not have a name, but its members had guns and courage. "When I got word my house was going to be shot into," recalled Charles Young, "everyone would be alerted and prepared with rifles and shotguns. There was no set number. My neighbors Lonnie Edwards and Rudolph Rairly used to help when I was threatened too. They sat in the upstairs windows of their homes. Sometimes they stayed with me when I sent my family away for safety."

Most often, they got the call to turn out to protect Reverend Porter's First Union Baptist Church, which was so well guarded that it escaped damage. Charles Johnson's church, Newell Chapel Methodist, was not so fortunate. It had a wooden parsonage and Johnson, recalling how the Klan destroyed it in 1967, said, "They attempted to burn it, but a neighbor got up early, saw the fire and called the fire department and they put it out. The second time, they torched it."

Porter's men were also called on with some regularity to protect Bill Ready, who was the only white in the self-protection group. Ready liked to joke about surviving eighteen death votes in different klaverns in east Mississippi and Alabama, but there was no denying his life was in constant danger. "My preacher friends guarded my house for five years," he said. "We used to sit up all night many a night, waiting. Our wives had learned to make us all-night meals."

If the black community was armed and ready, the Jews of Meridian were dozing under a false sense of security. After the bombing of Rabbi Nussbaum's house in Jackson, Rabbi Milton Schlager warned members of his Meridian congregation that their synagogue—also named Temple Beth Israel—might well become a Klan target too. Like Nussbaum, however, he was an "outsider," a native of Revere, Massachusetts, who had served Northern congregations until arriving in Meridian five years earlier. His warning was ridiculed. His congregation told him he did not understand that the Klan would not dare attack Meridian's Jews because Jews had helped found and build the town. Schlager's insistence that the danger was real only intensified their scorn; he was labeled an alarmist, a pinko, a Communist, a homosexual—even a Yankee. His warnings were upsetting the applecart, members of the congregation told him, and could only cause problems for the Jewish community by calling unwanted attention to it.

Anyone who had examined the argument of Meridian's Jews might have realized that because Sam Bowers was not from Meridian, he was unlikely to draw a distinction between the Jewish communities in Jackson and Meridian just because a statue of Israel Marks stood on a pedestal in Highland Park on land Marks had given the city of Meridian.

Some of those who saw no threat represented a particular irony. Paula Ackerman had fled Germany with her late husband, Rabbi William Ackerman, in the late 1930s. The rabbi was hired by Temple Beth Israel and served until he died in November 1950. Paula Ackerman served the temple for more than a year as an acting rabbi. Although she was not ordained and not educated as a rabbi, she was a strong personality and had learned the tenets and many of the rituals of Judaism from her husband. Having found refuge in a friendly Southern town, Paula Ackerman refused to believe that Meridian's Jews were in any danger.

Another who had escaped the Holocaust and found a haven in Meridian was Mrs. Nellie Kass, whose daughter was married to the Ackermans' son. Mrs. Kass scoffed at Schlager's warning. A widow who operated a needlepoint store, she dismissed the idea that her beloved Meridian could experience the kind of violence that had struck the synagogue and the rabbi's house only eighty miles away. It was as though she and other Jews in Meridian refused to believe the Jackson bombings had occurred.

"That kind of thing may happen in Germany," Mrs. Kass told Schlager, "but not here."

It was like the denial of death, Schlager thought: it couldn't happen to you, only to the other person. Or was it like the refusal of many German Jews to believe that they, with such deep roots in Germany, would be harmed by the Nazis?

I. A. Rosenbaum, a prominent businessman who had become a close friend of Schlager's and later was mayor of Meridian, never doubted that the Klan was capable of attacking the Jewish community. He tried to reassure the rabbi, but out of what he considered an abundance of caution, Rosenbaum and his wife prepared for the possibility of violence: he had a rifle; she carried a small pistol in her purse.

As Frank Watts saw it, the Roberts brothers were FBI's best hope. If they could be turned into informants, that could open the way to ending the violence and breaking up the Klan. To do it Watts needed the help of Tom Hendricks, who had retired from the FBI in 1962 after twenty-five years' service. Hendricks, a native of Bolivar County, Mississippi, lived on his pension and meager law practice. Tall, slender and bespectacled, he was a nervous man who handled mostly divorces and small-time criminal cases. He did represent the notorious Robertses, however. That and the fact that Hendricks was known as a man always on the lookout for a buck is what made Watts think of calling him.

If any Klansmen in Meridian had credibility with Sam Bowers and could penetrate the curtain of secrecy that surrounded the innermost councils of the White Knights, it was the Roberts brothers—especially Alton Wayne, who was free on an appeal bond after his conviction in connection with the killing of Schwerner, Chaney and Goodman.

Trying to turn the Roberts brothers, Watts knew, would be a dangerous maneuver. But he wanted to close in on the cold-blooded killers, people, he knew, who were "planning to do a Number Four on somebody—a complete elimination."

The Roberts brothers came from a dirt-poor family that lived in a shack of a house down by South Sowashee Creek—the only whites who lived in the area. Their father, Cockie, was a city sanitation worker. In addition to Raymond and Alton Wayne, there was a brother named Lee who was a member of the Meridian police force. A fourth son, Lloyd, had been a likable, easygoing boy, but he was sickly most of his life and had died of leukemia in his early twenties.

Alton Wayne, a hulking six-foot-two-inch, 250-pound nightclub bouncer, was the meanest and toughest of the Roberts clan. Given to violent explosions of anger, he constantly picked fights and got into trouble. "He was a firm believer in the axiom that whoever gets in the first punch wins the fight, so whenever he would get into arguments he would haul off and sock somebody in the face with no warning," said one of his former high school teachers.

As a senior he played tackle on the Meridian High School football team, which was generally one of the best teams in the state. Although a ferocious tackler, he got into so many fights and cost Meridian so much yardage in penalties that at least one of his coaches considered him a net liability. He and another coach tried to talk with Roberts, but they concluded it was an exercise in futility. He did not want to be, or could not be, helped.

One night following a game in Vicksburg, Alton Wayne spotted a youth sitting on the curb near the school gym where a dance was being held. Recognizing him as a player for the Vicksburg High Green Wave, Roberts said, "Hey, you're a Greenie, aren't you?" The youth stood up and said he was. With that Alton Wayne smashed him in the face and knocked out several teeth. Before leaving Vicksburg that night, Alton Wayne beat up another Vicksburg youth. His savage brawling created bad feelings between the two communities that lasted several years.

In high school Alton Wayne would go to almost any length to get attention—once he just sat sprawled out on the classroom floor in the eleventh grade to create a ruckus. Although hardly anyone remembers him ever doing anything admirable, a former teacher recalled an incident in which a girl in his class suffered a diabetic seizure and Alton Wayne picked her up and carried her to a teachers' lounge for treatment. "He was really proud of that, the one thing you could say he was really proud of," the former teacher said.

After high school, Alton Wayne joined the marines, but in less than two years he was booted out with a bad-conduct discharge for drunkenness, fighting and being AWOL. He later married and went to work for a window company. In the summer of 1964, when he was only twenty-six, he and his wife already had three small children, and some acquaintances were hopeful that the town's bully might be on the verge of settling down. But he took a job as a bouncer at the Skyview nightclub, a redneck hangout frequented by Klansmen and other racists and toughs. In his new job he was exposed to a pamphlet Bowers was circulating to recruit new members for the White Knights.

"It is clear now that if communism is to be defeated in America it will be done in the South, and primarily in Mississippi," Bowers wrote. He said he was looking for

ONLY: ... American white me... ...asic fact that their ... bound up with th... ...t accept Jews, bec... ...nations of their i... ...nter of what we ... ...Papists, because th... ...of the First Com... ...espon-sible, indiv... ...ls, Tar-tars, Orie... ...native background... ...tem of governmen...

For Alton W... ...ng of an exciting period. With... ...at thousands of youths would be inva... part of Freedom Summer and with Meridian slate... a major staging center for voter registration drives and the organization of black community centers, Roberts saw an opportunity for the kind of action he craved.

Unlike his brothers Lee and Alton Wayne, both of whom were big, broad-shouldered, outgoing ladies' men, Raymond was tall but thin and had a bad complexion. He made poor grades in school and dropped out in the ninth grade. The Selective Service board classified him 4-F, according to an FBI document, "for reason of being substandard mentally." But he had a cunning side. And he did not mind night riding. He talked tough, too, although he generally left the fisticuffs to Alton Wayne.

Violent and dangerous as Alton Wayne and Raymond Roberts were, both needed money and both had been involved in so much racial violence that threats of prosecution could be held over their heads.

Watts had a special reason for tackling the Roberts brothers. While Chief Gunn and his men believed they were involved in the rash of local bombings, informants among the rank and file of the White Knights had told the FBI that the key to recent violence, especially the attacks on Jews, was someone from outside the area who had linked up with Bowers and had no real ties to the regular Klansmen. Indeed, they did not even know his name; he was referred to simply as "the Man."

If that was true, Watts reasoned, the tactics the bureau had been using—the incessant questioning and harassing of known Klan members—might never get anywhere. True, without those efforts, the bureau would not have developed the informants who were now telling them of "the Man's" existence. Catching him, however, would require a new approach.

Meridian Jews could go on insisting the Klan would never dare attack them personally, but the violence in January and February had alarmed and incensed some of them, and much of the rest of the community too. Joe Clay Hamilton, the Lauderdale County attorney, recalled that "the time was so tense and potentially explosive that people were afraid to speak up." Hamilton, a leader of a committee to keep the public schools open during the confrontation over desegregation, received threatening telephone calls that usually began, "You nigger-lovin' son of a bitch, you better get your ass out of Mississippi." He believed most of the people who disapproved of what was going on were afraid to speak out except to their closest friends because they never knew what connections other people had to the Klan. Likewise, political leaders feared alienating Klan sympathizers. And while many people did not condone violence, he said, "they acquiesced in the Klan's actions because they felt that might help preserve the status quo and keep the blacks in 'their place.' "

Still, more than in Jackson, religious leaders spoke out against the violence. Strikingly, the Lauderdale County Baptist Pastors Association led the way by issuing a statement deploring the "burnings, bombings, shootings, which have plagued our community in recent weeks."

Shortly after that statement was issued, fire destroyed another black church—the Mount Pleasant Baptist Church.

Two days later, an interracial group of religious and business leaders in the Meridian area formed the Committee of Conscience to raise funds for the rebuilding of the churches that had been damaged or destroyed. A white minister, Reverend Harold O'Chester, pastor of the Poplar Springs Baptist Church, was named chairman of the group.

The violence continued. The Klan now targeted members of the Committee of Conscience. There was the attack on Dr. Kornegay, who was a member of the committee but was also involved in Head Start and civil rights activities. A graduate of Morehouse College in 1945 and the dentistry school at Meharry Medical College in 1948, he had also begun to train local blacks to pass job examinations. More important than any of this, Kornegay was on good terms with Chief Gunn and other Meridian leaders. He was targeted almost on general principles, the FBI concluded—to serve as a warning to other blacks.

Raymond Roberts and other Klansmen kept two other committee members—a white couple, lawyer Lawrence Rabb and his wife, Clo Ann—in a constant state of fear with threatening calls and messages. A menacing Raymond Roberts terrified Mrs. Rabb by following her home every night after the adult extension classes she was taking at the University of Southern Mississippi. "It was just awful," Mrs. Rabb recalled. "He would follow me home in his car and then park and just sit there to intimidate me. We were so afraid with all the bombing and shooting that was going on that at night we would get down on the floor to watch television so if someone shot through our window we wouldn't get hit."

Rabbi Schlager had first tried to avoid the issue of civil rights, but he had not entirely succeeded and now felt exposed and vulnerable.

When the latest round of church burnings had begun, he played a quiet role in organizing the Committee of Conscience—in fact, he had come up with the name. Since then, he and his wife had gotten a number of threatening telephone calls. And he and several other prominent Jews, including I. A. Rosenbaum, who also was a member of the Committee of Conscience, had received through the mail a stream of anti-Semitic literature, including copies of *The Thunderbolt*, the hate sheet published by J. B. Stoner's National States Rights Party. Raymond Roberts served as chairman, and Mrs. Alton Wayne Roberts as secretary, of the party's local chapter.

Moreover, Schlager had always known that for all the seeming acceptance of Jews in Meridian in the past, a stream of anti-Semitism now coursed beneath the surface. (Shortly after moving to Meridian, on June 13, 1963, he had been shocked one morning to learn that Dr. William Ackerman, son of Rabbi William Ackerman, who died in 1950, had arrived at his dental office to find a large swastika painted on the building.) Almost everyone in Meridian had been aware that two of the three civil rights workers killed in nearby Philadelphia—Schwerner and Goodman—were Jews. And on June 19, 1964, only two days before they disappeared, Schlager had met with Schwerner and the third victim, Chaney.

After a chance encounter with Schlager on a street in downtown Meridian, Schwerner had tried to persuade the rabbi to join him in protesting the denial of voting rights to blacks in Mississippi. The rabbi opposed the demonstrations. He was concerned that instead of promoting civil rights for blacks, the protests would arouse the passions of violent racists. Hoping he might be able to persuade Schwerner to return to his home in New York, Schlager invited the youth to his house to discuss the issue.

Schwerner, accompanied by Chaney, showed up the next day. It was a hot, muggy afternoon. The three stood in the shade of tall pine trees in the rabbi's front yard and discussed the matter for a half hour or so. Chaney said he was protesting because he wanted "the right to vote." Challenged, perhaps spuriously, by Schlager to say whether he had ever actually tried to vote, he admitted he had not. After that Chaney fell silent while Schlager and Schwerner talked about the pros and cons of the civil rights demonstrations. Schwerner stressed the importance of bringing justice to blacks in Mississippi and told the rabbi it could be done only by confronting whites with the injustices of their system. A rabbi, of all people, should be involved in a campaign for equal justice, he maintained. Schlager argued that the civil rights workers were "underestimating the deep-seated feelings of white Mississippians and their commitment to segregation." Confronting them with demonstrations, he said, would only antagonize them and provoke them to seek retribution. And if he got involved, the rabbi said, it might endanger his congregation.

"I told Schwerner he probably would get killed if he kept on because he was miscalculating the feelings of the people in Mississippi," Schlager recalled. "I told him, 'You're banging your head against an iron curtain and getting nowhere, and it seems to me you're taking the wrong approach. You're just a fly-by-nighter and ought to go on back home.' But he said, 'No, I brought my wife with me and what I'm doing is meaningful.'

"There he was in his overalls and sweatshirt with a beard, and I thought to myself he was like an Old Testament prophet, he was going for justice, he was going for human dignity. I admired his courage. He never wavered, never changed his course. He dismissed the idea of being killed. He never dealt with negatives. He showed a spiritual stubbornness for justice and human dignity."

On June 21, when Chaney, Goodman and Schwerner disappeared after being jailed in Philadelphia, some people held out hope they would be found alive. Not Schlager.

"I had seen some of the raw hatred in Meridian and I knew how dangerous it was," he said.

In December of 1962, when William Ackerman and Al Rosenbaum arrived in Dover, New Hampshire, to interview Schlager about becoming Meridian's new rabbi, they found a young man who had no experience in the South, was chronically ill, and considered himself a physical wreck. They took an immediate interest in him.

Partly it was because Schlager, a Reform rabbi, seemed to be ministering successfully to an Orthodox Jewish congregation. Most of the Jews in Meridian were Reform, but some—including the influential Meyer Davidson and his brother Sammie—retained an Orthodox heritage. How had Schlager bridged the gap? "The most amazing thing," he told them, "is that I get along splendidly with the congregation as long as I don't use the word *Reform* or *liberal*."

Schlager was astounded that his visitors had any interest in discussing the job with him. He was thirty-seven years old and scrawny, five feet nine inches tall but weighing only about 125 pounds. He had lost most of his hair in 1947–48, apparently as a result of malnutrition suffered when he was a student at the University of Jerusalem and got caught up in the Arab-Israeli War.

Schlager had eventually returned to his normal weight of about 170 pounds, but in 1958, while serving as a rabbi in Glen Cove, Long Island, he suffered a severe stomach disorder with internal bleeding. Surgeons removed part of his stomach. "I began calling myself 'the gutless rabbi,' " he joked, "but it was very serious. From a blood transfusion, I got hepatitis, and it has to some extent always remained with me. My weight dropped below one hundred eighteen pounds. I was a living freak. I was so thin that the hat I wore would fall over my eyes and make people laugh."

Luckily, Schlager's wife, Bette Lee, whom he had met and married in Cincinnati in 1954 after graduating from the Hebrew Union College of the Jewish Institute of Religion, was a registered nurse. She carried him through a long and painful convalescence.

When Ackerman and Rosenbaum offered him the job, Schlager was eager to accept. He had grown weary of the New Hampshire winters and a warmer climate was appealing. Schlager's first years in Meridian were generally quiet, but members of the congregation remember one episode that showed their rabbi was not quite as washed out and spiritless as his appearance might have suggested. When the Meridian *Star* ran an editorial calling kosher food "a rip-off for the Jews to make money," Schlager went to the newspaper's offices in downtown Meridian and stormed into the office of James Skewes, the *Star*'s eccentric publisher. Banging on Skewes' desk, the rabbi declared that the *K* on food packages stood for "kosher" and the *U* for "Union of Orthodox Rabbis." Food so marked was authentic kosher food, Schlager told the publisher, and any attempt to call it a rip-off was wrongheaded. Skewes hastily apologized and wrote a correction that was immediately published in the *Star*. Schlager was pleased with his triumph, though he considered the correction to be "more foolish than the original editorial."

Skewes, who usually wore a derby and by turns drove a Rolls-Royce or an old Bentley convertible, had inherited the Meridian *Star* from his father and used the newspaper as his father had— to promote conservative causes and defend segregation. He helped found Lamar Academy, a White Citizens Council school established as part of a statewide network of private schools set up to evade federally mandated desegregation of the public schools. A nervous man with a stutter, Skewes took almost no part in Meridian's social life.

While he generally left direction of the editorial side of the paper to others, under his ownership the *Star* flew the "Southern way of life" banner and ran scathing editorials blasting the federal government for trying to promote desegregation. The news columns routinely carried stories supporting white supremacy and published articles about the Klan and the National States Rights Party as though they were ordinary civic organizations.

When President Johnson dispatched J. Edgar Hoover to Mississippi to open the FBI's new Jackson field office, the Meridian

Star editorial said that Hoover's "real" mission was to "add to the to-do the government is making out of the disappearance of the three civil rights workers," and that "the big Philadelphia show goes on and on—the student volunteers, the beatniks, the wild-eyed left-wing nuts, the unshaved and unwashed go on meddling and muddling. The poison pen sweepings of the gutters of journalism go on printing their lying trash."

The newspaper, Rabbi Schlager thought, belonged at the top of any list of things that held the city back and suppressed new ideas.

At the beginning of April 1968, J. B. Stoner visited Meridian to conduct rallies of his National States Rights Party. Local Jews paid little attention. The FBI, aware of NSRP links to the White Knights and to incidents of racial and anti-Semitic violence in the 1950s and early 1960s, carefully monitored his activities. As it happened, the bureau's offices in the Meridian Post Office Building overlooked Bill Gordon's barbershop across the street, a notorious gathering place for the Klan.

On the evening of April 4, Jack Rucker, Frank Watts and several other FBI agents turned off their office lights to observe an organizational meeting Stoner was conducting in the barbershop. All of a sudden, as they looked out the window at Stoner standing under a huge banner emblazoned with the NSRP thunderbolt, word came over the FBI office's radio that Dr. Martin Luther King, Jr., had been assassinated in Memphis.

"Damn," Rucker exclaimed, "J. B. Stoner's got an alibi. If he wasn't down there right now, he'd be tops on our list of suspects." Stoner, a short, pudgy lawyer who walked with a limp as a result of childhood polio, had delivered bitter diatribes against King.

Word of King's death quickly reached Gordon's barbershop. Stoner and several Klansmen erupted into whoops of joy. "He's been a good nigger since he got shot," chortled Stoner, who later would represent James Earl Ray, King's assassin. Joining in the laughter at the barbershop were several Klansmen, including Raymond Roberts. And upon hearing the news at his mountain hideaway, Tarrants danced for joy.

While Stoner's anti-Semitic activities had caused relatively little concern among Meridian's Jews, he was the subject of a bulging dossier at ADL headquarters in New York. He had been a Ku

Klux Klan organizer as a teenager, formed the Stoner Anti-Jewish
Party at the age of twenty-three, wrote and distributed a pamphlet
declaring "the Satanic Jews must be put to death" and for more
than two decades had been one of the nation's most notorious
hatemongers. (Lawmen tried repeatedly, but without success, to
link Stoner to the 1963 Birmingham church bombing that killed
four black children. Not until 1980, when he was brought to trial
in Alabama and convicted in the 1958 bombing of another black
church in Birmingham, did Stoner finally go to prison. At his
trial, where he was sentenced to ten years, John Yung, the prosecutor, characterized him as "a professional hater, a cold-blooded
bomber and a bald-faced liar.")

Rabbi Schlager's reaction was an exception to the indifference
with which Meridian's Jews met Stoner's visit. He saw Stoner's
appearance as part of a larger pattern of growing intolerance. He
urged the congregation to organize for its own protection and to
install a security system for the synagogue.

In late May 1968, Binder was invited to speak at a Meridian
B'nai B'rith meeting and used the occasion to deliver a warning:
"Listen to your rabbi, take him seriously. He knows what he's
talking about. I know from my experiences in Jackson."

Meridian's Jews tried to shrug it off. Badgered by the rabbi,
the temple's board of trustees finally agreed to discuss hiring a
guard, but ultimately decided against even that precaution. Schlager was left to find what reassurance he could in a pledge from
the chief of police: "We won't let the bastards bother you," Roy
Gunn said. "We won't put up with Klan violence."

In a night rider attack late on the night of May 2, a machine gun
was fired into the home of Flossie Lindsey, a black woman active
in the NAACP who had been employed by a Head Start program
in the Sandhill community in rural Rankin County just northeast
of Jackson. Mrs. Lindsey's six-year-old niece, Betty Jean McLin,
was wounded in the leg by a bullet.

Tarrants, commuting in Danny Joe Hawkins' dark green Buick
back and forth to the area from his mountain hideout, had struck
once more.

On May 26, 1968, a Sunday, several area churches observed a
"Restoration Day" to raise funds for the rebuilding of six black

churches that had been burned in Lauderdale County in the preceding months. The appeal had been organized by the Committee of Conscience.

Two evenings later, Rabbi Schlager and his wife got home late from visiting a young couple who had just become engaged. The three Schlager children—Lennie, eleven; Helaine, six; and Davita, four—as well as Mrs. Schlager's mother, Ida Baren, who was living with the Schlagers, were all asleep. The rabbi and his wife were preparing to go to bed themselves when, about 12:15 A.M., a thunderous explosion in the distance shook the china in their kitchen closet.

The synagogue was three miles from Schlager's house, but from the moment he heard the sound, there was never any question in his mind that it was the temple.

"I knew it, I knew it, they've blown up the synagogue," he cried.

The Meridian temple was a modern three-building complex of glass, brick and concrete block. The sanctuary stood at the center, joined by glassed-in walkways to a religious education building on one side and a recreation building on the other. It had been built four years earlier, the year after Schlager came to Meridian, and was located on a sprawling wooded lot at the end of a dead-end street in the fashionable Broadmoor area. The nearest house was 150 yards away.

A powerful bomb made of fifteen sticks of dynamite had been placed on the concrete floor in an alcove at the front door of the religious education building. It had blown a hole in the roof, shredded the walls of the building, shattered the windows of the sanctuary, and rocked homes for blocks around. The thick glass wall panels of each of the education building's eleven classrooms were shattered. Chairs and tables from the two classrooms nearest to the explosion were blown out of the building.

The blast was so powerful it warped the foundation of the education building, left a gaping crater at the front entrance and draped the tops of hundred-foot-high pine trees surrounding the synagogue with the tattered remains of curtains and drapes.

Tarrants and Danny Joe Hawkins had driven quietly into the sleeping neighborhood and crept across the broad lawn carrying submachine guns along with the explosives.

To reach the front entrance of the education building, they had passed a memorial given to the temple the year before by a group of Meridian Christians. Six large gas lights burned perpetually in memory of the six million Jews slaughtered in the Holocaust; the lights surrounded a stone tablet on which was engraved the question:

"Am I My Brother's Keeper?"

8

Roy Gunn was in the hospital with a recurrent hip problem. He was asleep when a telephone call from the desk sergeant at police headquarters woke him with the news that the synagogue had been dynamited. True to form, the chief flew into a rage. He instructed the sergeant to get the department's top officials to his room immediately.

As his lieutenants and an FBI agent filed in, Gunn was still barking orders on the phone. The agent, in a Teletyped message to Hoover, said the chief was "visibly upset and highly emotional as a result of bombing and ordered his staff to commence this date an around-the-clock close surveillance of principal Klansmen in Meridian. Their activities will be closely watched to create the opportunity for an immediate arrest for any local violence regardless of how minor. Chief Gunn hoped to put constant pressure on suspects to ferret out any weak links on the hard core Klansmen."

Gunn's fury had a personal edge. The Meridian bombing was a territorial challenge. It made a mockery of his pledge to Rabbi Schlager that he would keep his people safe. If he could not protect the Jews, what about others? As Gunn knew, his own name headed the White Knights' hit list.

Reverend Harold O'Chester, pastor of the Poplar Springs Baptist Church, was awakened by a telephone call from the police department. The desk sergeant thought the pastor, as chairman of the Committee of Conscience, would want to know about the bombing. O'Chester was an unabashed conservative and segregationist who had declared, "I do not preach any social reform,

I preach the Bible." But the racial violence sickened him. As pastor of Meridian's third-largest Baptist church he had announced, "it's time to get rid of the Ku Klux Klan, the National States Rights Party, Americans for the Preservation of the White Race and all other hate-type organizations."

Shortly after the call from the police notifying him of the bombing, the telephone rang again. This time it was a voice he did not recognize.

"Do you know what happened?"

"Yes."

"You're next."

Jewish leaders in Mississippi expressed outrage at the latest bombing of a synagogue and vowed to raise whatever amount of reward money it might take to bring the terrorists to justice.

The attack on the temple prompted state and local officials to issue statements of shock and outrage similar to those expressed after the bombing of the Jackson synagogue and Rabbi Nussbaum's house.

Mississippi's new governor, John Bell Williams, accompanied by staff members and several reporters, flew to Meridian to inspect the damage and offer the state's full support in the investigation. "What kind of mind could get satisfaction from something like this?" he asked, standing amid the bricks, broken glass and rubble.

Though Williams had been silent while at least two hundred black churches in Mississippi were bombed or burned during his time as a congressman and then governor, he now declared that "it defies the imagination of civilized people to understand a mind so depraved as to destroy any house of worship." Ignoring the fact that six black churches in the Meridian area alone had been burned since he had become governor five months earlier, the governor called the bombing of the temple "the first" terrorism at a house of worship during his administration.

The Meridian city council labeled the bombing "a cowardly assault," called the terrorist acts "merely symptoms of a disease that plagues us all" and urged citizens to cooperate in the investigation. County sheriff Alton Allen, in a local television appeal, also urged public cooperation in the probe, saying, "We cannot and we will not tolerate chaos and violence in this county."

The Chamber of Commerce adopted a resolution calling on the majority to "assert itself to do whatever may be necessary to apprehend and convict those who destroy places of worship," and, paraphrasing Edmund Burke, it declared, "All that is necessary for evil to prevail is for good men to do nothing."

Even the Meridian *Star*, which had ignored most of the black church bombings, denounced the temple assault as "disgraceful" in a page-one editorial headlined "We Are Outraged." On the editorial page of the same issue, the *Star* denounced another "outrage"—the U.S. Supreme Court's decision striking down the freedom-of-choice plans that Mississippi officials had adopted to avoid desegregation.

The local business community was more responsive than its counterparts in Jackson had been to the bombing there. A group of businessmen that included Christians as well as Jews visited the Meridian *Star*, and the FBI later sent a Teletype to Washington saying they had gone "to impress upon the editor the need for more favorable publicity in regard to law enforcement agencies and less favorable publicity for J. B. Stoner and NSRP."

Binder and other Jewish leaders in Jackson, after conferring with Moore, decided to make their own reward funds available for the Meridian investigation, since the bombing there appeared to be the work of the same hands.

The Meridian temple's board of trustees appointed Meyer Davidson chairman of a committee to raise reward money. Meridian and Jackson newspapers quoted him as saying that as much as one hundred thousand dollars was being collected to pay informants.

The ADL's A. I. Botnick, who had driven to Meridian as soon as he learned of the bombing, assured Jewish leaders that enough money would be raised to solve the case. He also told Chief Gunn and Meridian mayor Al Key to call on him and the ADL for any assistance they might need in the investigation.

In Jackson, Joe Harris, Binder and George Mitchell, a Jackson businessman who was the state president of B'nai B'rith, scoffed at Botnick's assurances about the reward money. They said most of the money was raised by Jewish leaders in Jackson and neither Botnick nor the ADL had any role in raising it. Mitchell had led a drive that netted about forty-five thousand dollars, mostly in

donations of about five thousand dollars each from various B'nai
B'rith chapters.

Most of the money went through B'nai B'rith, Harris said,
"because that way it was tax deductible. All the ADL wanted was
the glory. Botnick talked too much. We told him to get his ass
out of Jackson and keep it out. But you couldn't insult Botnick."

To some extent, they were selling Botnick short. Jewish leaders
in Meridian felt his close working relationship with the FBI was
helpful. And in Washington, the ADL kept the political pressure
on the FBI to make sure agents in the field had whatever mandates
and resources they needed for the investigation.

Like most Southerners, Gunn had grown up an unquestioning
believer in segregation. And, like many Southern law enforcement
officers of his time, his instinct was to rely on force or physical
brutality when it came to dealing with blacks. In the early days
of the civil rights movement, his sympathies often had been with
the Klan. For years, Gunn's approach to racial justice was summed
up in his famous dictum: "The only thing we need to enforce the
law around here is a bunch of burrhead sticks."

Gunn often called himself a graduate of the school of hard
knocks. Born on July 1, 1904, Columbus Leroy Gunn quit school
in the seventh grade and went to work as a laborer on the Gulf,
Mobile and Ohio Railroad to help provide for his family. He
worked his way up to brakeman, but his railroading career was
ended by an almost fatal accident. One day, while riding on the
outside of a moving train, he lost his grip and fell between two
cars. Only quick reflexes saved him from being crushed to death.
He rolled himself into a ball as the train passed over him, but his
left leg was mangled and he was left with a permanent limp.

Gunn joined the Meridian police force as a motorcycle officer.
With his impaired leg, he had trouble at first keeping his balance
and frequently fell off. He took so many spills that he would joke
that "that son of a bitch will throw me and then come back around
the block and chase me." He was never seriously hurt, but one
of the spills reinjured his leg and made it worse.

Eventually, he joined the detective bureau. He spent fifteen
years there before being named assistant police chief and finally,
in 1965, taking over the department. An imposing figure, he stood
just over six feet tall, weighed 240 pounds and spoke in a loud

voice that some called authoritative and others called authoritarian. His daughter Amelia said he was "the kind of person that when he came into the room you either liked him a lot or hated his guts."

One who hated him—and the feeling was mutual—was Sam Keller, the assistant police chief Gunn beat out for the top post. Keller was a known Klan sympathizer whose brother Harold, a city fireman, was a Klan member. Another brother, Everett, was a Meridian policeman who was neither a Klansman nor a sympathizer, but because of Harold's Klan membership, Everett was turned down for police training at the FBI National Academy.

Everett Keller admired Gunn despite his brother Sam's feud with the chief. "There was never a time I didn't respect Gunn," Everett Keller said, "but for him there was only one way to do things and it was his way. He had guts, though, and if he told you to do something he'd back you to the hilt. He was an egomaniac and he had a strange religious bent. He could go from religion to vulgarity in a flash. He would say, 'I fought the good fight and Goddamn it, I'm gonna keep on doing it.'"

Gunn considered himself the keeper of the morals of all his men. More than once, when he found that an officer was having an affair with another officer's wife, he would call in both couples and counsel them. He disliked Everett Keller's brother Sam as much for his dubious morals as for his Klan ties. Sam moonlighted as a country music disc jockey on a local radio station and was widely known as a ladies' man. Around the police station they jokingly referred to him as Killer Keller because one of the women he went out with had been shot to death with his gun while he was in her apartment. Keller claimed the gun had gone off accidentally while she was sewing a tear in his uniform. He was never charged.

Gunn was in the habit of going to bed early, usually by eight o'clock, but frequently he would wake up after midnight and summon a patrol car. Then, dressed in his pajamas, bathrobe and slippers, he would have the patrolmen drive him around town so he could check on officers working the eleven-to-seven shift. It was a way of making sure they did not shirk their duty. Whenever he found an officer missing from his assigned post, the chief assumed he had slipped away for a tryst, most likely to meet a waitress from one of the local cafés or truck stops.

"He's just out fooling around with the damn chili dippers,"
Gunn would say. "You'd better watch out for those chili dippers,"
he lectured his men. "They love that uniform and they'll stay after
you, so don't let them lead you astray. Now, don't go messin'
around on your wife."

Gunn's moral concern extended beyond the police department
and included what people saw at the movies. He shut down the
Royal Theater when it attempted to show an R-rated film called
Bloody Mama, based on the gangster exploits of Ma Barker and
three of her four sons in the 1920s and 1930s. The marquee let
Meridianites know: "CHIEF ROY GUNN SAYS MERIDIAN CAN'T SEE
BLOODY MAMA." Gunn acknowledged that he had not seen the
film but he had been told it included "one nude scene and two
nudes from the waist up, and was vulgar and indecent." A court
overturned the ban and the movie played to packed houses, but
Gunn was proud of his stand and kept a clipping of the Meridian
Star's article on the controversy in his scrapbook.

"The law to him was black and white and he had no philosophy
to him whatsoever," said Elsie Logan, a Meridian stockbroker
who served with Gunn on the board of stewards of the Hawkins
Memorial Methodist Church. Gunn was chairman of the board.
"He never had any question about what he was doing. He was
adamant about the rightness of his actions. He was absolutely
sure that every word of the Bible was true. He never had any of
the doubts about that that some of the others of us had."

Gunn's certainty reinforced his legendary temper. Many recall
the time the Atlas Roofing Company was embroiled in a labor
dispute and a striker fired a shot that shattered a truck driver's
windshield. The chief ordered so many officers into the three
available patrol cars that they were virtually hanging out the windows as they raced to the scene. Gunn rode shotgun in the lead
car.

When the cars screeched to a halt at the roofing company, Gunn
jumped out with a megaphone. He climbed on the hood of the
second patrol car, held out his arm to look at his watch and
bellowed: "All right, I'll give you just five minutes to get your
asses out of here. You can leave two pickets, but they can't sit
down. If you're not out in five minutes, your asses have had it."

The crowd instantly dispersed, leaving two pickets standing
alone holding signs. "If they had not left, he would have shot

them, I have no question about that," said John Proctor, the resident FBI agent in charge of the Meridian office.

On another occasion, when tensions flared in Meridian's black neighborhood and there were rumors the Meridian police might be the target of violence, Gunn showed up at a noisy demonstration. "I'll do what I can to see that there's no violence, and I'll sit on a curb and negotiate with a nigger prostitute," he told the crowd, "but the first son of a bitch that throws a brick at one of my police officers is dead." There was loud murmuring among the demonstrators, but the crowd dispersed.

Gunn's disregard for due process was reflected throughout the department. When Meridian police lacked evidence to make arrests, they would simply book suspects on charges of "D and S"—dangerous and suspicious—and hold them for as much as seventy-two hours.

During the early part of Gunn's tenure as a top police official, the department was riddled with Klan members and went in for brutality. "A den of hatred," Elsie Logan called it. The detectives' interrogation room was a torture chamber. The "lie detector," a two-foot-long black leather strap with a metal spring in it, was used in questioning blacks, and an electric cattle prod and a contraption rigged up with wires and two batteries were used to shock recalcitrant suspects.

Marie Knowles, the detective bureau's secretary, never got used to the sound of the clubs smashing against skulls and prisoners screaming in pain. "They would pop them with anything that was handy," she said, "and sometimes just backhand them."

When she had taken the job three years earlier, she was twenty-four years old and had six children to help support—three from her first marriage and three from her second husband's first marriage. At first, she had found the rawness of the life hard to take. The officers' conduct had shocked her nearly as much as the crimes. Rough-natured men with little formal education or professional training, they lived hand to mouth on low wages and met violence with violence.

Knowles had a close-up view of "the rotten side of life," as she put it. She knew "who was going with who and when they were doing it and what night of the week they were doing it." And when the detectives were using the "burrhead sticks" or "nigger knockers" on some poor black, she would have to leave the bullpen. "Just go take a coffee break 'til we're done," the detectives would tell her.

Some FBI agents made it their business in that period to avoid the detective bureau when they thought suspects were being interrogated. The agents reasoned that, since they had to work with the local police, they had best avoid situations that might require them to investigate the detectives.

On one occasion, Everett Keller decided to "play a joke" on a new FBI agent assigned to Meridian. "Keller got a young black to go into the interrogation room with a policeman and act like he was being beaten," recalled John Proctor. "While the policeman pounded the desk with a leather strap, the youth hollered, 'Don't hit me no more! I did it! I did it!' When he heard that, the young agent turned and ran out of the police station."

Somehow, during the rise of the civil rights movement and the resurgence of the Klan, Gunn underwent a dramatic conversion. He began to take seriously his obligation to enforce the law evenhandedly. He turned against racial violence, and, as much as any man in the state, he dedicated himself to ridding Mississippi of the Klan. In doing so, he set off a virtual blood feud with the White Knights and made himself the indispensable man to the FBI and its allies in the Jewish community.

The change seems to have begun with Jack Rucker and Frank Watts. The agents, who had been sent to Meridian in 1964 as part of "the new Southern FBI," knew that unless they could persuade Gunn to change his own attitude and clean up his department, the bureau stood little chance of breaking the back of the White Knights in an area that was fast becoming its main battleground.

Watts remembers that he and Rucker spent "hours on hours" with Gunn in an effort to change him. "In a way he was honest as he could be. I don't think he'd ever told a lie. But he was hardnosed and uneducated like so many of the police officers in Mississippi and it was tough convincing him that he needed to be professional and needed to make his police force more professional. The Meridian police force was like a lot of the other local police departments—it was pathetic. They didn't have any training, and if you were a big, burly guy and could stand up and breathe and knock the hell out of somebody, then they'd give you a badge and a gun. That's the way Gunn was brought up and a lot of police in his department, too. We had to persuade him you couldn't go around slapping handcuffs on suspects and then pulling guns on them."

For instance, if the FBI agents told him they wanted to interview someone, the chief would say, "go out and get the son of a bitch and handcuff him and bring him in." For all the patrolmen knew, the subject might have just robbed a bank, so they would go out and slap handcuffs on him and take him to the police station, only to find they had brought in a respectable businessman who could ill afford to leave his business and who might not even have the information the agents needed. Watts and Rucker advised Gunn that it would be much better for the officers and that they would get more cooperation out of the subjects if they treated them courteously and gave them the benefit of the doubt.

"Gunn was the kind of guy who would give you the shirt off his back, but he was high tempered and wouldn't take anything off anybody," Watts said. "He didn't forget anything and he didn't forgive anything."

For all of Gunn's hardheadedness, the efforts of Watts and Rucker gradually began to have an effect. Signs of change began to appear. The chief stopped talking about "niggers" and began talking about how he wanted people to respect the police department.

It was one morning while sitting in church that Gunn had the experience that strengthened his determination to change. Reverend William Apperson, a member of the Committee of Conscience, remembered Gunn coming to see him about the experience. Apperson, the pastor of First Christian Church in Meridian, had become something close to a father confessor for Gunn. First Christian Church's approximately five hundred members were as open-minded a Protestant congregation as any in Mississippi. And Apperson was no stranger to racial violence. He had been in Kentucky when Governor Happy Chandler had called out the National Guard to quell violence over school desegregation, and in Meridian a rock had been hurled through his window bearing a message to him, his wife and their two young daughters: "You and your family will get yours."

On this occasion, Gunn had attended a Sunday evening service that Apperson had conducted. It was a warm summer night. As other members of the congregation drifted away to their homes, Apperson and Gunn stood under a streetlight on the sidewalk in front of the church.

"I've reached a crossroads and now it's do or die," Gunn told Apperson. "I've got to do something about enforcing the law for everybody and I've got to do something about the police department." He did not go into details; he didn't have to. He and Apperson had talked before about Gunn's growing frustration at not being able to trust some of his own men because they were Klansmen. "We both knew what he meant," Apperson recalled. "It seemed to come to him as a conversion experience. It was a real about-face. He said, 'I can't carry water on both shoulders anymore.'

"After he shared this with me," said Apperson, "I simply made a couple of comparisons. 'Well, Chief Gunn,' I told him, 'you are doing the right thing. Your own Wesley went through the experience of having his heart strangely warmed, and many years before that Martin Luther, confronting the princes of Catholic tradition at the Diet of Worms, said, 'Here I stand. God knows I can do no other.' "

"That's about where I am," Gunn responded.

The next day Gunn sought out Bill Ready. Ready's father and Gunn were close friends, but the young lawyer had often argued with Gunn about the police department's treatment of blacks. Gunn, repeating what he had told Apperson, said, "Ready, I don't think I had a religious experience, but something happened sitting in church yesterday. I decided that I'm the damn law in Meridian, Mississippi, and if the law doesn't apply to everybody, it doesn't apply to anybody. I think you're right. If they start killing off the black folks, next they'll get all the Jews, and then they'll get the Catholics—and that means you. And you and me are friends."

Soon after, Gunn assembled the police force and issued an edict: "You can be a member of the Meridian police force or you can be a member of the Klan, but if you're a member of the Klan you can't be a member of the Meridian police force."

He required the eighty-five members of the force to sign a loyalty oath denying that they were or ever had been members of the Communist Party or other "subversive groups," which according to Gunn's decree included the Ku Klux Klan and other hate groups. Several officers quit outright; several took early retirement. "Some of the others just lied and signed it," Gunn told a local reporter. By some estimates, more than half and perhaps as many as two thirds of the members of the department were Klan sympathizers.

Gunn decreed that there would be "no more nigger talk" in the department and that henceforth the law would be applied equally to all people. To show he meant business, the chief ordered the arrest of several Klansmen on misdemeanor charges of trespassing and disturbing the peace after they were caught burning crosses in the yards of members of the Committee of Conscience—offenses the police had previously winked at. Columnist Tom Etheridge ridiculed the arrests in the Jackson *Clarion-Ledger* and likened the cross burnings to flashing the "V for victory" sign during World War II. Ken Fairley, then a *Clarion-Ledger* reporter, watched Gunn read the column then angrily telephone Etheridge and one of the Hedermans who owned the paper. "He was furious and told them, 'I've read that crap in the paper about the arrests for burning crosses and I want you to know that if you come down to Meridian and I can find a way to do it, I'll throw your ass in jail.' "

At the urging of Watts and Rucker, Gunn sought to upgrade the outdated equipment of his force, and in February 1968, in an open letter to voters supporting a bond issue to finance improvements, he maintained that the department was "40 years behind times in techniques and equipment." He wrote that in the thirty-five years he had been on the force, the number of officers had increased from seventeen to eighty-five, but the department still had the same work space and "deplorable jail cells, only one small cell block for female prisoners with no accommodations whatsoever and no cell at all for juveniles, they have to be placed with hardened criminals, the perverts, robbers and other assorted professional crooks."

There was a touching side to Gunn's efforts to follow the FBI's lead. He issued a strict dress code requiring that detectives wear black shoes and the broad-brimmed felt hats that had been—but no longer were—the FBI's trademark. They were ordered to wear them at all times when on duty, regardless of season. The hulking figure of Gunn limping down the corridor to the bullpen, intoning, "Yea, though I walk through the valley of the shadow of death I will fear no evil" as he was wont to do, could strike fear into the hearts of the most hardened detectives. They knew that if he caught them bareheaded more than once, they would be suspended without pay for three days—no small matter, considering the officers' modest pay. Spotting violations of his hat decree, Gunn would order Marie Knowles to type up a succinct memo— "Detectives have been observed bareheaded!" The chief of detectives would immediately take names and order, "Everybody get your hats on!"

Sloppy dress and uncleanliness were likewise grounds for suspension. Once, when a young rookie patrolman who moonlighted as a "shade-tree mechanic"—fixing automobiles in his yard— showed up for work with grime under his fingernails, Gunn told him, "I'm gonna suspend you for three days to give you time to get that grease out from under your fingernails."

Spotting an officer with his shoes scuffed up, Gunn ridiculed him: "Look at him. His shoes don't match. He's as worthless as teats on a boar hog."

To the White Knights, Gunn's about-face was more than an outrage. It was dangerous. Bowers' lieutenants did their best to punish and intimidate the chief and all who supported him. There were death threats, harassing telephone calls late at night and more.

Gunn responded by organizing trusted police officers into the blackshirt squad, which began using some of the Klan's own tactics against it. In addition to gathering information about Klan activities, the blackshirts waged their own "COINTELPRO" of anti-Klan harassment, sometimes going so far as to set off small explosions outside Klansmen's houses or shooting into their homes to intimidate them.

The chief felt he had almost a divine mandate to stop the violence in Meridian, and he agonized over his inability to do so. His war with the Klan put tremendous strain on him and his family. On those nights when Klan threats had been received, police cars were stationed in his neighborhood. Gunn would eat supper and climb the stairs to the upstairs bedroom in the front of his modest frame house at the corner of B Street and Twenty-fourth Avenue near downtown Meridian. There, in the hot, humid darkness, he would sit for hours with the shotgun across his lap, looking out the window at the empty street and waiting for the Klan.

With all the strains on his department, Gunn felt there was not enough manpower to keep a permanent guard outside his house, and one night when he had removed the police watch and was standing watch himself, the Klan set off a powerful stink bomb in front of the house. The wind was blowing away from the house so it caused only a minor problem for the Gunns, but the foul odor permeated a hospital several blocks away and caused such discomfort that the patients had to be evacuated.

Gunn's daughter Amelia saw her father become "so frustrated he would get very emotional and cry like a baby." At Hawkins Memorial Methodist Church, he broke down and wept while telling the congregation he had failed in his mission to stop the terrorism. "He often would cry while praying if he happened to be frustrated over not being able to solve the latest case of racial violence," Elsie Logan recalled. "They were terrible times and it just killed him he couldn't have things his way. He was determined that there would be no killings by the Klan and he yearned to stop the violence."

To drive his point home, Gunn made a speech at the weekly meeting of the Meridian Kiwanis Club and startled the members by waving a shotgun around. Declaring that he had been subjected to threats and that two "known Klansmen" had circled his home and planned to attack him and his family, he said, "This is what a man is subjected to if he's got guts enough to stand up for law and order. But it will not deter me personally or my department from doing our duty, but will increase our efforts fourfold. And I pray to God to spare my life long enough that I can be a pallbearer to these people's funeral so as to send them to hell where they belong."

The club gave him a standing ovation.

Early in June, soon after the Meridian synagogue was bombed, Al Binder and George Mitchell drove to Meridian to meet with Watts and Rucker. With the bombings in their own city still unsolved, both of the Jackson Jews had begun to carry guns wherever they went. The Hinds County sheriff's office, agreeing with the concern expressed by the Jewish community that any activist might become a Klan target, had deputized them—along with Joe Harris and several other Jackson Jews—so that they could legally carry firearms.

Binder was armed with a gleaming new Colt .38 with his name engraved on it, presented to him by Detective Luke Scarbrough on behalf of Chief Gunn and the Meridian police force. Although Binder did not consider the detective as "necessarily a sympathizer with the Jews," Scarbrough endeared himself to the lawyer by taking him out to a firing range and teaching him to shoot the pistol.

At their meeting in Meridian, Mitchell asked the two FBI agents: "What do you need that the government's not providing?"

"Money to buy information," said Watts, echoing Roy Moore of the Jackson FBI office.

"You'll get it," Mitchell said.

At his office, Moore had immediately decided to mount a full-court press in Meridian. He had ordered additional agents to the city and dispatched a cable to Hoover saying the FBI laboratory and identification facilities already had been made available to local and state authorities. Military intelligence, the Secret Service and other relevant federal agencies were being alerted. Agents had been instructed to contact all "Klan and appropriate informants" immediately.

The questioning of known Klansmen turned up nothing fruitful; one Klansman reminded the agent that "Jews are the biggest nigger-loving people in the world" but disclaimed any knowledge of the bombing. Nor did the FBI's thorough canvassing of persons living near the synagogue turn up anything; one man said he had heard a car go past on the street a few minutes before the explosion but had not seen it. And the crime scene yielded little: no bits of wire or fragments of detonator caps that might be traced.

They were not quite up against a blank wall, however. At long last, they were zeroing in on the shadowy figure known as "the Man." He and Danny Joe Hawkins had become the bureau's prime suspects.

According to FBI informants, "the Man" reported only to Bowers and dealt with almost no other members of the White Knights. He was extremely careful. He never showed up at Klan rallies. He guarded his identity. He was cautious about using telephones. And he struck with lightning speed, then disappeared from the area.

The bureau did not yet know who the mysterious figure was, but it was finally on the right track.

9

Early in the second week of June, the ADL's Bee Botnick met with Ken Dean and his wife, Mary, in a passenger lounge of the New Orleans airport. Dean had received an urgent telephone call from Botnick and had agreed to meet him during a layover. Botnick looked greatly alarmed and more nervous than usual when he rushed up and declared, "Something almost beyond belief has happened."

Chief Gunn and Mayor Key had come to see him in New Orleans on June 2, Botnick told Dean, and had identified Raymond and Alton Wayne Roberts as the ones responsible for the Meridian synagogue bombing and most of the other Klan violence in their area. Botnick said Gunn and Key had asked him if the Jewish businessmen who were putting up the reward money "would be willing to purchase bodies and not testimony."

And, according to a Dean memo recounting his meeting with Botnick, they also asked Botnick "if he would make a contact somewhere in the North, such as Chicago, to have two Klansmen liquidated. The two Klansmen were Raymond Roberts and Alton Wayne Roberts. The mayor and the chief assured Botnick that if he could make the arrangements, there would be no investigation."

While Gunn was widely known as a hot-tempered zealot capable of violence, Algreene Earl Key was a gentle, friendly man and a local hero; for the mayor to be party to such a proposal would be staggering. A famed aerial stuntman during the barnstorming era in the 1920s, he and his brother Fred had set a world's record for endurance flying, keeping their plane in the air nonstop over Meridian for twenty-seven days and nights—a record not broken until the *Skylab Two* spaceflight in 1973.

Botnick, according to Dean's memo, told Gunn and Key he could not do what they had asked. The mayor then asked what he would suggest they do. "Botnick said that he told the mayor that rather than shoot the Roberts brothers, it would be better to get them to talk. He said he told the mayor and the chief to take the two Roberts brothers out on a dark road at night and beat the hell out of them to within an inch of their lives. He said that if they would do this and then offer money that the Roberts brothers would talk."

For all Botnick's alarm at their proposal, he told Dean he brought it up at a meeting of Jewish businessmen and, far from rejecting it, they had indicated "they didn't give a Goddamn how the mess was cleared up, but only that it was."

Gunn was acting out of fear as well as anger. He told Botnick that he and Key had seen a Klan assassination list and both he and Key were on it, along with eight Mississippi Jews. Meridian police had picked up rumors through Klan informants that the Roberts brothers were personally pressing for Gunn's assassination. A Scarbrough memo quoted two different confidential sources as saying Raymond Roberts "contacted Sam Bowers and wants to eliminate Chief Gunn and possibly two FBI agents."

Like Gunn, Watts and Rucker were focusing their attention more and more on Raymond and Alton Wayne Roberts as the keys to ending the wave of violence. But they were also still trying to pin down the identity of the elusive terrorist they knew only as "the Man." Their first break came when news of the hunt for the Meridian synagogue bombers prompted a report about a "Tommie Tarrance" who had desecrated a synagogue and made anti-Semitic threats in Mobile. When agents followed up on the tip, they learned that Tarrants had been indicted on federal charges of possessing a machine gun after his car was pulled over the previous December in Collins, Mississippi. The incident linked Tarrants to Sam Bowers, who was his passenger that night.

In a teletyped message to FBI headquarters on May 30, three days after the synagogue bombing, the FBI identified "the Man" as a fugitive from Mobile named Thomas Albert Tarrance. Another FBI memo noted that he should be "considered armed and dangerous" and that agents were searching for ties between him and Meridian Klansmen.

The Meridian police had their own network of informants, and they too were coming around to the view that Tarrants was responsible for the synagogue bombing. Detective Scarbrough dictated a detailed memo headed "Wanted as Fugitive," which spelled Tarrants' name the same phonetic way the FBI had in its report to Hoover:

> Thomas Albert Tarrance, aka Nick Allen, WM, 21, DOB: 12/20/47. Subject was arrested in Collins, Mississippi, 12, 22, 1967 with Sam Bowers and had in his possession a machine gun and was in a stolen car. He went to Mobile and threatened a rabbi and also a civil rights worker. He told an informer that he had robbed a supermarket of $4,000 and that a klansman in Mississippi was going to hide him out. Subject has boasted that he knows how to use explosives. At this time he is driving a 1954–56 blue and white Pontiac with Webster Co., license 78————.
>
> Last fall subject went to Laurel and worked as a Masonite employe from August until April of this year. He is a big braggart and tells people he enjoys killing; also curses a lot. On March 26, he was known to possess a 30.36 rifle, an automatic pistol and a machine gun. At the time Sam Bowers was arrested it was known that Tarrance was in the area of Laurel and was also known that Raymond Roberts met with Sam Bowers and expressed to him his dissatisfaction that "enough is not going on." L. E. Matthews, who is supposed to take Bowers' place [as imperial wizard of the White Knights] when he leaves [for prison], came to Meridian and when he returned he said they had a man in Meridian that was capable of handling the job well and is named Raymond Roberts. Roberts told Matthews that he had to go down South to get somebody to pull a job.

Tarrants himself had been in hiding since March. Out on bond on the illegal machine gun charge, he had enrolled at Mobile College in January, hoping to present a better image to the authorities. But with a federal indictment being prepared in the case, he doubted he could get off this time as a wayward youth. So in March, facing the indictment and almost certain conviction, he decided to go underground. He immediately set out on a trip to the West, visiting the anti-Semitic Dr. Wesley Swift of Lancaster, California. Tarrants would later testify he bought a rifle from Swift with plans to use it to shoot Dr. Martin Luther King, Jr. "That was my ambition, to shoot Dr. King," Tarrants said later. "I hated Dr. King."

On March 23, when he returned to his home in Mobile, he found the FBI waiting. Teams of agents were sitting in two cars parked outside his house. He spotted them before they recognized him, however, and escaped.

Within a week, Tarrants was in a safe house located in the mountains near Franklin, North Carolina, staying with friends who were followers of Swift and connected with right-wing radicals in Miami. Months later, FBI agents backtracking on Tarrants' trail interviewed a neighbor of the family. The neighbor said the house was used for meetings of extremists from Mississippi, Alabama, Georgia and Florida as well as North Carolina. He described the host family as "extremely antiblack and anti-Jewish" and one member as "crazy enough to blow up the White House." The area behind the house was used frequently for target practice with firearms ranging from pistols to automatic weapons. Using the North Carolina house as a base, Tarrants was soon making forays into Mississippi for meetings with Bowers and new attacks on Klan targets. He saw himself as a patriot and closely identified himself with another notorious felon and anti-Semite on the run, Robert DePugh, head of the paramilitary Minutemen.

In his notebook one night, Tarrants wrote a memo that he thereafter carried with him everywhere he went. The note stipulated that it was to be made public, but Tarrants never released it.

"Gentlemen," the memo read,

> Please be advised that as of March 23, 1968, I, Thomas Albert Tarrants III, was forced to go underground or be arrested and imprisoned on framed Federal charges of violation of National Firearms Act and other misc. charges. My decision to make this announcement was in part influenced by a similar announcement by that great patriot Robert DePugh of the Minutemen. In that

my situation is very similar to his I have decided to make public this announcement.

I will further state that I have always believed in military action against the common enemy. I have committed myself totally to defeating the communist jew conspiracy which threatens our country—any means necessary shall be used. On March 23, 1968, I was forced to go underground or face framed federal charges of possession of a submachine gun in Collins, Mississippi, on 21 December 1967.

Please be advised that since March 28, 1968 I Thomas A. Tarrants have been underground and operating guerrilla warfare.

At least once, Tarrants turned to robbery to finance his activities. He proved a calm, cool holdup man. He remained in the back of a Kroger supermarket in Jackson after closing time on a Friday night until only a clerk doing last-minute chores remained in the store. Pointing a .45-caliber semiautomatic pistol at the clerk, Tarrants said, "Don't act like a hero, just open the safe."

When the terrified clerk told him that only the manager and assistant manager had the combination, Tarrants ordered him to summon the manager by telephone: "Make up a good story, because if he brings someone with him, there will be a shoot-out with you in the middle." The clerk made the call with the steel of the pistol's barrel on the back of his head, the safety clicking off and on. He told the manager he needed him to come help because the water pump had broken and it was flooding the produce area. As soon as the clerk completed the call, Tarrants locked him in the meat cooler.

About thirty minutes later the manager arrived, a smooth-faced young man who looked to be hardly in his twenties. As the manager walked toward the back of the store, Tarrants stepped slowly from behind a food display, pointed the pistol at his head and said, "Hold it. If anyone is with you or if the police come up, there will be a shoot-out and you'll be in the middle." Tarrants forced the young manager to open the safe, them made him transfer $4,279 from a cash drawer to a paper sack.

"Aren't you a little too young to be a manager and won't this cost you your job?" Tarrants asked.

The manager agreed that he was young for the job and that the robbery probably would result in his being fired.

"I'm sorry," said Tarrants as he herded the manager into the meat cooler, "but it has to be done."

Tarrants' partner, Kathy Ainsworth, meantime, was continuing to live her bizarre double life—devoted grade school teacher and model citizen by day, right-wing radical by night. She taught her classes, helped her husband, Ralph, with his health club business and played the role of typical young homemaker.

With the help of her mother, for example, she had gone to the Kennington Company, a Jackson home-appliance dealer, and arranged to buy a new kitchen range, a new refrigerator and a washer and dryer on the installment plan. The total bill came to $937.33, a considerable amount for a schoolteacher in the 1960s, but she put down $50 and agreed to pay $78 a month until the balance was retired. Her mother cosigned the contract.

The secret to her success seemed to be that she never let her two worlds overlap. Going back even to her own school days, she had seldom allowed anyone from her daytime world to glimpse the depth of her racist and anti-Semitic feelings.

In fact, Kathy Ainsworth was a second-generation hater.

Along with an older brother, Anthony Capomacchia, Jr., Kathy had been raised in Miami. Her mother, born Margot Marshon in Los Angeles of Hungarian immigrant parents, was a follies dancer who married Antonio Capomacchia, a circus juggler twelve years her senior, in Juárez, Mexico, in 1939. They later moved to Los Angeles, where Antonio junior was born in 1940; subsequently the father joined a traveling vaudeville show, and on July 31, 1941, Kathryn Madlyn Capomacchia was born in Chicago.

During World War II, the USO hired Antonio Capomacchia as an entertainer and he traveled from one army camp to another, always taking his family along. Finally, in 1945, they settled in Miami, where he found work at resort hotels. The marriage, apparently never very stable, began to crumble. Mrs. Capomacchia constantly ridiculed her husband, often in the presence of others, and he would sometimes react violently. A childhood friend of Kathy's was quoted in *The Miami Herald* as saying, "Mrs. Capomacchia used to ridicule Kathy's father all the time in front of the children. It was like she hated all men. I can still remember her standing in the kitchen, drying the dishes with us, and saying that Kathy was just the product of an accident on a cold Chicago night."

Kathy's father doted on her, but she sided with her mother in their many domestic quarrels. Her father, speaking in broken English, told *The Miami Herald*, "She was an angel. Great big brown eyes and everyone on the block adore her. Always so sweet. She always stay aroun' the house . . . never, never go out in street to play like a bad girl." But the deterioration of his marriage also cost him his relationship with his daughter. "My wife become very cold to me," he said. "I learn to live with her like that, but soon I become a stranger in my own house. I come home from work and say to Kathy, 'Kathy, you come with me to the movie, huh?' But Kathy, she run to her momma and say, 'No, momma, I don't want to go with him!' Her momma always there. . . ." In 1954, Mrs. Capomacchia ordered her husband out of the house; later, she was granted a divorce and given custody of the children.

Mrs. Capomacchia had little formal education, but she was determined that her daughter would be well schooled. Working as a cleaning woman, she managed to put Kathy and Antonio junior through high school. Kathy was considered highly intelligent by both classmates and teachers at Coral Gables High, where she graduated with honors and was a member of the Cavalettes, an elite marching group selected on the basis of popularity and scholastic ability.

Although eligible for scholarships at several Florida schools, Kathy chose to accept a scholarship to attend Mississippi College, a rigidly segregated institution in the small town of Clinton. Her racism and anti-Semitism were reinforced at the college. Dr. W. M. Caskey, a hard-line segregationist and adviser to Governor Ross Barnett, was one of her favorite professors. Dr. Caskey lectured students about "outside agitators" coming into Mississippi and trying to destroy the state's white Christian culture.

Kathy shared a room with Bonnie Barnes, whose father was Sidney Crockett Barnes, widely known as an extreme racist and anti-Semite. A fat, balding and boisterous housepainter, he was an avid follower of several hate propagandists, including Wesley Swift, the head of the Church of Jesus Christ, Christian, in Lancaster, California. Barnes often gathered friends together at his house to listen to tape-recorded messages from Swift. Mrs. Capomacchia and Kathy attended many of the sessions.

Although Kathy openly expressed her extremist views only rarely, some of her friends in Mobile began to notice a strain of anti-Semitism. She reacted coolly when Shirley Fulcher, a teacher whose brother dated Kathy and who "would have been happy if they had married," told her how much she enjoyed teaching at the predominantly Jewish Miami Beach High School and how much she admired the students' talents and abilities. At first Fulcher was puzzled by Kathy's reaction, but she understood it better after a mutual friend told her Kathy expressed disappointment that her friend Shirley seemed to enjoy teaching at a school attended by so many Jews.

In 1964, Barnes and his family moved from Miami to Mobile. Kathy and her mother continued to visit them, and it was on one of their visits that Kathy met Tommy Tarrants. Both considered Barnes their mentor and thought of themselves as Christian soldiers pursuing a holy cause.

Tarrants called their dedication "a passionate devotion" and said the depth and intensity of it was hard for the average person to understand. With unselfconscious irony, he cited what he said was a letter written by an American Communist breaking off an engagement with his fiancée as perhaps the best expression of such commitment among all radicals, left or right: "We have a cause to fight for, a specific goal in life. We lose our insignificant identities in the great river of humanity; and if our personal lives seem hard, or if our egos seem bruised through subordination to the Party, we are amply rewarded—in the thought that all of us, even though it be in a very small way, are contributing something new and better for humanity."

Kathy's radicalization had reached the point where she embraced such fanaticism wholeheartedly. She joined the White Knights and the Americans for the Preservation of the White Race. She began dating a young farmer in Mendenhall, not far from Jackson, and fell deeply in love with him, but it was a one-sided affair and the couple broke up after a brief romance.

Not long afterward, Kathy had taken a temporary job at the Universal Health Club in Jackson and begun to date Ralph Ainsworth, the club's amiable young manager. He adored Kathy, but was appalled when she pledged him to secrecy and told him she was in the Klan. Her commitment to the Klan was so strong that she would break a date with him to attend a nighttime rally.

Despite the many hours she spent every week on Klan-type activities, Kathy's associates outside of the hate groups had little inkling of her state of mind. She was known as a segregationist, but that did not set her apart from most Mississippi whites. She was not generally considered an extremist at Duling Elementary School, where she and eleven other women taught about 360 students. Except for one black girl, all of the students were white. When the black girl was assigned to Kathy's fifth grade class, by all accounts she treated her the same way she treated the white students.

Her fellow teachers considered her mild-mannered and pleasant, although naive and easily influenced. At Duling, she organized and published a mimeographed cookbook entitled *Favorite Recipes of the Mothers of Our Fifth Grade Class*. Included were two of her own recipes: "Miss Kathy Capomacchia's Brunswick Stew" and "Miss Kathy Capomacchia's Fig Cake." It was quite a different individual who attended meetings of the White Knights and the Americans for the Preservation of the White Race. At one APWR meeting, she vehemently denounced "the Communist/Jewish conspiracy" and declared she was being required to teach from textbooks containing "Communist propaganda."

On only one recorded occasion did she let her religious views slip into her schoolwork: she wrote a playlet that evoked the name of Christ so many times in connection with secular events that it caused a minor flap among parents of the several Jewish students attending the school. In the end, the school principal decided the playlet was too difficult for the children to perform as written so the script was rewritten and the numerous references to Christ omitted. It was the only time anyone there could recall Miss Capomacchia getting involved in anything controversial.

Kathy and Ralph Ainsworth were married in August 1967. A beaming Sidney Barnes gave away the bride. Mrs. Capomacchia was not particularly happy about the wedding—she had hoped her daughter would marry someone who shared their views on race and religion—but she continued to play a dominant role in her daughter's life, even selecting the site of the couple's honeymoon. For their wedding trip, they traveled to Arkansas to visit the Christ of the Ozarks, a monument erected by Gerald L. K. Smith, the notorious anti-Semitic radio preacher from the 1920s and 1930s. Kathy and her mother had once worshiped there.

If Ralph Ainsworth ever attended any Klan rallies or other meetings of hate groups, the FBI was not aware of it. An inform-ant told the bureau that Kathy always attended alone and that Klan members considered her husband to be "both a square and unenlightened."

Ainsworth was madly in love with his wife but disapproved of her membership in the White Knights. He did not disagree with the Klan's goal of preserving segregation, but he opposed its tactics and was so concerned about Kathy's safety while she was traveling alone to attend nighttime rallies that he bought her a six-millimeter Browning automatic pistol to carry in her purse.

10

The strain of the bombing investigation and the demands of protecting Mayor Key, Chief Gunn and several Jewish residents was proving too much for the Meridian police. They decided they needed outside help. Scarbrough suggested that Gunn get help from a special unit known as "the goon squad" that the state highway patrol used to harass hate groups. At Gunn's request, the highway patrol assigned a six-man squad to Meridian.

Gunn supplied the squad with photos of suspects and Scarbrough noted in a memo, "We fully explained to them what we wanted done and left it in their judgment when and how to carry it out."

The FBI also had decided it was time for more extreme measures—as Frank Watts put it, it was "time to fight fire with fire." Even though he had no hard evidence, he was convinced that Tarrants had bombed the synagogue, and he felt the quickest way to nail Tarrants would be to lay a trap for him. To do that would involve the unpleasant chore of recruiting the Roberts brothers as informants, but Watts figured, "You just have to deal with the scum of the earth to catch the scum of the earth."

The bureau had been gathering evidence linking the Roberts brothers to attacks on some of the black churches, but the priority now was not the church burnings. It was the bombing of the synagogue. "Once the Jews were attacked," Watts said, "it was a different ball game. This wasn't just a local across-the-railroad-track case. It involved the whole United States." People were putting pressure on senators and congressmen in Washington and demanding that action be taken against the terrorists. As a result of that pressure, Hoover decreed that every morning, seven days a week, Watts was to file a Teletype to Washington keeping the director abreast of every development.

Watts' boss, Roy Moore, summed up the most threatening situations: "There were four things that they had on the drawing board. There was the killing of the chief, doing away with me, placing a case of dynamite in a synagogue over there when all the congregation was in it, and the fourth thing they had on the drawing board—there were four of them—they planned to get one of the prominent Jews who was collecting the reward money for the city fathers."

While Watts and Jack Rucker pressed their plan to turn Alton Wayne and Raymond Roberts into informants, Chief Gunn turned his attention to a third brother, Lee, a policeman and a known Klan sympathizer who was believed to have a drug problem. He was a large man with a bullying nature. Once, after spotting Reverend Charles Johnson, a young black minister, making an illegal U-turn in downtown Meridian, he rushed up, put a pistol to Johnson's head and shouted: "You don't do that, nigger, or I'll blow your brains out."

Gunn, looking for a way to get rid of Lee Roberts, assigned Scarbrough to work up a case against him based on rumors that Roberts had falsified prescriptions for drugs. Later, Marie Knowles typed up a report of Scarbrough's investigation.

Armed with the report, Gunn told Roberts, "You can resign or I'm gonna put your ass in Parchman state prison." Roberts resigned.

To unnerve Raymond and Alton Wayne, Watts and Rucker began to dog their footsteps everywhere they went. The agents arranged to run into them on the street in Meridian. They dropped by the 49 Club South, where Alton Wayne was a bouncer. They made a point of seeing them at the Davis Grill or sidling up to them at Widemann's Restaurant, where the brothers frequently went for coffee. It got so that wherever Raymond and Alton Wayne went, whenever they looked around there would be Watts and Rucker watching them. And whenever circumstances permitted, one of the agents delivered a cryptic warning: "Time is of the essence," the agents would say. Or, "If you know what's good for you, you'll meet with us privately."

The encounters usually resulted in little more than verbal sparring; the brothers insisted they had nothing to say to the FBI.

Watts and Rucker were not discouraged. They saw this shadowboxing as an exercise in preparing the Klansmen mentally for the idea of associating with the FBI. The real approach would come through Tom Hendricks, the brothers' attorney. Ironically, the Klan itself had softened up Hendricks for the FBI's approach. Though he had represented members of the White Knights, recently he had experienced two nasty encounters with Klansmen that were followed by anonymous calls threatening his life. One involved his decision to represent a black youth involved in a fight with a young white boy. That led three hard-eyed Klansmen to confront Hendricks at the courthouse and demand, "You gonna represent that nigger against our boy?" The other situation grew out of Hendricks' refusal to represent a Klansman who wanted to bring charges against Meridian police for harassing him.

Initially, Hendricks had rebuffed the FBI's overtures. Now, alarmed at the Klan's threats, he sought out both Watts and Scarbrough and told them what had happened. If he could remain absolutely anonymous, Hendricks said, he would act as the go-between with the Roberts brothers. He wanted no one in the FBI, outside of Watts and Rucker, to know the role he would play. And within the Meridian Police Department, he would work with no one but Luke Scarbrough. Watts assured Hendricks on both points. Then he told the lawyer that he wanted the Roberts brothers to attend "a prayer meeting" at his house and that if they failed to show "their asses are going to be in big trouble." Scarbrough filed a report saying Hendricks was ready to "help us any way he could."

Though he did not know it, Hendricks' stipulation about working only with Scarbrough matched the agents' thinking perfectly. They had already learned that the soft-spoken Meridian detective was a man they could rely on. They had begun building a special relationship with him months earlier, when they first learned that the White Knights were shifting their focus from Jackson to Meridian. Another plus in Scarbrough's favor was that in 1964 he had attended the FBI National Academy's sixteen-week training program for municipal police officers.

The FBI agents began by having coffee with Scarbrough at

Widemann's. Soon the three of them were going fishing together and discussing mutual problems—first and foremost, the Klan. Watts considered Scarbrough a natural for the team, someone who "would go along with what Roy Gunn wanted, but at the same time was a real professional."

Solidly built, five feet eleven inches, 185 pounds, with wavy salt-and-pepper hair, Scarbrough had the clean-cut, neatly dressed image the FBI liked. He was a hard worker, and despite his low-key manner he was tough and resourceful. Recalled to active duty in the marines during the Korean War, he had been among those cut off at the Chosin Reservoir in the bitter cold of winter. The marines fought their way out, bringing their dead and wounded with them, and Scarbrough, his hands and feet frostbitten, was sent back to the naval hospital in Pensacola, Florida. At Christmas his condition was judged too serious for him to travel, but he persuaded a doctor to approve a three-day leave and he hitchhiked the more than two hundred miles to Meridian; let out on the highway almost two miles from his house, he hobbled the rest of the way to see his wife and newborn baby.

Later, in 1951, Scarbrough became a Meridian policeman at $270 a month. Though he got only two days a month off, he earned extra money by parking cars at ball games and driving mental patients to the state sanitarium at Whitfield, ninety-five miles away, for $10 a round-trip.

Watts and Rucker also knew they could count on Scarbrough when it came to the Klan. As a kind of test, they had asked him for help when J. B. Stoner's National States Rights Party scheduled a rally near Meridian. Scarbrough talked to the owners of the land where the rally was to be held. The rally was canceled.

With Scarbrough as a trusted ally and Hendricks offering to cooperate, Watts decided it was time to strike. He confided in Hendricks his plan to use the Roberts brothers to lay a trap for the two top hit men in the White Knights—Danny Joe Hawkins and Thomas Tarrants.

And the softening up of the Roberts brothers had apparently worked. When Hendricks approached them, the two Klansmen agreed to meet with the FBI agents.

At Watts' instructions, Hendricks drove the brothers to Watts' split-level house late one night. The lawyer drove directly into the garage and Watts quickly pushed the button to bring down the automatic door. He ushered them into a den that adjoined the garage, and the agents got right down to business.

"The FBI wants your cooperation to get those responsible for blowing up the synagogue," Watts told the Robertses. "And this is a fair warning. We know you've been involved in some of the violence around here and if you don't cooperate we're going to hold you responsible. You son-of-a-bitches are gonna to have to answer for it."

It was not like an interview, Watts said later, "it was more of a 'you are going to cooperate' meeting." He assured the brothers that if they delivered Hawkins and Tarrants, they stood to get the reward money collected by city officials and the Jewish community, as well as recommendations for lenient treatment in any future criminal cases. Failure to cooperate, they were warned, would make them the focal point of investigations that already had linked them to Klan violence.

The FBI's immediate goal was to nail Tarrants and Hawkins, but it also hoped to persuade Raymond and Alton Wayne to testify against Sam Bowers and perhaps L. E. Matthews. Both the bureau and the Meridian police had compiled intelligence indicating that Matthews, a well-to-do Jackson electrical contractor, was prepared to replace Bowers as imperial wizard of the White Knights when Bowers began his ten-year prison sentence in the Philadelphia case.

Although convinced that Matthews was the White Knights' chief bomb maker, the FBI had not been able to bring a single charge against him. In fact, Matthews boasted that he had never spent a day in jail despite the FBI's constant attention. The bureau was so frustrated that at one point officials arranged for three carloads of agents to maintain thirteen straight days of around-the-clock open surveillance of his house in a rural area near Florence, about ten miles south of Jackson. When Matthews' mother, then in her mideighties, encountered the agents and asked what they were doing, one of them replied, "We're watching your son, he's a dangerous criminal."

Although obtaining evidence against Matthews and others was high on the FBI priority list, negotiating with the brothers to get testimony was not without its risks. "Dealing with Wayne, who'd killed two people, was weird," Watts said, "but we had to do something to protect innocent people that were being targeted. I figured I sure deserved my paycheck. You had to stay one step ahead of them. You knew they were capable of doing anything."

At first, the Robertses refused to be pinned down on whether they would cooperate. Then they made it clear that if they did, they wanted ironclad guarantees that they would get the reward money and would not have to testify against Bowers and Matthews or any other Klansmen.

For almost three hours, until nearly 2:00 A.M., Watts and the two Klansmen talked back and forth. Finally, the brothers agreed to meet periodically with Watts, Rucker and Detective Scarbrough. But they angrily insisted they would not testify, that coming out in the open as witnesses was out of the question. The problem was not their Klan oath of secrecy. The barrier was fear. "I'd be as good as dead if I testified against Sam and L.E.," Raymond Roberts said. "I'd be signing my own death warrant."

The late-night meeting at Watts' house was one step in squeezing the Roberts brothers. A few days later, Watts and Rucker drove Alton Wayne into neighboring Neshoba County and stopped at the spot off Highway 19 near Union, Mississippi, where Schwerner, Goodman and Chaney had been pulled from their car four years earlier. Then the agents drove him to a spot closer to Philadelphia where the three civil rights workers had been killed.

Alton Wayne was not easily spooked, but Watts, watching him in the rearview mirror, saw him squirm.

The Meridian police were doing their part, too. One night two officers in a patrol car drove slowly by Raymond's house and fired into it, shattering a picture window. A panicky Roberts rushed to the FBI's office in the Post Office Building to appeal for protection. An agent told him he had nothing to worry about if he cooperated with the FBI, but if he did not, that was another matter.

Watts telephoned Roberts later that night and asked, "Who was that who shot into your house, Raymond?" Roberts responded with a stream of profanity, then hung up. He could not tell whether the Meridian police had shot into his house because he was not cooperating or the Klan had done it because he was. He could not be sure which was worse.

• • •

Hendricks advised the Roberts brothers that they had nothing to lose and everything to gain by cooperating with the FBI. The attorney insisted on a ten-thousand-dollar cut for himself, but he pointed out that if Raymond and Alton Wayne cooperated, they stood to collect tens of thousands of dollars in reward money— and they could probably count on the FBI and police to recommend leniency in court when it came to bringing any criminal charges. If they refused to cooperate, on the other hand, the FBI and police would make their lives miserable and they could expect to face stiff criminal charges and hard-line prosecution. Moreover, Watts and Rucker were likely to let word of their secret meetings with them leak out, and that could bring retaliation by the Klan.

The FBI could press Raymond and Alton Wayne, but they knew how to drive a hard bargain, too. Hendricks reported to Scarbrough that—among other things—the brothers wanted the full eighty-five thousand dollars in reward money the Meridian *Star* reported the Jewish communities of Mississippi had raised. They insisted, too, that they be granted immunity from having to testify. And Alton Wayne refused to cooperate unless Scarbrough pledged that the police would recommend reducing his ten-year sentence.

Then, on June 8, eleven days after the Meridian synagogue bombing, the brothers made what they said was their final offer. Hendricks delivered a two-part message to Scarbrough. First, Raymond Roberts was concerned for his life because a detective had threatened to kill him and police had shot into his house. Second, the brothers knew the names of the two men who blew up the Meridian synagogue and the same two were planning a murder in Meridian on the night of June 10—a plot unrelated to the conspiracy to dynamite Meyer Davidson's house. The brothers said if they could reach agreement with the FBI and Meridian police on their demands, they would be willing to disclose the terrorists' names.

Their offer did not end there. In a memo Scarbrough quoted Hendricks as saying the brothers could also furnish information on the synagogue bombing in Jackson, the bombing of a black residence in Florence and "nine open cases in the Meridian Detective Bureau involving damage to churches."

Scarbrough had asked Hendricks what evidence the brothers could furnish. The lawyer said that it would be enough to eliminate any doubt as to who the guilty parties were, and that Raymond and Alton Wayne could also tell them where their dynamite was located and get them a statement from a woman who knew about the bombings.

By the morning of June 10, no deal had been struck. The brothers had not supplied the names of the two men they said were planning to commit murder that night in Meridian. With a life possibly at stake, the Klansmen were playing a game of cat and mouse that drove even the normally unflappable Scarbrough to fury. "I told him [Hendricks] that Raymond Roberts was dead and the only thing that would save his life would be to join forces with us and turn full state's evidence," Scarbrough reported in a memo. "I explained to him that he [Roberts] could be placed in another city and a job could be secured for him. I also advised the intermediary that if anyone was hurt in Meridian the night of June 10, 1968, that some asses would be in serious trouble. He told me that this information was supposed to have been in confidence and I told him that murder cases were not handled in confidence and that the only agreement that we could reach would be full state's evidence."

Scarbrough said he warned Hendricks that he was getting impatient and "other negotiations" were underway. If the brothers did not "come around quickly they would lose the money and any leniency that could be offered." Hendricks said he would relay Scarbrough's message right away and Raymond and Alton Wayne could "take it or leave it" because he was ready to wash his hands of the entire matter.

Hendricks was clearly shaken by Scarbrough's harsh tone. No more than two hours had passed when Hendricks telephoned the detective and told him the brothers were "ready to do business." By now it was midafternoon. Scarbrough had to move quickly if the terrorists who bombed the synagogue were planning to kill someone that evening. But where could he meet the brothers on such short notice? Watts' house was out of the question; there was no time to remove his family and there were too many other houses nearby. Then he hit upon the perfect place—his own small trailer on a patch of woodland he owned on a remote country road outside Meridian. He and Watts and Rucker would meet them there.

While Hendricks agreed to ask the brothers to go to the trailer, he insisted he would not go there himself. In fact, Hendricks had become so wary of the developing plot that he—as a Scarbrough memo made clear—did not even "want to know the content of the conversation in the trailer."

The old trailer sat alone in a clearing at the end of a narrow gravel track that led off Coker's Road. Dense pine woods with a scattering of hickory, oak and sweet gum trees pressed close around it, sealing off the sound of any cars that might pass along the road. The trailer was shabby, a one-room affair with no electricity or plumbing. Scarbrough had used his car to haul it from Meridian some years before. He worked a large vegetable garden on a twenty-acre plot nearby and used the trailer for storage and occasional shelter.

As Scarbrough and the two FBI agents pulled into the weedy clearing, they were surprised to find not only the Klansmen but also Hendricks waiting in their car. The brothers had insisted he come, Hendricks explained, and they were in no frame of mind to take no for an answer.

The six men clambered into the trailer. Inside, the air was stifling. Scarbrough, Watts and Rucker ordered the Roberts brothers to raise their hands so they could search them for weapons, The found a snub-nosed detective's special revolver tucked in Alton Wayne's belt under his jacket. A small but deadly derringer was concealed in Raymond's boot. Both weapons, along with the officers' own .38 revolvers, went into the drawer of a small dresser.

"Now we can talk," Watts said.

It took several hours, but finally the Roberts brothers confirmed what the FBI suspected: the Meridian synagogue had been blown up by Tarrants and Hawkins. The brothers said they still would not consider testifying because the Klan would kill them if they did. For the right price, though, they might be willing to act as informants and lay a trap for the Klan hit men.

Such talk unnerved Hendricks. He feared becoming involved in such a conspiracy. Yet he did not want to get out without a share of the reward money, which Scarbrough said totaled seventy-nine thousand dollars, not the eighty-five thousand dollars reported in the Meridian *Star*. The lawyer insisted he deserved a ten-thousand-dollar cut for acting as intermediary.

The purported plan to kill a Meridian citizen that night either had been a bluff or had been called off at the last minute. But, as a Scarbrough memo noted, the Roberts brothers were ready to talk about setting a trap: "Raymond told us it would take about three days to set up another job in Meridian and said that anything that happened in Meridian he has knowledge of because they trust him since he is a 'Roberts.' He also stated that Sam Bowers trusts him. He stated that when the next job is set up we would have to stake out three different places and said there is always two alternatives besides the real thing. The reason for this being Goddamn pimps like me."

Raymond told Scarbrough that the police on stakeout duty on the night of the bombing attempt should be hidden well because the hit men were "professionals and they are sharp as hell." When they pull a job, he said, they park two or three blocks away from the target and are always well armed.

"Can I get some of the pressure taken off of me?" Raymond asked Scarbrough.

"I don't set the policy, I just investigate," the detective replied, "but common sense would tell you, if you cooperate with us the pressure will let up."

Shortly after midnight, as the meeting was breaking up, Alton Wayne and Raymond complained bitterly that Scarbrough and the agents had brought none of the promised money.

"We'll see you out here again tomorrow night," Watts replied, "and we'll have some money then."

11

Somewhere along the line between the Philadelphia murders and the Meridian synagogue bombing, the FBI started playing by different rules. On the calendar, four years had passed. For many of the FBI agents and police officers involved in pursuing the Klan, however, it had been a single, uninterrupted surge of violence, frustration and danger. The White Knights' ceaseless attacks, the hit lists and brazen threats to law enforcement personnel and their families. The nights on stakeouts and the early-morning memos to Washington. The constant fear and the unrelieved pressure for results. All this had taken a toll, profoundly changing the men and what they were capable of.

From a distance, the first meetings with Raymond and Alton Wayne Roberts could have come from an FBI textbook on investigative procedure: the offering of rewards, the threat of punishment, the time-honored carrot-and-stick strategy for squeezing information from unwilling subjects. But the process that began in Scarbrough's lonely trailer outside Meridian went far beyond any textbook.

Frank Watts described it this way:

"My name was on the list and my house was being watched or protected because I had my wife and three small sons there—and that got my attention. Every time I looked at one of the Roberts brothers I would think that one of the places targeted to be blown up was my house with my wife and three children. And Meyer Davidson, one of finest guys anyone would ever want to meet, targeted too. And Chief Gunn, of course. People's sons and daughters who weren't harming anybody. And these animals, these mad dog killers, want to eliminate them. That gives you enough strength to look them in the eye and say, 'You son of a bitch, you're gonna tell me or I'm gonna get rid of you.'

"It changes your personality when you realize what you can do. You're sitting there and you know in your own mind you may have the key to aborting a multiple murder. And when you realize that you can accomplish what you set out to do, it's just a matter of making them understand you're capable of doing it.

"I was pretty active in the church in Meridian at that time and ninety-nine percent of the people in the church would say that Frank Watts is not capable of doing anything like that—it's not his personality. But when you think of what they're going to do and you think, I'm placed in a position, because of my job, to abort this if I do my job, then you're going to do whatever it takes to do it."

On June 11, the day after the first meeting in the trailer, Scarbrough, Watts and Rucker met with I.A. Rosenbaum at the Downtowner Motel. Rosenbaum was president of the Meridian Temple Beth Israel congregation and he told the lawmen arrangements had been made to fly twenty-five thousand dollars in twenty-dollar bills from Jackson to Meridian that day.

In the afternoon, on schedule, a courier carrying a briefcase stuffed with the money arrived at the Meridian Airport. He was met by Rosenbaum, Scarbrough and Sergeant Lester Joyner, the rough-talking leader of Chief Gunn's anti-Klan squad, "Joyner's guerrillas." Rosenbaum took the briefcase and drove with the two officers to a bank, where he put the money in a safety-deposit box. Concerned that he might someday face a tax problem if the money were traced to him, Rosenbaum consulted Watts, who helped him get a receipt showing that the funds had been contributed anonymously as reward money in the synagogue bombing case.

Scarbrough went back to the police department. He found Marie Knowles standing outside the detective bureau talking to one of the policemen suspected of being a Klan sympathizer. He called her off to the side and whispered that there would be a meeting at his trailer that night with the informants and he needed to dictate a memo for the files. He told her that he had been authorized to give the informants a thousand dollars as come-on money and that he would be traveling to the trailer in his personal car because the Roberts brothers had gotten skittish. They didn't want any more "city cars" around them.

Earlier that day in Jackson, Danny Joe Hawkins and L. E. Matthews had attended a National States Rights Party rally. With them was Raymond Roberts, making his debut as an FBI informant. Roberts did not get much information on his first try. Afterward, Scarbrough noted in a brief memo, "Matthews and Hawkins were talking in a low tone of voice and the informant overheard a man invite Matthews to a rally on Highway 11 South of Laurel the night of June 14th. Matthews is described as being a WM, DOB: 9/13/23, 6'3", 230 lbs., brown hair, balding, blue eyes, RFD Florence, Mississippi."

Jacksonians knew Matthews mostly as a businessman. Even though he was a top aide to Bowers and slated to succeed him as imperial wizard, Matthews had avoided publicity and managed to keep most of his Klan activities secret. He owned the nine-story 203 Capitol Building in downtown Jackson, which housed the offices of the Equal Employment Opportunity Commission and several other federal agencies. The FBI kept a close watch on Matthews, even having him followed at a convention of the National Electrical Contractors Association in Boston.

In preparation for the next meeting at the trailer, Watts drove out in the afternoon and hid a recorder in a cabinet beneath the sink. The Roberts brothers, distrusting the agents as much as the agents distrusted them, constantly complained that the FBI had their home telephones tapped, but apparently they never considered the possibility of tape recorders at the trailer.

Watts always denied tapping the telephones. "We don't do that kind of stuff," he told Raymond. "We just meet man to man." Raymond's wife was a telephone operator and Watts suggested he have her ask the company whether their phones were tapped. The phones were, of course, tapped: Watts was one of the FBI's "sound-trained" men, skilled in secretly installing recordings and telephone taps. That had been his specialty when he worked on Soviet espionage cases in New York.

About midnight on June 11, Hendricks and the Roberts brothers pulled into the clearing. Watts, Rucker and Scarbrough were already inside the trailer. Scarbrough held the briefcase. Scarbrough planned to spread the mass of bills out on the table for the informants to see, then give them a nominal down payment. He had already written out a receipt on a legal pad: "June 12, 1968 . . . Received this date from Luke Scarbrough the sum of $1,000 for services rendered."

As the two Klansmen entered, the FBI agents once again patted them down. Each was carrying a pistol. "Put 'em on the table," Watts instructed.

"We'll put ours up when you put yours up," Alton Wayne answered. Carefully, Scarbrough and the two agents drew their own weapons and waited for the Robertses to put their guns on the table. After a few tense seconds, they did, and the law officers laid their pistols beside them.

Then Scarbrough opened the briefcase and methodically began to spread piles of twenty-dollar bills out on one side of the table, opposite the five revolvers. Hendricks and his clients watched in wide-eyed silence. Finally, the last stack of bills was in place.

But the money was only half the equation. Watts, standing beside Scarbrough and almost close enough to the Robertses to touch them, looked directly at the two Klansmen and pointed to the currency. "Over here," he said, "you've got money coming in." Then he pointed to the guns. "Or over here you can have your ass shot off one night when you come out here. It's your choice. We expect your cooperation."

Tension seemed to suck the air from the tiny room. Scarbrough and the two agents stared at the brothers but said nothing. Raymond Roberts looked shocked. Even Alton Wayne, who was not used to being on the receiving end of threats, seemed stunned. The terms of the deal were not quite what they had seemed to be the night before. It was not a question of cooperate or face prosecution. It was help or die.

Scarbrough picked up one of the stacks of money. He counted out fifty bills and pushed them toward Alton Wayne, along with the receipt. The money was a down payment, he said, to be split with Raymond.

"You can get the rest of the money when Danny Joe Hawkins and Tarrants come down here," Watts said. Alton Wayne snickered nervously and stuffed the bills into his trouser pocket, then scrawled a signature on the receipt and handed it back to Scarbrough.

He had used a pseudonym, Bobby Komoroski, a name he thought sounded Jewish. Now he watched for Scarbrough's reaction. There was none. The detective only glanced at the signature before beginning to scoop the stacks of bills back into the briefcase. He laid the receipt on top and snapped the case shut.

They would meet at the trailer again in twenty-four hours.

The following day Scarbrough was with Watts and Rucker in the FBI offices in the Post Office Building when Hendricks burst in unannounced and without knocking. He was there on urgent business, he said. He was convinced that, for the right amount of money, the Roberts brothers would be willing to testify about Klan violence. The right amount of money, Hendricks said, was $150,000.

Scarbrough and the agents were intrigued but skeptical. They were not sure any amount of money could elicit testimony against Bowers and Matthews.

The next night, June 12, the meeting was again set for midnight. This time, Scarbrough and the two agents, accompanied by Hendricks, arrived at the trailer at 10:30 P.M. The Roberts brothers were already there, lurking in the woods. Watts sat down at the small table and was drinking coffee and looking out the window when he spotted Alton Wayne sneaking up along the side of the trailer, his hand cupped to his ear. Watts looked at Scarbrough and winked.

"You say you think you can get Raymond and Alton Wayne to testify against Bowers and Matthews?" Watts said in a loud voice. "You say you can get 'em to do it for about a hundred fifty thousand dollars?"

"No, Goddammit, you won't," Alton Wayne bellowed, barging through the trailer door. "I'm not gonna testify to anything, and if my brother does, I'll kill him before you do."

Hendricks, in Scarbrough's words, "like to shit when he heard that. It scared him half to death."

Scarbrough began to calm Alton Wayne down. Neither of the brothers would have to testify. No one could force them to do that. What they must do instead of testifying was persuade Hawkins and Tarrants to set up another job in Meridian. Guns on the table, the cat-and-mouse game began again.

It was to go on that way for two weeks, the strain steadily increasing. They would go to the mobile home out in the woods night after night until two, three or four o'clock in the morning, even though Watts and Rucker had to be in their office at the Post Office Building by eight o'clock every morning, seven days a week, to prepare a synopsis for Hoover of what they had learned during the previous twenty-four hours.

The two agents saw their negotiations with the Roberts brothers as "a touch and go thing. We had to make them believe that we were sincere, that we were capable of completely eliminating them one way or another if something happened," Watts recalled.

The Roberts brothers found it hard to understand—or believe—that agents of the FBI, considered the nation's most professional law enforcement agency, would be willing to kill them if they refused to cooperate. But Watts and Rucker were determined to make believers out of them.

The message did sink in. On June 13, two days after Scarbrough had spread the money on the table and Watts had spelled out the two choices, Raymond Roberts met with Danny Joe Hawkins at the Dog-N-Suds Drive-Inn in Brandon, Mississippi, a small town east of Jackson on the road to Meridian. Hawkins listened sympathetically as Roberts made his pitch for a favor to a Klansman. The FBI and police were putting tremendous pressure on him and his brother in connection with the synagogue bombing and the burning of black churches in the Meridian area, Raymond said. If he and Alton Wayne could just be somewhere else with an ironclad alibi when another major attack occurred in Meridian, it would help.

Whether it was sympathy that moved him or his appetite for violent action, Hawkins responded quickly. He contacted Matthews. The next day Matthews called Raymond Roberts, as Scarbrough noted in a memo, and told him that "the two hit men had gone after two cases of dynamite."

Later the same day Raymond Roberts rented a car in Meridian and went to Jackson for another meeting with Hawkins. They drove around for several hours discussing a possible bombing mission. While passing by Tougaloo College, Hawkins showed Roberts two houses the Klan had shot into and a house with a "PEACE" sign on it where Hawkins said the Klan planned to commit a Number Four—a murder. Trying to impress Roberts with his terrorist acts, Hawkins showed him a car riddled with machine-gun bullets that had been driven earlier by two blacks. Roberts later reported that as they looked inside it Hawkins said, "Brother, there is blood on the seat."

Back in Meridian, Raymond Roberts told Scarbrough that the only way he could get the Klan's hit men to tackle a job in Meridian would be "to set up" Wallace Miller, the former Klansman and Meridian police sergeant who had turned FBI informant and prosecution witness in the Philadelphia case.

"Hawkins wants to know what shift Miller is working and a description of his house and a map of the streets and avenues around his house," Scarbrough reported. "Hawkins wants to kill Miller with a machine gun, referred to by them as a 'chopper.' "

To Scarbrough the proposal sounded like a harebrained scheme dreamed up by the Roberts brothers to spook Miller rather than a plan crafted by Hawkins and Tarrants. But the detective was more interested in having the brothers continue with the plan for a trap than he was in ridiculing their proposal. And he knew the two brothers' minds never strayed far from the reward money. So he simply responded: "I don't advise that because you probably won't get any of the reward money if a Jew is not the bombing target. After all, the Jews put up the reward money."

The money argument was particularly persuasive with Raymond. So far, he had not received a cent. His brother had refused to split the thousand dollars Scarbrough paid him at the trailer. Raymond said he would do his best to get Hawkins and Tarrants to bomb the home of a Meridian Jew, though he again emphasized the importance of arranging an ironclad alibi for himself.

Raymond and Scarbrough agreed on a scenario. "At the time of the bombing," the Klansman said, "I want to be in a nightclub and start a fight so I'll have a witness to my whereabouts when the bomb goes off."

"That makes sense," Scarbrough said.

Roberts returned to Jackson once again to meet with Hawkins and later reported a strange episode in which Hawkins was seemingly on the verge of shooting a black at random but got distracted when he broke his sunglasses. Scarbrough duly reported: "Informant stated that while he was riding with Hawkins a Negro was standing in the middle of the street and Hawkins told him not to slow down, that he would kill the SOB and pulled a .45 automatic pistol from under the car seat. Hawkins broke his sunglasses as he pulled the pistol out."

Scarbrough had no way of knowing how serious Hawkins might have been about killing the man, but the detective was aware that Hawkins had a reputation for violent impulses and thought Roberts' description credible enough to include it in the memo.

In fact, the FBI and Meridian police tried to locate other sources to verify all crucial aspects of information the Roberts brothers gave them. "We didn't trust them and they didn't trust us and we kept our eyes on them the whole time and tried to verify everything they told us," Rucker said.

At one of the late-night sessions at the trailer, Scarbrough, Watts and Rucker interrogated Raymond Roberts at length as Hendricks looked on nervously. They drew out of the informant a detailed report of what he said was Hawkins' description of how he and Tarrants had bombed Meridian's Temple Beth Israel.

According to Roberts, Hawkins said he and Tarrants had pulled over to the side of the highway not far from the synagogue and, while moving the dynamite from the trunk of the car to the front seat, agreed that if a policeman showed up "they had nothing to lose and they intended to kill him." After parking their car in an isolated area, both men, armed with machine guns and carrying the box of dynamite, made their way through a thick wooded area to the synagogue. They placed the dynamite in a recessed door at the west end of the synagogue's religious education building and used a cigar to light the twenty-foot fuse, then ran to their car and headed for Highway 493. But Hawkins said they got lost in the Broadmoor subdivision of Meridian and heard the explosion at the synagogue several blocks away before finding their way out to the highway.

Roberts also quoted Hawkins as saying he did not like Matthews as well as he did Bowers because "Matthews talks too much, especially to his girlfriend." Bowers could never be accused of talking too much to a girlfriend because in addition to being extremely secretive, he stayed away from women. In contrast, Matthews was known to have had several girlfriends, and on one occasion, Roberts reported, "a strange woman" accompanied him on a trip. A Scarbrough memo indicated that Hawkins' concerns about Matthews talking too much were well founded; the woman was feeding information to the FBI.

Sometimes of course, there was simply was no way of verifying everything Raymond and Alton Wayne were telling the agents. Occasionally, the brothers would emphasize that Danny Joe Hawkins had indicated he was interested in killing FBI agents or policemen, and they quoted him as saying that it would be "easy to rig" a bomb to a police car and that if he got caught in a bombing attempt he had "nothing to lose" by shooting it out with police. Once, Scarbrough reported, Roberts said the hit men "cased the FBI parking lot in Jackson and know that they have a panel truck and fully intend to kill an FBI agent, preferably Mr. Roy Moore."

Scarbrough could never be sure how serious Hawkins was about such threats or whether he had actually made them. The Roberts brothers might be fabricating or exaggerating the story to encourage the police to kill Hawkins and Tarrants, thereby eliminating a possible threat of retaliation against themselves.

The law officers felt confident, however, that the brothers would be afraid to lie about their main mission of setting up another bombing attempt. Scarbrough figured they had the brothers "by the short hairs," that they would not dare double-cross the FBI and Meridian police.

On June 17, Scarbrough dictated a memo saying the Roberts brothers planned to meet that night or the following day with Hawkins to "attempt to set up a job on Al Rose's House." Rose, a Meridian jeweler active in Temple Beth Israel affairs, had not been identified with civil rights activities, but he was one of twenty-three white moderates in Meridian on a Klan blacklist. They were people said by the Klan to be "trying to destroy our southern way of life by meeting and working with Negros and Negro organizations trying to force integration upon us."

Scarbrough said he had promised to try to get money for Raymond after he complained that he needed $850 for current bills and that Alton Wayne had kept all of the initial $1,000 payment. The next night at the trailer, Scarbrough and the agents gave Raymond $850 as "part of the full amount to be paid." The receipt, which Scarbrough once more wrote out in longhand on lined tablet paper, read: "June 18, 1968 . . . Received this date from Luke Scarbrough the sum of $850.00 for services rendered." With a sardonic laugh, Roberts signed the receipt "Al Rose."

Scarbrough's writing chores were not finished, however. Roberts abruptly announced that he and his brother had a new deal to offer: if immunity could be guaranteed, they would disclose who was responsible for all the burnings of black churches in the area. When Scarbrough agreed, they demanded a written guarantee of immunity. Out came the tablet again. The detective wrote the requested statement, signed it and gave it to them.

"Hell," Scarbrough later said, "I would have signed anything to have caught Tarrants 'cause it wasn't worth a damn anyway. They had me signing all kinds of crap."

On the evening of June 19, Hawkins and the Roberts brothers agreed that Al Rose would not be the target of the bombing mission after all. Instead, they would go after Meyer Davidson. A member of the Committee of Conscience, he had been outspoken in denouncing the bombing of the synagogue. He had also been a leader in raising reward money among Jews all over the state to fight Klan violence. Hawkins and Tarrants had both read of his activities in the Meridian *Star*.

Scarbrough learned of the change in plans at ten the next morning when Raymond Roberts called and said the bombing would occur the following week. Hawkins and Tarrants planned to come to Meridian and check out the residence themselves two days ahead of time. The hit men were supposed to call Raymond the morning of the day of the bombing and meet with him and Alton Wayne at Akins trailer court to go over their plans, since they would need the Robertses as local guides.

The car to be used was Danny Joe Hawkins' 1966 Buick Electra 225. The agents were surprised. "Ninety-nine percent of the Klan used pickup trucks with a shotgun in back, and that's what we were looking for in our surveillance," Watts said. "Well, this green Buick appeared several times in FBI reports of interviews with persons living near the sites of earlier bombings, but we didn't pay much attention to it. It didn't look like a Klan car and it didn't look like Klan people in it. But it was being used to case these places in Meridian. A housewife would tell us, 'All I saw was a green Buick with a woman driving.' It turned out it was Kathy Ainsworth driving, but we didn't know it then."

Roberts also reported it was now doubtful that Tarrants would participate in the bombing because he was still in hiding. The FBI had been circulating his photograph as the chief suspect in the Kroger store robbery.

Scarbrough, Watts and Rucker were alarmed at the prospect that Tarrants might not participate, but the Klan—for different reasons—attached as much importance to having Tarrants take part as the FBI and police did. At a later meeting Hawkins told Raymond they had better get Tarrants out of hiding "because they cannot stand for a mess-up on the job."

Hawkins and Roberts planned the bombing for the night of June 27 because Dave Gardner, a comedian notorious for racist jokes, would be entertaining in Meridian that night; Gardner undoubtedly would draw a large crowd and perhaps distract the Meridian police force. Hawkins told Raymond that he and Tarrants intended to use ten cases of dynamite on the Davidson house. Roberts protested that ten cases "would blow up the whole block" and he opposed using such a large amount because he had a friend with children who lived near Meyer Davidson. The "friend" was Sam Keller, the assistant police chief, who lived across the street from Davidson. Because of Keller's known Klan sympathies, Chief Gunn had kept him in the dark about the ambush plans.

Hawkins told Roberts that since the bombing mission was planned "strictly as a favor" to him, he would use only twenty-nine sticks of dynamite. That was still enough explosives to destroy the Davidson house and cause damage to nearby houses. Hawkins asked which bedroom Davidson slept in. Roberts, who had cased the house, told him the bedroom was near the carport. Hawkins said the dynamite would be placed in the carport and timed to explode at 4:00 A.M.

Roberts said he was worried about having an alibi. Hawkins said they would work out something the following Monday or Tuesday, two or three days before the bombing. Hawkins told of receiving ten cases of dynamite and then having to get rid of it because it was old and dangerous. Then he laughed, according to Roberts, and said that at one time he used "a bottle of nitro that would have eliminated a block of Negroes in Jackson and stated that he was very nervous because it was his first job. He stated that he lit the fuse and it made a buzzing sound and went out and he lit it again and it made the buzzing sound again and he ran for two blocks. He stated that he knew it burned a lot but he was afraid to go back."

Roberts said Hawkins also told him that he was running low on money. He wanted to know of anyone who carried a large sum of money that he could rob. Scarbrough, in his memo, noted: "In the conversation Hawkins popped his finger and said that he knew a SOB in Meridian and he is Blackie Ramia."

Blackie Ramia, a bookie, was known to carry large sums of money, but he was never robbed. And police never discovered whether Hawkins robbed someone else instead.

Chief Gunn was keeping A.I. Botnick up to date on plans to lure the Klan members to Meridian. In turn, the ADL official was confiding in Ken Dean. Dean was told that the bombing attempt was now scheduled for the night of June 27. Botnick also told Dean that the FBI and some of the Meridian police would be waiting at the scene, and that Hawkins and Tarrants would be ambushed the minute their car arrived. Botnick reported he had provided Chief Gunn and the FBI with twenty-five hundred dollars in "come-on money" for the informants.

At the same time, the bureau was keeping at least some activist members of the Jewish communities in both Meridian and Jackson informed. Al Binder was in the thick of it, and he was briefing some other activists in the Jewish community.

"They were doing something that they had never done before. And we were doing something we had never done before," FBI agent Jim Ingram recalled. "So we had to give each other not only our word, because there was nothing on paper—it had to be strictly a handshake. We would carry out our part of the bargain and they were more than willing to carry out their part—and they did."

With the bombing attempt only three days off, the Roberts brothers insisted on payments of at least ten thousand dollars each in advance. Scarbrough promised to talk to the people putting up the money.

The next evening, at another lengthy session at his trailer, Scarbrough counted out twenty thousand dollars in twenty-dollar bills and spread it on the table. The Roberts brothers "went apeshit over the money," Scarbrough said. "They'd count their damn money and each would accuse the other one of having twenty dollars more than him. It was a scream."

By now the trailer sessions were occurring almost every other night. Usually Raymond Roberts was the only informant present, and he had begun to drink heavily, apparently to calm his nerves. One night, when he arrived drunk and still drinking beer, Scarbrough, in his own words, "reamed him a new one." With so much at stake, he told Raymond, such drinking could not be tolerated.

Hawkins, meanwhile, had supposedly secured a fresh supply of dynamite through an employee of a dirt-hauling firm in nearby Philadelphia, who had been indicted in the federal civil rights case that resulted from the murder of Schwerner, Chaney and Goodman but who had been acquitted. Scarbrough reported that the employee obtained the dynamite for Hawkins through his firm by signing out for more dynamite than he actually needed to blow up trees and tree stumps. He would frequently use only ten sticks after signing out for fifteen, for example, and would store the other five.

The scenario for the Davidson bombing kept changing at the last minute. Hawkins told Roberts that because Tarrants was still in hiding in the North Carolina mountains, another Klansman would be accompanying him on the night of the twenty-seventh. They planned to use fifteen sticks of dynamite with a timing device, Hawkins said, and the dynamite would be placed in the carport by 11:30 P.M. Roberts said Hawkins told him that on the night of the bombing he and Alton Wayne should go to the Dave Gardner show and shake hands with ten or fifteen people, then go to a nightclub and drink four or five beers so they "would sleep good and would be asleep when and if the police come for them."

Shortly thereafter, Hawkins relayed another change in plans. Sam Bowers had given Tarrants permission to leave the mountain hideaway. Tarrants would accompany Hawkins on the bombing mission after all. And they would carry a more powerful bomb, composed of twenty-nine sticks of dynamite.

The FBI and Meridian police began preparations in earnest. At the Holiday Inn South, where officers met to discuss plans, Chief Gunn offered members of the blackshirt squad a final chance to drop out of what everyone knew would be an exceedingly dangerous encounter. Tarrants and Hawkins were expected to be armed with hand grenades as well as machine guns. And twenty-nine sticks of dynamite packed enough explosive force to kill at a considerable distance. No one took the offer to drop out.

At the FBI's request, the Office of Naval Intelligence at the Meridian Naval Air Station made arrangements for an army demolition team from Fort Benning, Georgia, to be on hand the night of the twenty-seventh. The Fort Benning team members would use an unmarked car so local people would not know they were in town.

On June 24, Scarbrough received the news that Hawkins and Tarrants had arrived in Meridian. They were sighted in a Buick at 9:15 P.M. They had coffee at the Torch Café and remained in Meridian until about 3:30 A.M. The detective filed a memo saying the hit men planned to strike Thursday night, June 27, and would plant the bomb shortly after dark. It would be set to explode around midnight. Tarrants would set the timer while Hawkins circled Davidson's block. "Tarrants will then get out of the car and walk to the target checking clearance," Scarbrough's memo said, "and then go back to the car and get a machine gun and the dynamite. Hawkins will circle for three minutes."

The next day was uneventful, but on the eve of the scheduled bombing, the level of tension shot up. Another Klan informant in Jackson turned in an alarming report: "Something is going to happen in Meridian Thursday night and it is a known fact that they have twelve clocks," the informant said, referring to the number of separate timing devices the terrorists possessed. The report, coupled with earlier indications of the acquisition of massive amounts of dynamite, raised the possibility that multiple bombs might be planted in one night.

Scarbrough, in a memo dictated to a nervous Marie Knowles, said, The following is the list they have the clocks prepared for:

1. Meyer Davidson.
2. C. L. Gunn.
3. Rabbi Nussbaum.
4. Judge [Harold] Cox [of the U.S. District Court]
5. Sam Jennings [FBI agent].

Might Hawkins and Tarrants opt for trying to bomb someone other than Davidson? If so, would the FBI and police find out soon enough? These thoughts raced through Scarbrough's mind as he contacted Watts and Rucker. After interviewing Raymond Roberts and being told that Davidson's house was the only site that had been thoroughly cased by the Klan, the agents decided it remained, at least for the time being, the only feasible target.

At about eight thirty on the night of Thursday, June 27, a squad of black-clad Meridian police officers arrived in the Davidsons' neighborhood in unmarked cars. They began taking up positions on the embankment across from the Davidsons' house, in a ditch behind the house, in the woods up the block from the house and in several cars parked strategically in driveways in the neighborhood to cut off any escape attempt by the terrorists. Watts and Rucker, along with the army's demolition team, occupied a house on top of the embankment across from the Davidsons'. Several other agents were in cars parked in secluded areas of the neighborhood.

They waited anxiously throughout the evening, stirring nervously and fingering their weapons when an occasional car passed by. The green Buick never appeared.

The next morning Scarbrough filed a report: "Stake-out was placed in the immediate area of the home and an outer perimeter was formed in case of an escape. This stakeout lasted from 8:30 pm until 5:00 AM Friday, June 28th. Subjects did not show."

Later that day, Tarrants and Hawkins drove to Meridian and picked up Raymond Roberts, who was as mystified as the FBI and police at the failure of the hit men to show up as promised. The two hit men told Roberts they had not executed the bombing plan because they had been pressed for time and needed to get some money. Also, Tarrants explained, he was concerned that the FBI had been tailing him in Jackson. Roberts told Tarrants and Hawkins it was important for them to proceed with the bombing mission without further delay. He appeared so eager to have it carried out that Hawkins finally asked, "What's the rush?" Roberts said he was afraid a Lauderdale County grand jury was preparing to indict him the following Monday in church burning cases. He said he figured that if a bombing took place before the grand jury convened and he had an alibi, it might stave off an indictment.

"We'll do it before the weekend's out," Hawkins said.

"They said they would pull the job before Monday and it will probably be Sunday night," Scarbrough said in a memo. "Before they pull the job, they will call and meet with informer at the service station and from there he can go to an all-night cafe for an alibi."

Roberts told Scarbrough that the Buick Hawkins was driving contained two machine guns, several hand grenades, a .45-caliber pistol in the glove compartment, approximately twenty sticks of dynamite in a brown grocery bag and a small box, about six inches by six inches, containing a timing device.

12

It was nearly eleven o'clock Saturday night when Tommy Tarrants and Kathy Ainsworth got to Meridian. Tarrants found a pay telephone near a hamburger stand at the edge of town and called Raymond Roberts. Fearing that Roberts' telephone might be tapped, Tarrants arranged to meet Raymond and Alton Wayne at a truck stop on Highway 20 near the Akins trailer court several miles east of Meridian.

Under the circumstances, it might have seemed a reckless rendezvous. Police pressure on the White Knights had been mounting since the Philadelphia slayings and the Akins trailer court was a known Klan rendezvous point. But Tarrants was feeling close to invulnerable. He considered the night's work "something of a routine procedure." Besides, he prided himself on his meticulous preparations. Elements of the bomb had been carefully separated. The dynamite was in a cardboard box in the trunk and the four electric detonator caps were on the front seat between him and Kathy. There would be no accidental explosion. Tarrants also made it a rule to keep the plans of his operations secret from everyone except the few directly involved. And the trustworthiness of Raymond and Alton Wayne Roberts seemed beyond question.

The decision to use Kathy Ainsworth instead of Danny Joe Hawkins was a last-minute change in the plans, but it represented an added security precaution because Hawkins' activities were often monitored by the FBI. Tarrants had borrowed Hawkins' car and driven to Ainsworth's house to enlist her help. Her husband was away for two weeks of National Guard training at Camp Shelby, near Hattiesburg. Kathy was preparing to take a vacation in Miami, where her mother lived. Tarrants had sketched the plan and promised he would drive her on to Florida afterward.

At the truck stop, Tarrants and Ainsworth waited in the parking area with the Electra's headlights turned off until the Roberts brothers arrived in a white 1965 Chevrolet. Raymond and Alton Wayne were startled and disturbed to see a woman with Tarrants; they had been expecting Hawkins. To ordinary Klansmen, the idea of involving a woman in Klan violence was almost unthinkable. Raymond protested that the mission was too dangerous for a woman and too important to involve someone he did not even know. Tarrants brushed the objections aside. He insisted that Kathy Ainsworth knew what she was doing and was one of Sam Bowers' best and most experienced people. Raymond grudgingly gave in; he did not want to abort the mission.

Tarrants and Ainsworth followed behind as the brothers drove to the Travelers Club, a bar attached to a Meridian motel, where they planned to establish their alibi by staging a fight. They parked the car and Alton went into the club. Raymond climbed into the backseat of the Buick. He would ride with Tarrants and Ainsworth through the Davidsons' neighborhood to acquaint them with the scene and make sure all was clear before rejoining his brother.

Davidson's house, L-shaped and built of mustard-colored brick, was located on a large lot at the corner of Twenty-ninth Avenue and Thirty-sixth Street. The yards of the neighborhood were filled with clumps of shrubbery and what real estate agents called "old shade"—huge oak trees, sweet gums and pines.

It was getting close to midnight now. There was no moon. The neighborhood was pitch black except for a streetlight here and there. The streets were empty. It was almost eerily quiet. Tarrants thought conditions were ideal.

"This one is going to be easier than the last two," Ainsworth said.

They took Raymond back to the Travelers Club. He immediately telephoned police to alert them that Danny Joe Hawkins was not in the car and that Tarrants was accompanied by a young woman wearing shorts. Raymond said he had not seen the woman before and did not know her name.

Patrolman Mike Hatcher and his partner, Tom Tucker, sat in a darkened squad car tucked back at the far end of U.S. Circuit

Court judge Benjamin Cameron's driveway. Their role, they thought, would be anticlimactic. In theory, they would roll down the driveway and block Twenty-ninth Avenue if the Klansmen should break free from the cordon of police hidden around Davidson's house. In practice, Tucker and Hatcher thought, they would probably be dealing with crowd control: keeping the curious away from the scene after it was all over.

Earlier that night, in the final meeting at the Holiday Inn South, Chief Gunn, Captain L. A. Willoughby and two FBI agents had laid out the plan for the twenty or so assembled members of the blackshirt unit. Then the officers were given their assignments, with Hatcher and Tucker, who were only acquaintances, paired together for the night. Like all Meridian policemen, they earned less than one hundred dollars a week regardless of their assignments, and, like most of the other officers, they held down second jobs to make ends meet at home. Tucker moonlighted as a butcher, Hatcher as a salesman for a car-parts firm.

Hatcher, an eight-year veteran and father of three, was a member of "Joyner's guerrillas" and a veteran of Chief Gunn's private war against the White Knights. Tucker, though a member of the department for five years, earlier had been under suspicion as a Klan sympathizer. FBI agents had trailed him constantly and questioned him repeatedly about his engagement to marry a Philadelphia woman named Patricia Beard. Finally, the FBI had concluded Tucker was not involved with the Klan and he was invited to join the blackshirts. Only later did Tucker learn that his fiancée was a niece of Edgar Ray (Preacher) Killen, a rural minister who was a defendant in the Philadelphia case; the jury had been unable to agree on a verdict and a mistrial was declared.

At the Holiday Inn meeting, the two officers had made a pact: each would give first priority to completing the mission; if one of them should get hurt, the other would forge ahead with his assignment. It was a tense business. And it got more tense shortly after 11:00 P.M., when a disturbing message came over the radio: Tarrants would be accompanied not by Hawkins, but by a woman, and every effort should be made to avoid harming her.

"Here we are out here having to worry about all sorts of things and the possibility of getting killed ourselves," Hatcher thought, "and we're told there's a woman in the car and to be careful and not hurt her."

• • •

Ken Dean may have been the only one who wanted to stop what was about to happen in Meridian that night, but the usually decisive director of the Mississippi Council on Human Relations could not decide what to do.

A fearless and untiring champion of human rights for blacks, Dean nonetheless maintained close ties with many segregationists, even some members of the Klan. Thanks to Botnick, he had gotten the drift of what was planned and he was shocked at the idea that a death trap was being set. In other circumstances, he might have hurled his burly physical presence into the middle of the action; he had done that more than once in the past.

This time, however, he was uncertain. In a sense, he had fallen victim to his habit of trying to talk to people on both sides of the street. He and his wife, Mary, had driven to Meridian that night to visit Reverend Duncan Gray, an Episcopal minister who was president of the Mississippi Council on Human Relations. In 1962 Gray was a campus chaplain at Ole Miss during the rioting against James Meredith's enrollment. A quietly courageous man, Gray had tried unsuccessfully to persuade students who were being whipped into a frenzy by rabid segregationists to return to their dormitories. For that, as well as for sermons advocating racial justice, Gray himself had been a target of Klan harassment. It was natural for Dean to choose Gray when he needed someone to talk to about right and wrong.

Yet when Dean poured out what he had heard, Gray dismissed the whole thing as "preposterous."

Concerned that Dean had succumbed to emotional stress, Gray recommended that he get away for a bit. Dean acquiesced; he and Mary drove north to Maryville, Tennessee, to spend the night with his mother. As he thought over the scene with Gray, he felt increasingly embarrassed. Maybe his information had been wrong. Perhaps the plan was so bizarre it had been dropped.

In a house across the street from the Davidson residence, members of the bomb disposal squad were ready but worried. They were confident they could disarm the explosive device if it could be retrieved, but what might happen if an exchange of gunfire should erupt was anyone's guess: there was an even chance the device would explode if hit.

And if the device consisted of twenty-nine sticks of dynamite, as the FBI's information said it did, then it was almost certainly powerful enough to destroy not only Davidson's house but the house across the street, where the bomb squad members and Watts and Rucker were positioned. The explosion probably would also kill Scarbrough and two other detectives and a patrolman who were concealed behind bushes on a bank in the side yard.

The two officers sheltered in a drainage ditch behind the Davidson house might survive, but the four positioned in clumps of bushes across the street might not, though they were forty feet or so from the end of the Davidsons' driveway.

"The only thing you can do if you hit that dynamite is pray," one of the demolition experts said.

Tarrants and Ainsworth headed for a wooded area several miles north of Meridian on U.S. 45 to make their final preparations. Tarrants pulled off the road and parked beneath the dense boughs of a clump of large pine trees. He stepped out into the hot, humid night and opened the trunk of the car. The temperature had soared to one hundred in Meridian that day and still was in the high eighties. It was now about 12:15 A.M., and as Tarrants lifted the brown Clorox box containing the dynamite from the trunk, he was dripping with perspiration. As always, he handled the box gently.

Next he turned to the detonating device. In the past, he had always relied on simple fuses cut to lengths that would burn fifteen or twenty minutes. They were simple to ignite with a match or cigarette lighter and left behind no telltale evidence. This time, however, he had decided he and Ainsworth would need more time to flee the scene after the explosion. And because a fuse with more than twenty minutes' burning time was impractical, he had decided to get Matthews to rig an electrical detonating device with a clock.

Tarrants checked the circuitry and set the timer for 2:00 A.M.—time enough for him and Ainsworth to be well on their way to Florida before the minute hand clicked upward for the last time.

He placed the Clorox box on the front seat of the car between Ainsworth and himself.

Although they were not necessarily expecting trouble, she carried a .25-caliber pistol in her purse and Tarrants had a nine-millimeter Browning automatic pistol on the seat beside him. A German Schmeisser nine-millimeter submachine gun lay within easy reach under the front seat.

At the Travelers Club, Raymond and Alton Wayne Roberts spent a little time drinking at the bar. Raymond made a point of greeting shouting acquaintances in a loud voice. Then the brothers launched into a violent quarrel with a hapless patron, stirring such a commotion that there would be no shortage of witnesses to testify about where they had been at the time of the explosion.

At about 12:45 A.M., Tarrants drove slowly north on Twenty-ninth Avenue, passed the house and continued up a hill for a full block. Then he turned around and let the heavy car creep back down the hill.

Watts and Rucker watched from a bedroom window of the house opposite Davidson's, broadcasting a description of the car's movements on a portable police radio. "There's a black Buick headed this way," Rucker said, mistaking the color in the darkness.

Another FBI agent, Larry Brock, was positioned in a car a block away on Poplar Springs Drive, one of several agents and police officers assigned to interception duty on the perimeter. "How many people?" Brock asked.

"Looks like two," Rucker replied.

"Are they both males?"

"I can't tell."

Charles Johnson, a pleasant-faced officer with brown hair who moonlighted as an upholsterer, was desperate for a cigarette. As a security precaution, the men stationed outside had been told not to smoke. Johnson, who was lying in a ditch behind the house, found the order impossible to obey. "It was as stressful as waiting at the hospital for your wife to deliver a baby," he said. "I dug me a hole about six inches deep and put the cigarette in the hole and smoked it. I was facedown, and suddenly Moore says, 'Here it comes.' I looked up and saw the car coming with no lights on. I snuffed out the cigarette in the hole real fast."

Tarrants pulled the car to the curb and stopped near a huge oak tree about fifty feet from the broad driveway that led to Davidson's double carport. The driveway was some fifty feet long.

"Hold it, he's stopping," Rucker breathed into the radio; he moved to the living room window for a better view.

Behind the bushes on a bank forty feet from Tarrants, Detectives Scarbrough, Willoughby and Ralph McNair and Patrolman Andrew (Bo) Partridge, dressed in black T-shirts and trousers and armed with shotguns and rifles, watched as Tarrants opened his door and stepped into the street. He reached back into the car for the Browning automatic and tucked it into the waistband of his trousers. Then he took the bomb from the front seat and closed the car door. Ainsworth remained in the passenger seat; the officers could not see her clearly.

Tarrants, cradling the box in his left arm, holding the automatic in his right hand, moved cautiously around the front of the car, crossed a small section of Davidson's yard and stepped onto the driveway heading for the window of the bedroom where the Davidsons ordinarily slept. To Rucker, Tarrants seemed to be moving on tiptoe.

"We'd better stop him here," Rucker commanded.

Scarbrough heard the order on his radio and acted at once. "Halt! Police!" he shouted.

At the sound, Tarrants whirled around and Scarbrough, seeing what he later described as two flashes from the automatic pistol, opened fire with a shotgun. The night erupted in a fusillade of firing. Willoughby and Partridge opened up with shotguns and McNair cut loose with a rifle. "Frank and I were ducking all over the place," Rucker remembered, "because suddenly it sounded like a war down there. Everybody was unloading."

Tarrants dropped the bomb and his pistol on the driveway. He ran dancing and zigzagging back toward the green Buick through a hail of bullets. Buckshot struck two of the sticks of dynamite. Almost miraculously, the bomb did not explode.

As Tarrants reached the front of the car, a load of buckshot from Scarbrough's shotgun tore into the upper part of his right leg. He staggered and almost fell but grabbed the side of the car. Ainsworth, frantically trying to help him, leaned over and opened the door on the driver's side. Two loads of buckshot caught her in the shoulder.

"Tommy, I've been hit," she gasped. Then a rifle bullet tore into her spine. She fell back. There was a gaping wound at the base of her neck.

With blood gushing from his leg and bullets still hammering against the car, Tarrants struggled to get behind the steering wheel, turned the ignition key and jammed the accelerator to the floor. The car took off with a jerk, tires screeching, and hurtled south on Twenty-ninth Avenue.

A block away, sitting in their white, unmarked 1966 Ford patrol car in Judge Cameron's driveway, Tucker and Hatcher heard the gunfire. A minute later, Scarbrough's excited voice came over the radio: "They've broken out, headed south. Try to stop them!"

Tucker wheeled the patrol car onto Twenty-ninth Avenue as the Buick, with Tarrants bent low over the steering wheel and Ainsworth crumpled on the floorboard, whizzed toward him. The police car blocked the street. Tarrants swerved up into Judge Cameron's yard, through a clump of azaleas and back onto the roadway beyond the cruiser. Tucker swung after him in hot pursuit. The lighter, faster patrol car quickly began to overtake the Buick. Hatcher leaned out the window on his side of the car. A blast from his shotgun shattered the Buick's back window. He kept firing.

Tarrants slammed on the brakes and turned sharply right on Twenty-first Street. They were now fifteen blocks from Davidson's house. With Tucker right behind him, Tarrants made another right at the next intersection, then a left. But his front tires had been hit and his car skidded to a halt in a yard at the corner of Twenty-first Street and Thirtieth Avenue. Tucker rammed the patrol car into the back of the Buick, knocking it into a fireplug a few feet away and slamming Tarrants against the steering wheel.

Shaking his head clear, Tarrants got out of the wrecked car, brandishing the submachine gun. He whirled and began firing, raking the front of the patrol car with bullets. Tucker ducked out of sight beneath the dashboard. Hatcher pushed his car door open and started to raise his shotgun when three bullets tore through the windshield and into his chest. Still clutching his shotgun and desperately trying to avoid being shot again, Hatcher fell from the car and rolled under it, collapsing in shock. One of the bullets had hit him in the ribs, traveled around the rib cage and stopped in the right ventricle of his heart.

Tucker raised his head and peered over the dashboard just in time to see Tarrants desperately trying to slide another clip into the Schmeisser. Tucker fired his .38-caliber service revolver and hit Tarrants in the upper left leg, staggering him. Tarrants screamed in pain and dropped the machine gun. But somehow he turned and began to run, dragging his left leg and leaving a trail of blood on the grass as he plunged away toward a nearby house.

Snatching his shotgun off the floor of the patrol car, Tucker fired a load of buckshot. Tarrants also seemed to fire again. Despite the darkness, Tucker could see a figure fall. He ran toward it, thinking Tarrants had gone down, but realized to his horror that "it was another white male I didn't recognize." Robert Burton, a sailor who had stepped off the porch of the house after hearing the commotion, had been shot and critically wounded.

Left behind at the Davidson house, Sergeant Joyner and Officer David Sessions had commandeered a fire department car. "Run this thing," Joyner ordered the driver, "and if you can't, move over and let me drive!" The driver nodded and the three men piled into the car.

The sound of the shooting had immediately been reported to police headquarters by alarmed neighbors. The radio dispatcher that night had been excluded from any knowledge of the ambush plan. Passing the neighbors' report along over the police radio, he said, "Send somebody out there. Some kids must be playing with firecrackers."

Instantly another voice came over the air, countermanding the astonished dispatcher: "It's the Goddamned police. Stay away from here."

Detective Charles Overby and two other blackshirts, following the confusing radio traffic as best they could, arrived in the general vicinity of the spot where the wounded Tarrants had disappeared. Sprinting down the street, they saw what they thought was the fugitive in an abandoned automobile in a vacant lot. A head popped up from the backseat of the car and the officers raised their guns to fire. Overby drew a bead with his .357 Magnum. Suddenly, they heard the sound of gunfire half a block away. Overby and the other two officers turned and ran in the direction of the shooting, saving from almost certain death a black man who had been sleeping in the old car.

The shots the officers heard were aimed at Tarrants, who had eluded Tucker and hobbled some fifty yards from his wrecked car before coming up against a chain-link fence. He tried to climb over it, but the top strand of wire was electrified—thanks to a white property owner who was concerned about black neighbors. The electricity knocked Tarrants to the ground, and he lay sprawled there in a clump of bushes when pursuing officers spotted him and opened fire again with their shotguns. Officer Partridge, dropping to the grass and sliding toward Tarrants on his belly, fired his shotgun from a distance of only fifteen feet.

Sergeant Joyner had found his way to the scene at last; he and three other officers shone their flashlights on the crumpled figure, then turned out the lights and fired again at the same close range. "All four of us were firing shotguns from about fifteen feet away," Joyner recalled. "We had in mind killing him, I don't mind telling you."

Two shots tore into Tarrants' right arm, almost severing it. Two others struck the ground inches from his chest. An officer again turned a flashlight on Tarrants.

"Is he dead?"

"No, the son of a bitch is still alive."

They dragged the gasping, bleeding figure out of the bushes onto an open plot of grass that quickly began to turn dark crimson. The "double-ought" buckshot had ripped him open. Lead pellets the size of marbles traveling at fourteen hundred feet a second and designed for deer hunting caused gaping injuries similar to war wounds. Blood gushed from Tarrants' right arm and from both legs, and a stream of blood coursed down his abdomen.

One of the officers cocked his gun and aimed at Tarrants' head.

"Shoot him, shoot him!" someone shouted.

"Don't shoot," another voice said. "The neighbors are here."

Officer Partridge, dazed and trembling, stood over Tarrants with his shotgun aimed at the crumpled figure's head. But for a quirk of fate, a final shot might have finished Tarrants off. In the Meridian Police Department's arsenal, some of the shotguns were double-barrels and some had magazines. Most of the latter held five shells; one held six. For years, Partridge and officer Glenn Miller had vied for the gun that held the extra round. On this night, Miller had gotten to the police station first and taken the prized weapon with him to his assignment—guarding Chief Gunn's house. In the shooting in the yard, Partridge had fired five times. Now, his shotgun was empty.

It was a nightmarish scene Partridge would never forget. Neighbors, some in pajamas and robes, scurried forward from all directions. The night was filled with the scream of sirens as ambulances and more police cars arrived.

Tarrants had fallen in the backyard of 2117 Thirtieth Avenue. In the front yard, twenty-five yards away, Robert Burton, the sailor who had been shot in the liver while frantically trying to crawl away from the gunfire, lay motionless on the ground. Keith Garrity, another sailor visiting that house, remained hidden under a car parked in the yard, where he had crawled when the shooting started. A third sailor had rushed back into the house and called an ambulance when Burton fell.

About seventy-five yards farther on, at the corner of Twenty-first Street and Thirtieth Avenue, officers were gently preparing to load the gravely wounded Hatcher into an ambulance that had pulled alongside his bullet-pocked patrol car.

Back at the detective department, Marie Knowles' heart was pounding. From the excited exchanges between officers on the radio, it was clear a policeman had been shot. So had a woman in the car with Tarrants. Mrs. Knowles would remember "something inside of me saying, 'You shouldn't be part of this. It's almost like you were the one that was planning a murder even though it was Klansmen.' "

There had never been any question in her mind about the object of the police mission that night. She had heard Gunn and others spell it out too many times during the meetings at the Holiday Inn. One order stuck in her mind: "Drop 'em, drop 'em." And when she had been taking down Scarbrough's reports of the sessions with the Roberts brothers at his trailer, she had felt a nervous quiver every time she typed the word *set-up*.

Suddenly the telephone on her desk rang. It was Sergeant Willoughby calling from the house on the embankment across the street from the Davidson house. He told her Tarrants had escaped, "but everything's okay out here."

"Everything's *not* okay, Hooky, it's *not* okay," she shouted into the phone. "I've been listening to this wild chase and an officer's just been shot and there's a woman shot in that car they were chasing. Don't stay on this phone telling me everything's okay because it isn't and I've got to get back to the police radio to see what's happening now."

• • •

Paramedics from the first two ambulances concentrated on Hatcher and Burton. Both were critically injured, but they would survive. The sailor could be treated in Meridian, but Hatcher required open-heart surgery to save his life. Arrangements were quickly made for a navy plane to fly him to Emory Hospital in Atlanta. Chief Gunn, his face wet with tears, accompanied him.

Tarrants was barely conscious when medics finally reached him. As they loaded him into the ambulance, he became aware of another bloody figure sprawled on a stretcher that had already been loaded into the vehicle. "The woman's dead," he heard an attendant say. Not until then did he know for certain that the wound at the base of Kathy Ainsworth's neck had been fatal.

Watts, having raced to the scene with Rucker, took one look at Tarrants and said, "I don't think there's a way in the world he can live." Turning to Dan Bodine, another FBI agent, Watts said, "He hasn't got long. Get in there and go to the hospital with him and see if you can get a dying declaration. See if you can get him to talk about all those other jobs. Ask him about Sam Bowers and Danny Hawkins and L. E. Matthews."

Bodine jumped into the back of the ambulance between Tarrants and the body of Kathy Ainsworth. With a burst of its siren, the ambulance lurched off toward Mattie Hersey Hospital four miles away. Bodine leaned over and tried to talk with Tarrants, but the Klansman groaned and turned his head away.

Of the five big hospitals that made Meridian an important regional medical center, Mattie Hersey stood near the bottom of the social totem pole. Police called it "a charity hog slaughter," meaning it treated the city's poor, regardless of their ability to pay. Like many such hospitals, however, its clientele made it the best place in the city to be treated for trauma, especially gunshot wounds; Mattie Hersey had seen more than its share of those. The emergency room was swarming with medical personnel, police and FBI agents when attendants wheeled Tarrants in on a stretcher, with Bodine following close behind. Nurses used scissors to cut away Tarrants' blood-soaked shirt and trousers. A doctor examined him quickly and announced, in a voice loud enough for everyone present to hear, that he probably had no more than forty-five minutes to live.

The medical team labored to stem the flow of blood and prepare

Tarrants for surgery. Bodine bent close to his ear and whispered: "The doctor said you aren't going to make it. You ought to talk while you can get it off your conscience."

Tarrants groaned, but did not answer.

Undeterred, Bodine ran through the list: the Meridian synagogue bombing, the bombing of the Jackson synagogue, the bombing of the Jackson rabbi's house, Sam Bowers and Danny Joe Hawkins and L. E. Matthews.

The agent's face was only a blur and his words seemed to run together as Tarrants slipped in and out of consciousness. Still, he heard enough of Bodine's entreaty to understand the underlying message: make a deathbed confession and save your soul. If Tarrants believed he had a soul, he had long ago given it to the Klan and remained true to its code of secrecy.

As he was wheeled into surgery, heavily armed police officers took up positions outside the operating room and began patrolling the hospital's corridors and grounds. There was concern that the White Knights might try to do what the police had failed to do. Tarrants knew so much about the Klan's operations that he could put away its top leaders and hit men for a long time. Killing a fellow Klansman who possessed that kind of information and who might be tempted to talk was part of the Klan's code, too.

Ironically, some of the same policemen who had tried to kill Tarrants now were protecting him. In fact, the FBI and Meridian police were pulling for Tarrants' recovery, hoping he would crack and implicate Bowers and Hawkins, as well as Matthews.

Throughout the night, Mattie Hersey's surgeons worked to save Tarrants' life. They ordered blood transfusions and removed buckshot from his abdomen, legs and right arm. The damage was not confined to the impact of the lead pellets. The shotgun blasts had struck with the force of explosions, blowing away whole sections of bone in his right arm and large areas of tissue in the arm and in his legs and abdomen. For the moment, doctors could do little more than cover the massive wounds with gauze soaked in a saline solution to guard against infection.

Whether or not Tarrants would make it, they could not say.

In the bloody Buick Electra, police found a nine-millimeter submachine gun with three clips, a nine-millimeter Walther automatic pistol with a loaded clip, a loaded six-millimeter Browning automatic, a hand grenade, a cannister of Mace in a holster, more than two hundred rounds of assorted ammunition, fourteen blasting caps, a seven-foot length of fuse and a pair of handcuffs.

Along with several books, including *Anatomy of Spying, Gray Ghosts of the Confederacy* and *School for Spies,* they also found the stenographer's notebook in which Tarrants had carefully penned his note of March 23, 1968, saying he was "forced to go underground or be arrested and imprisoned on framed Fed charges."

On another page he had written a jumble of phrases, many with a biblical ring: "Brother . . . kinsman . . . Melchezidec . . . Without mother without father . . . having neither beginning of days, nor end of life; but made like unto the son of God . . . abideth a priest continually . . . order of Melchisdec . . . a brother of race . . . what seek ye? . . . Peace, order, observers of the laws of YAWVEH."

And on yet another page, under the heading "Prima Facia Considerations," he had scribbled his own rambling thoughts about operating as a terrorist:

> Not a game—this is war—must start to get and think like military men. Caution—demoralizing effect of capture, defeat— depriving cause of strength.
>   Selfishness in action by doing small insignificant acts.
>   Change of attitude to passive.
>   Necessity of being face in crowd . . . inconspicuous.
>   Don't let people know what to expect.
>   Practice self-control and will power.
>   Cover-story methods.
>   Attempt to draw out and identify militants demon etc.
>   Observant . . . explosives . . . assassinations . . . funds . . .
> sanctuaries, etc. etc.

On a slip of paper found in Tarrants' wallet, he had written the names of eighteen other potential targets, mostly Southern civil rights activists, including Charles Evers and Aaron Henry, the NAACP leaders in Mississippi, and two Selma, Alabama, ministers, Fred D. Reese and L. L. Anderson.

There were several Klan identification cards in his wallet, as well as a draft card identifying Tarrants as 4-F because of his criminal record. That would have surprised his former co-workers at the Masonite plant in Laurel; there he had bragged that, as a soldier in Vietnam, he had killed more than seventy Vietcong.

In Kathy Ainsworth's tan wicker handbag, police found a Belgian-made .25-caliber automatic pistol containing five bullets, as well as a variety of other items that reflected the bizarre split in her life as a teacher by day, terrorist by night. She had two shopping lists, one for Oil of Olay and Lemon Jelvyn skin freshener and another for gunpowder, primers and bullets.

Also in her purse were: two photos of her students, one of a little girl in a red dress signed, "With love, Gail Wang," the other of a boy in a white cap and gown; prescription sunglasses; a perfume atomizer and a gold compact with mirror and Avon face powder; a contract for the $937 balance she owed on four Whirlpool appliances—a range, a refrigerator, and a washer and dryer she had purchased with a $50 down payment; a calling card from "L. E. Matthews, Your Candidate for State Senator"; a red, white and blue calling card from "Sam H. Bowers, Jr., Political Investigations, Christian, American, Whig"; a membership card for the Ladies' Auxiliary of the Americans for the Preservation of the White Race, signed by Johnnie Mae Hawkins, secretary; and a $78 receipt for the purchase of munitions.

There was also a card from the Christian National Crusade, Los Angeles, that read:

> No man escapes when freedom fails,
> The best men rot in filthy jails,
> And those who cried, "Appease! Appease!"
> Are hanged by those they tried to please.

13

As doctors struggled to save Tarrants' life, the FBI and the Meridian police—along with Jewish leaders in Jackson and Meridian—braced for Klan retaliation. How could the White Knights let the ambush pass unchallenged?

The day after the shoot-out, Watts told Raymond Roberts to contact Bowers and find out his reaction and his plan for responding. Raymond and Alton Wayne met with Bowers later that day in Laurel. That evening, the brothers, accompanied by Tom Hendricks, met once again at the trailer with Watts, Rucker and Scarbrough. The lawmen wanted a detailed briefing of their conversation with Bowers. What had he told them? Was he angry? Was he looking for revenge?

Raymond said Bowers was enraged, expressed intense hatred for Officers Tucker and Partridge, and complained bitterly that Partridge had shot Tarrants while he was helpless on the ground. Bowers told Roberts, "We've lost a good soldier in Kathy. She's as good as Tarrants or any of the rest of them."

More Klan action was being prepared, Raymond said. "They are planning a Number Four and are going to start daytime action instead of night riding."

The Roberts brothers were unusually nervous during the session at the trailer and accused Scarbrough and the FBI agents of double-crossing them. They were angry that they had been paid only eight thousand of the promised seventy-five thousand dollars. They had risked their lives to help arrange the trap. They had expected no survivors, knowing that if Tarrants survived he would soon figure out who betrayed him. Immunity from prosecution was all very well, but if they were exposed as informants the Klan might turn its fury on them. What's more, they were still playing a dicey game by continuing to inform on Hawkins and Bowers. What if the hit man and the imperial wizard suspected them?

The brothers said they were sick and tired of putting their lives on the line to gather information and then being stiffed. As Scarbrough later noted in a memo, they were "very unhappy" and said they would not talk anymore "unless we keep our end of the bargain and for us not to contact them again unless we have the money. An offer of $150,000 was made for testimony—they refused."

Finally, Scarbrough decided to dole out some more cash. He opened his briefcase and took out a pile of twenty-dollar bills. To prevent squabbling, he carefully counted out two stacks of four thousand dollars each. Each brother received one of the stacks. Then Scarbrough counted out two thousand dollars and handed it to Hendricks.

Raymond used the pseudonym Alfred Roseburg in signing a receipt for eight thousand dollars. Hendricks signed his two-thousand-dollar receipt James Overeaugh.

"That's all for now," Scarbrough told the informants. "There'll be more if you do what we tell you. If you don't, it's like I said before, your asses will be in big trouble. We want you to stay after Bowers and Matthews and Danny Joe Hawkins. Get us everything you can."

Altogether, the Robertses had now received a total of $29,850 or less than half of the seventy-five thousand dollars they had been promised to set up Tarrants and Hawkins. And Hendricks had received only two thousand of the ten thousand dollars he had been promised to get the Roberts brothers' cooperation. Hendricks felt the FBI had double-crossed him as well as the brothers.

Despite his anger, Bowers limited his immediate public reaction to words. He sat down at a typewriter in his office at the Sambo Amusement Company and typed a five-page, single-spaced letter to Officer Tucker complaining that the police had killed "a Christian, American patriot . . . doing her best to preserve Christian civilization by helping to destroy the body of an animal of Satan's synagogue . . ."

Bowers wrote that he had seen Tucker's photograph on page one of the Jackson *Clarion-Ledger,* and "my impression of this

picture was that of a sincere law enforcement officer who had
performed his duty as he saw it with diligence and courage,
and who, afterward, could see the horrible consequences of his
actions. As one who has been repeatedly accused of having
blood-stained hands himself, Mr. Tucker, I can say with candor
that I know how you must feel. And my heartfelt sympathy goes
out to you for the horrible experience which you have undergone."

It was a typical Bowers epistle, except for such self-deprecating
comments as "I realize I have been presumptuous to address
myself to you, and I confess that my witness is damaged by the
fact that I am an ignorant filthy and dishonorble sinner, and actually deserve more criticism than I have received, and I humbly
bow to any low opinion you may have of me."

Bowers wrote that he did not address himself to J. Edgar
Hoover or Roy Gunn because he considered "that their depraved
sense of justification and righteousness under law has hardened
their hearts to the point where the witness of a sinner as ignorant
and as incompotent as myself would have no more effect upon
them than the beating of a butterfly's wings upon a solid steel
door."

"Mr. Tucker," Bowers wrote, "the principle of law as it has
been twisted and abused by the animals in the synagogue of Satan,
one of which you were guarding and protecting on the night when
young Kathy was killed, and one of your fellow officers was
wounded nigh unto death, is not the Law of our Father; it is the
law of Asiatic, cannabalistic slavery."

Instead of mailing the letter that evening, the next day Bowers
gave it to Byron de la Beckwith, the man accused of assassinating
Medgar Evers, and told him to pass it on to Raymond Roberts
and ask him to deliver it to Tom Tucker. Roberts dropped it into
a Meridian mailbox and Tucker received it the next day.

Two weeks after the shoot-out, with Hatcher out of danger, Chief
Gunn was ecstatic over what his department and the FBI had
accomplished. He dictated a letter to Roy Moore hailing the joint
effort of "your men working side by side with the Detective department and the police officers who were involved." Although
the FBI would insist it was strictly a local operation, Gunn told
Moore

there were many nights when they did not get to even go to bed, neither your men nor ours. Roy, words cannot express my feelings toward your fine men and also to you, personally. This type of team work and a few more buckshots I believe, will bring people to realize that crime does not pay, especially in our area, I hope. As you know, we are not blood thirsty, but when you are dealing with vicious animals, you have to play their game on their own terms. We hope that this type of action will not be necessary again, but if it becomes necessary, we stand ready and willing to do what we have to to preserve law and order in our city. The days do not get too hot or the nights too dark for us to come to your aid any time and any where we can serve your organization.

Moore's reply was as bureaucratic as Gunn's letter was rhetorical: "We were glad we could be of assistance and we stand ready and willing to be of aid in any way possible in matters of mutual interest. You are to be commended for your unequivocal stand on such acts of violence."

Discussing the case with his superiors in Washington, however, Moore insisted it was "strictly a local show from the word go." That was for the files and for "plausible deniability."

In a letter to Hoover, Gunn ignored such pretense: "Mr. Hoover, words cannot express how I feel about your men here in Meridian. These men, along with ours, on several nights did not even get to go to bed. Mr. Roy K. Moore gave us every assistance that was requested or needed. Without this kind of help, I am sure we could not have made the progress we did."

At Mattie Hersey Hospital, Tarrants' vital signs finally stabilized despite his massive wounds and enormous loss of blood. The doctors who worked to save him concluded—to their own amazement—that, barring complications, he probably would pull through.

Tarrants' right arm was so shattered—with a four-inch section of the ulna just below the elbow shot away—that doctors at first considered amputation. Instead, they decided to transfer him to Meridian's Rush Memorial Hospital, where an orthopedic surgeon, Dr. Leslie Rush, agreed to make a last-ditch effort to save his arm. Dr. Rush had been a pioneer in using stainless-steel pins and screws for bone surgery and was considered one of the foremost specialists in his field.

Three days after the ambush a convoy of police and FBI agents escorted the ambulance carrying Tarrants to Rush Memorial Hospital. At the same moment, an even larger convoy, this one headed by a long black hearse, traveled to a little cemetery on the outskirts of Magee, a small town about sixty miles southwest of Meridian. At the cemetery scores of mourners stood perspiring in the ninety-five-degree July heat as two black workmen lowered the mahogany coffin containing Kathy Ainsworth's remains into the sunbaked earth.

Her husband, Ralph Ainsworth, so distraught he could hardly talk, kept repeating to a reporter, "She was just an angel, an angel, that's all I can say."

The Klan, intent on making her a martyr to the cause of white supremacy, had tried to take control of her funeral, sending dozens of red, white and blue floral crosses to the chapel. Mrs. Capomacchia, stoic and dry-eyed, greeted dozens of Klansmen at the funeral with assurances her daughter had died for a worthy cause.

"Kathy was put here for a purpose and she died for that purpose," Mrs. Capomacchia whispered to one of Kathy's fellow teachers. The teacher later burst into tears, declaring, "It was madness, madness . . . this sweet girl dying for madness."

Ralph's father, Richard Ainsworth, a car dealer and retired army colonel, was shocked at Mrs. Capomacchia's attitude and called her "anti-Negro and anti-Semitic—just the worst you ever saw. She was just as satisfied at the manner in which Kathy died as if she had died in the middle of church," he said. Several times Richard Ainsworth ordered the Klansmen to leave the services at the funeral-home chapel, but they refused and followed along to the graveside rites.

In the back window of a white Cadillac, one of the last cars to leave the cemetery, was a sign: "This Car Is Protected by the Ku Klux Klan."

Several hours after the funeral, FBI agents interviewed Ralph Ainsworth at his house and asked for permission to search the premises. Ainsworth agreed. He told the agents that he knew his wife was a radical segregationist and that while they had political

The White Patriot—a hate sheet distributed by Americans for the Preservation of the White Race—helped create the atmosphere of violence in which the Klan terrorized Jews. The FBI labeled the organization a front for the notorious White Knights.

Kathy Ainsworth was a teacher by day and a Klan bomber by night. She was highly regarded at the elementary school where she taught and where no one suspected her virulent anti-Semitism.

Thomas Albert Tarrants III, who was known as a "mad-dog killer" and "the most dangerous man in Mississippi," at his trial in Meridian. Tarrants pleaded insanity to a charge of placing a bomb outside a businessman's home.

4

Rabbi Perry Nussbaum and wife, Arene, survey damage the morning after terrorists bombed their house in Jackson. They narrowly escaped death. Mrs. Nussbaum emerged from the house crying hysterically with splinters of glass in her face and hair.

5

Tarrants' device for a "Number Four," a murder—a Clorox box containing a timing device and dynamite. He planned to detonate such a device at Meyer Davidson's house in Meridian.

A portrait of the family the FBI labeled "the meanest Klan family in Mississippi." Hit man Danny Joe Hawkins, right; his father, Joe Denver; mother, Johnnie Mae; and son, Jefferson Davis.

Imperial Wizard Sam Bowers after his civil rights conviction in the case of the three murdered reformers (Michael Schwerner, Andrew Goodman and James Chaney) at Philadelphia, Mississippi. The FBI said Bowers masterminded nine murders and three hundred bombings, burnings and beatings.

8

Alton Wayne Roberts, right, and Deputy Sheriff
Cecil Price after their civil rights convictions in
the Philadelphia murders. Roberts and his
brother Raymond later became FBI informants
and helped set up an ambush of Klan terrorists
in Meridian.

9

Marie Knowles, secretary
of Meridian detectives,
stands near file cabinets
where she kept secret
police reports of the
informants meetings
with Klansmen.

LEFT
Meridian police chief Roy
Gunn. He fought a deadly
war with the Klan and
vowed to "send them
straight to hell where
they belong."

10

1

Ken Dean, executive di-
rector of the Mississippi
Council on Human Rela-
tions. He learned in ad-
vance of plans for the
ambush and tried without
success to head it off.

Detective Luke
Scarbrough met with
informants and helped
plan the ambush.

11

ABOVE
Roy Moore, agent in charge of the Jackson FBI office, told Jewish leaders that it would take money and informants to stop Klan violence against Mississippi Jews.

When police arrested Klansman Danny Joe Hawkins, they seized a small arsenal, as well as a Klansman's robe and hood, a hangman's noose, a Confederate flag and a pile of anti-Semitic literature.

15

Jackson attorney Al Binder, a Jewish leader who worked with the FBI to end Klan violence against the Jews.

BELOW
Raymond Roberts, crucial in setting up the ambush in Meridian, flies a Confederate flag outside the courthouse where his brother Alton Wayne was being tried on charges stemming from the Philadelphia case.

ABOVE   16
FBI agents Frank Watts, right, and Jack Rucker used tough talk and a big payoff to pressure the Roberts brothers into becoming informants and setting a trap for fellow Klansmen.

Thomas Albert Tarrants III after police arrested him in Collins, Mississippi, in December 1967. He was charged with possession of an illegal weapon—a submachine gun.

Thomas Albert Tarrants III in 1992.

differences on the subject, they had agreed not to discuss them or let them interfere with their marriage. He had tried several times to persuade her to quit the Klan, he said, and she had promised him she would discontinue her Klan activities by the following September.

As for his own attitude, Ainsworth pointed out that A. I. Bronstein, a close friend and owner of the Universal Health Club, where he worked, was Jewish. Prior to his marriage to Kathy, he and Bronstein were roommates. "He stated that he is aware that his wife had been very anti-semitic," and FBI report noted, "but she did not interfere with his friendship with Bronstein nor with his employment, and in fact, had indicated that in order to spend more time with her husband during the remainder of the summer, she would work gratis at the health club."

At the Ainsworth home, the agents confiscated a high-powered rifle that had been given to Kathy by the Klan, as well as a large quantity of Klan materials and hate literature. Among the printed matter were an antiblack, anti-Semitic survival manual entitled *We Will Survive* and a folder of news clippings on the bombings of the Jackson synagogue, the dean's residence at Tougaloo College and the Nussbaum and Kochtitzky residences.

Danny Joe Hawkins did not go to Magee for Kathy's funeral. Instead he telephoned Raymond Roberts at his house in Meridian and asked if he knew why the police had been waiting in ambush for Tarrants and Kathy. Roberts said he could not afford to talk about it over the telephone because the FBI probably had it tapped. He suggested they meet in Jackson at the Alamo Plaza Hotel on Highway 80.

Hawkins agreed to the meeting and apparently was not too concerned about an FBI tap. He told Roberts, "We have lost two of our most important underground people."

Later, at a bar at the Alamo Plaza Hotel, Roberts told Hawkins he was prepared to join other Klansmen in retaliating for what had happened to Tarrants and Kathy Ainsworth. The two men agreed that they were prepared to carry out any order from Bowers. And the impetuous Hawkins telephoned Bowers for instructions. The imperial wizard, however, "instructed that no additional acts of violence should be conducted at this time," according to an FBI report.

• • •

At Rush Memorial Hospital, Dr. Rush used metal pins to replace
shattered bones below and above the elbow of Tarrants' right arm.
A half-dozen police officers armed with machine guns and sawed-
off shotguns remained at his side even in the operating room.
Aware of Tarrants' extensive contacts with the Klan, the Minutemen and other violent right-wing organizations, they feared an
attempt to abduct or kill him. Tarrants himself would later say
that being liquidated by the Klan would not have offended him
"because we regarded everyone as expendable for the cause."

As he lay in the hospital bed recovering from the surgery and
slowly learning to regain some use of his right arm, Tarrants began
to concentrate on questions that had bothered him ever since the
ambush: How had the FBI and police known about his plans?
What had gone wrong? Did an informant penetrate Bowers' innermost cell? Did someone get careless? Did the FBI pick up
something in a bug or a telephone tap? He knew he had been
careful, but what about Danny Joe Hawkins and Raymond Roberts? Had Hawkins and Roberts slipped up in selecting Davidson's
house as the target?

He first dismissed out of hand the possibility of a well-placed
informant. Everybody who knew anything about the Davidson
job was so involved in other acts of violence that the idea of one
of them cooperating with the police or the FBI seemed preposterous. Gradually, however, Tarrants' view began to change. In
the quiet of his hospital room, he heard snatches of conversations
among the policemen guarding him. Over several days, the snip-
pets began to add up to a disturbing fact: the police and FBI had
been alerted long in advance about the Davidson site. The officers'
conversations contained no hint about the source, but Tarrants
could think of only one explanation: an informant.

Meridian police kept the hospital and especially Tarrants' room
under constant guard. Now that he was able to stand and walk,
a piece of tape was attached to the sill of his door and the order
to the guards was blunt: "If he puts one toe across that tape, kill
him."

One day hospital officials made an exception to the no-visitors
rule and permitted Percy Quinn, an attorney from Laurel, to visit
Tarrants. Bowers had dispatched Quinn to check on Tarrants'
condition, assure him of Klan support and learn as much as Tar-

rants could tell about the ambush. Bowers, like Tarrants, was trying to put all the pieces together. He, too, had concluded that there must have been an informant, and he wanted to know who it was.

Raymond Roberts, increasingly nervous and eager to demonstrate he had a continuing commitment to the Klan, again sought out Danny Joe Hawkins and pressed his argument that the Klan should retaliate. Hawkins seemed receptive, but suggested Roberts would need training with a machine gun. Roberts readily agreed and drove Hawkins to a city dump just south of Jackson that Klansmen used for target shooting.

There Hawkins instructed him in the use of the nine-millimeter machine gun. Roberts fired off two clips of forty shots each, blasting cans, bottles and other targets. The shots were loud enough to be heard clearly in homes a quarter of a mile away. The two men practiced for about an hour, long enough for the State Highway Patrol to be alerted. A patrol car containing three state troopers intercepted them as they were driving away from the dump.

The troopers ordered the Klansmen out of their car, then took the machine gun and a .45 automatic out of the car and put the weapons on the hood. One of the troopers radioed a message naming Roberts as the owner of the car, then, without explanation, put the weapons on the backseat of the car and said, "Okay, you boys get on out of here and don't cause any trouble around here."

"Why do you reckon they let us go?" Hawkins asked as they drove away.

Roberts said he did not know, but the question rang in his ears. Was it an innocent question or had Hawkins surmised that the troopers had made no arrest because they knew an informant was involved? Later, as they drove toward downtown Jackson, Hawkins resumed the unsettling line of questioning. Why were the Meridian police staked out around Meyer Davidson's house? Had an informant tipped them off? And had Alton Wayne talked to the FBI to get his ten-year sentence reduced?

Raymond told Hawkins that his brother would never talk, and that if he thought his brother had talked, he would kill him himself. As for the stakeout, he said, everyone knew that in the wake of the synagogue and church bombings the Meridian police had staked out several sites. It was ridiculous to think an informant was involved. The answers seemed to satisfy Hawkins, but he expressed concern that if the FBI investigated Tarrants' background, they would find that both he and Tarrants had been "deeply involved in various shootings in Jackson."

Despite Bowers' decree to halt the violence for the time being, Hawkins insisted on action: "We have to do something to show them how we feel about them taking two of our best soldiers."

By Raymond's account, Danny Joe was in a wild mood. He allegedly vowed "to go to the outskirts of Jackson and call a nigger cabdriver he knew and when the cabdriver came to that vicinity to pick up 'a customer,' he would then shoot him and hang him from a bridge."

The following day FBI agents intercepted Hawkins' car in front of the governor's mansion in downtown Jackson. They found a length of rope tied in a hangman's noose, two high-powered rifles, an automatic pistol, more than a hundred rounds of ammunition, two billy clubs, a Klan robe and a piece of paper on which was printed "Tarrance was here." Earlier Hawkins had told Raymond Roberts that he intended to try to help Tarrants escape from Rush Memorial Hospital and leave a note in his bed saying, "Tarrants was here."

The agents arrested Hawkins and charged him with having robbed a branch bank in Memphis the previous June 11. Although the FBI could never make the charge stick, the arrest took Danny Joe out of action for a while.

With Hawkins in jail, Raymond Roberts focused on Sam Bowers. After spending most of a day in Laurel with him, Raymond told Detective Scarbrough the imperial wizard was once again talking about revenge, including "plans to kill an FBI agent to set an example."

Bowers also showed Roberts how to make a timing device for a bomb, according to Scarbrough, "by taking a clock, driving a hole in it and placing a screw in the hole. When the big hand on the clock moves and makes contact with the screw it sets off an electrical charge."

Roberts told Scarbrough he and his brother Alton Wayne wanted another twenty thousand dollars to keep providing information on Bowers. The detective was noncommittal, but guaranteed the brothers more money if they would testify against Bowers, Matthews and Hawkins. Again Raymond refused. Bowers and Matthews, he said, kept coming back to him with questions that gave him chill bumps. One night about two weeks after the ambush they had telephoned and asked him to meet them at about 9:30 P.M. on rural Highway 84 west of Laurel. He was afraid to go—and more afraid not to go.

He went. The meeting started well enough. Talking in the darkness on the side of the highway, away from their cars in case the FBI had bugged them, Bowers, Matthews and Roberts agreed that with so much pressure being applied by the FBI, the time was not right for more terrorist attacks. When the subject turned to informants, Roberts was initially relieved that their suspicions seemed to be directed at Kathy's husband and not at himself or his brother. Bowers, in fact, suggested that Ralph Ainsworth had learned of the Davidson plan through Kathy and—not knowing she would be involved—had tipped off the Meridian police.

Matthews said a friend had told him that a woman and her husband in the Klan were talking to the FBI. Raymond Roberts hastily declared that he had heard the same thing at a conservative rally in Brandon—though he could not recall who had told him because he talked to several hundred people that day.

Bowers, however, raised the same question Hawkins had asked Raymond earlier: was Alton Wayne talking to the FBI to get his ten-year sentence reduced?

The question struck so close to home that Raymond once more fell back on an answer he had given Hawkins: "If so, I will kill him myself."

In Jackson, Al Binder and George Mitchell decided that since the Jewish community was putting up the money for the informants, they wanted to see the Roberts brothers for themselves. "We're paying for it," Binder told Roy Moore, "so I want to see where the money goes. I want to be eyeball to eyeball with them when they get paid."

Watts and Rucker arranged another meeting at the trailer, where Raymond and Alton Wayne would each receive ten thousand dollars. Mitchell, the chief fund-raiser and president of Jackson's B'nai B'rith chapter, was dispatched to the Deposit Guaranty National Bank to withdraw twenty thousand dollars in twenty-dollar bills from the special account he had set up to pay informants. Ben Keutzer, an FBI agent who had worked with Klan informants for several years, was assigned to drive Binder and Mitchell from Jackson to the meeting at the trailer.

The new payments would bring the Robertses' grand total to $49,850—more than half the $75,000 Raymond and Alton Wayne had been led to believe they would divide. Hendricks was still waiting for the rest of his money—he had been promised $10,000 and paid only $2,000—but the FBI and Meridian police were unwilling to pay him more.

No one wanted to terminate the relationship with the Roberts brothers—not Watts and Rucker, not Scarbrough and not the Jewish community. All continued to hope that Raymond and Alton Wayne might be persuaded to testify. Without continuing intelligence from the brothers, there might be no warning if Bowers and Matthews should hatch new plans for revenge. This would be the final payment for having set up the Meridian ambush, however. Future payments would depend on what the brothers might deliver down the road.

Binder was nervous. In the security of his own office, he had felt no qualms about demanding a meeting with the two Klansmen. But now, as Keutzer drove through the deserted countryside and the darkness that had shrouded so much violence in the past, the attorney was having second thoughts. He asked Keutzer to stop at a wholesale tobacco outlet. Though the lawyer had been chain-smoking all day, he was not out of cigarettes; in fact, he had just opened a fresh pack. But his nerves were on end, he explained to Keutzer, and he wanted to make sure he had plenty of cigarettes for the rest of the night. Like Keutzer, Binder and Mitchell carried .38-caliber pistols in shoulder holsters. Keutzer also had put three shotguns and three high-powered rifles in the back of the car. After what Raymond Roberts had reported about his conversation with Bowers, a Klan ambush did not seem likely, but Keutzer was ruling nothing out.

It was 10:30 P.M. and a lamp was burning in the trailer when they arrived. Scarbrough, Watts and Rucker were already there, a welcome sight to Binder and Mitchell, who were sweating profusely. The agents assured them they would be protected and that helped. But for the first time, the full weight of what he was doing hit Binder: he and Mitchell were not only paying out thousands of dollars from the Jewish community to men who hated Jews, but in Alton Wayne's case the money was going to the man prosecutors believed had personally executed the two Jewish civil rights workers in Philadelphia. "You think you're tough," Binder thought, "but I just never considered I'd come face to face with one of these guys. And out in the woods at night, too."

They had been in the trailer only a few minutes when the headlights of another car lit up the trees that separated the clearing from the road. Moments later, Raymond Roberts came in the door, wearing a peaked cap with gray trousers and shirt; the outfit reminded Binder of a Nazi uniform.

"See you brought the Jews with you," Raymond said.

Alton Wayne, wearing combat boots and a hunting cap, followed Raymond through the door. "The Goddamn Jews are taking over the whole world," he said, laughing.

"Screw 'em!" Raymond said, staring at Binder.

Binder tried to keep a poker face, but admittedly was "scared half to death."

"Cut the shit," Scarbrough snapped. "You know what you came here for. Let's get on with it."

"Yeah, where's the money?" Raymond demanded, looking at Binder. "You got it in that briefcase?"

Binder opened the case and pulled out a brown sack. He poured the money onto the table. The two Klansmen grabbed fistfuls of bills and began counting. They were soon shouting, calling each other "son of a bitch" and accusing each other of cheating. Finally, they finished dividing up the money, but complained that altogether they had been paid less than what they had been promised.

Scarbrough cut them short. The deal had been for the delivery of two hit men, not a man and a woman. There was a lot more money to be had for testimony against Bowers, Matthews and Hawkins, he reminded them again.

Once more they refused, saying it would be suicidal to testify against the Klansmen. But they did agree to keep feeding information to the FBI.

Almost three weeks after the ambush, Bowers was still agonizing over what had happened to his two "soldiers" and threatening retaliation. A Scarbrough memo noted: "Bowers told informant that the Meridian Police Department is expecting retaliation at this time, but he was going to let things cool off and then give them some sure enough hell. Informant stated that they intend to kill a lot of Jews and that at this time their attention is not focused on Negroes. . . . Four men have volunteered to take the place of Ainsworth and Tarrants and to carry on their work."

About four weeks after the ambush, an unannounced visitor walked into Tarrants' heavily guarded room at Rush Memorial Hospital. Tarrants, his general health stabilized and his right arm slowly mending, was startled at the sight of a man he did not recognize.

The man, reaching over the bed past Tarrants' heavily bandaged right arm, shook his left hand and introduced himself: "I'm Officer Mike Hatcher, the policeman who took three of your machine-gun bullets in my chest, including one in my heart."

Tarrants was speechless. Finally, he asked Hatcher how he was doing.

"Fine," Hatcher said. His voice had a pronounced country twang. "And I just wanted you to know I'm a better man than you are."

With that, Hatcher turned and walked away.

As the summer stretched to an end, the threat of renewed Klan violence seemed less imminent, but the FBI and the Meridian police pressed their quest for evidence against Bowers, Matthews and Hawkins. Bowers was the prime target; they held him responsible for nine murders and at least three hundred bombings, beatings and burnings, although only in the civil rights case growing out of the Philadelphia murders had he been convicted. He remained free on an appeal bond in that case. The FBI gave Matthews high priority because he was the Klan's chief bomb maker, although agents had not been able to make a single charge against him stick. Hawkins continued to spout threats of violence and remained, as Watts and Rucker saw it, the Klansman most likely to turn word to deed.

The FBI and police still had not given up on getting the Robertses to testify. Scarbrough spent two hours with Tom Hendricks urging the lawyer to persuade them to testify against Matthews and Bowers. Finally Hendricks agreed to arrange another meeting with the informants. It turned out to be a fiasco.

Scarbrough reported the brothers "were very hostile because we did not have the long-promised money for them. Informer stated that he was going to call the Jews and also that if he were Meyer Davidson he would get his money and go back to Israel."

Watts warned Davidson to feign ignorance if anyone called him asking about reward money. He briefed Moore, too, and later reported that the Jackson FBI chief had "decided each informer should be paid $10,000 for testimony and if they were not agreeable to this, there would be no further money paid to them."

If the Roberts brothers would not talk for money, Watts decided, maybe they could be subpoenaed and compelled to testify as hostile witnessses. He consulted George Warner, the Lauderdale County district attorney, who said that if the brothers were subpoenaed "they would have to testify or be locked up." If the threat of jail were to work, Warner did not want Scarbrough around to testify that they were paid informants. "Mr. Warner suggested that I not be available at the time of the hearing since he prefers not to have paid information brought into the trial and I would be subjected to testify regarding paid informants," Scarbrough said in a memo.

In the end, sounder legal judgment prevailed against the plan to compel testimony by the brothers. To use hostile witnesses to bolster part of a case was one thing. To rely on them as the core of what was sure to be a difficult prosecution was another.

That left Tarrants. Since he faced the possibility of a death sentence for attempting to commit murder with a bomb, Scarbrough and the FBI agents thought he might be ripe for a deal.

After thirty-one days of hospitalization, Tarrants had recovered sufficiently to be transferred to the Lauderdale County jail to await trial. Dressed in pajamas and robe and wearing slippers, he had been escorted out of the hospital by Sheriff Alton Allen and several deputies. They put him into a waiting car for the five-minute ride to the sprawling five-story gray stone building that houses the courts and the county jail in downtown Meridian. Police sealed off traffic on the main street leading to the courthouse for the move and city police and highway patrolmen carrying shotguns and high-powered rifles guarded the way. An entire cellblock had been reserved for him on the fourth floor.

Tarrants' stay in the hospital had done nothing to change his attitude. If anything, he was more implacable than ever. Largely alone and surrounded by concrete and steel, the "mad-dog killer" became, in his own words, "hard, cold, unfeeling, pessimistic, short-tempered, irritable, moody and preoccupied with violent and conspiratorial thoughts." His parents, Thomas and Doris Tarrants, faithfully traveled 145 miles up from Mobile to see him once and sometimes twice a week at considerable emotional and economic cost, but Tarrants later wrote that he was "insensitive to what my parents were going through and had gone through. Their heartaches and agonies were beyond my comprehension and of little concern to me."

During one of his visits to the jail, Tarrants' father complained loudly that the police had set up his son. Word quickly got back to Chief Gunn and he ordered the father put under surveillance. On a later visit, Tarrants' father drove his car into a small creek in Meridian; he was arrested for driving under the influence of alcohol and carrying a concealed weapon, a .30-caliber carbine that was found in the car. Police then went to his room at the Lamar Hotel, searched his briefcase and found Danny Joe Hawkins' name and telephone number in Jackson on a piece of paper.

The arrest, one of three run-ins the elder Tarrants had with police during several visits to Meridian, made no apparent impression on his son, who later called this period "the lowest moment of my life, a time of moral insanity and psychotic radicalism."

Shortly after his father's arrest, Tarrants was visited in his cell by Watts and Rucker. For more than an hour they discussed the hopelessness of his position and the potential advantages of helping them pursue Bowers and the others. They came away hopeful. Scarbrough reported that Tarrants "appeared to have a good attitude." Tarrants had said he knew the location of a large quantity of weapons and ammunition and knew how to locate Minuteman leader Robert Bolivar DePugh. Labeled "armed and dangerous" and under indictment on a bank robbery charge, DePugh was one of the FBI's most wanted fugitives.

"Tarrants is presently deciding if it will be to his advantage to give information and stated that he does not want to talk to an audience," Scarbrough reported. "Tarrants is of the belief that I shot and killed Kathy Ainsworth and prefers not to discuss the case with me any further at this time. Tarrants stated that he was shot 19 times, not including his arm. At a later date Agents Watts and Rucker will again interview subject and advise me of his position."

Watts, who was active in Meridian's First Baptist Church, believed he was dealing with "a vicious animal," and had referred to Tarrants that way in public. Nevertheless, the agent felt that a religious appeal to Tarrants might be helpful. At the FBI agent's request, Reverend Beverly Tinnin, the First Baptist Church's pastor, went to the county jail and conferred with Tarrants for about three hours.

"The Christian thing to do," Tinnin told Tarrants, "would be to cooperate with the FBI and police."

Tarrants promised to give the matter serious consideration, but told Tinnin he did not want to be "another Judas."

In fact, Tarrants was conning them, tantalizing them to lead them on. None of what he told them was meaningful. He had no intention of revealing where they could find DePugh or the weapons and ammunition he had mentioned. Matching wits with his adversaries was the one bright spot in his life. And it was more than a diversion. Once his health was restored, Tarrants had decided, he must escape and resume his work. He knew who his real friends were—Bowers, Matthews and Hawkins. Had not Bowers already sent a lawyer to see him in the hospital and assure him of the Klan's support? If he could just get a confidential message to them, he would let them know he was healing nicely and eventually would be looking to them for aid. Meantime, he would fence with the FBI agents, probing for clues to the ambush.

"I'll bargain with you," he told Watts. "I'll tell you what you want to know if you'll tell me who your informants are. I know you had informants or you wouldn't have gotten me."

Now that he was convinced he had been betrayed, he slowly combed his memory. The identity of the informants became clear: they had to be the Roberts brothers. The evidence was so plain he could not understand why he had not figured it out before. It was Raymond Roberts who had conferred repeatedly with Danny Joe Hawkins on the bombing mission. It was Raymond who had insisted they act no later than Saturday, June 29. It was Raymond who had argued—how ridiculous and transparent the reasoning looked now—that another bombing in Meridian would take the heat off him. The FBI had no doubt paid for the betrayal. And

Alton Wayne Roberts no doubt traded information for a reduction in his ten-year sentence.

If Tarrants had seen how the Roberts brothers were behaving, he would have been even surer of his conclusion. The two Klansmen had been repeatedly warned by Scarbrough and the FBI that any sudden display of wealth could give away their roles as informants. "Hell, we preached to the informants day and night not to spend the reward money for a while," Scarbrough said.

Self-control was beyond them, however. Almost immediately, they bought new cars—Raymond a Thunderbird, Alton Wayne a Cadillac. And they flashed rolls of bills around the Travelers Club and other places. Soon rumors were flying that they were the ones who had betrayed Tarrants and Kathy Ainsworth.

Raymond, suddenly aware of what he had done, panicked. He bought a watchdog, erected a high chain-link fence around his yard, illuminated the house with floodlights at night and hung a huge warning sign on the gate: "Beware of Dog."

14

The trial of Thomas Albert Tarrants III began in November of 1968.

In October, his frantic parents had arranged for him to be represented by the family attorney, Thomas Haas, despite their son's objections that Haas was too moderate on race and civil rights issues. Haas, a former assistant U.S. attorney from Mobile, concluded that there was only one possible defense: not guilty by reason of insanity. Tarrants' parents agreed. Their son had been caught in the act of placing a bomb outside a residence—a capital offense in Mississippi. He had shot and nearly killed a policeman. And the Lauderdale County district attorney had already made clear that he would seek the death penalty. The idea of pleading insanity infuriated Tarrants; he was perfectly sane, he said, and such a defense would mock everything he believed in, everything he had fought and risked his life for. And he knew that plea would mean his mother was ready to testify that she had doubted his sanity since his early teenage years. In the end, realizing the insanity defense offered his best hope of escaping the gas chamber, Tarrants gave in. If the jury rejected the argument, it still might deter them from recommending death.

In his opening statement to the jury of nine white men, two white women and a black man, Haas declared that the defense would prove the defendant suffered from "a severe case of paranoia, a form of schizophrenia," and that a hereditary element "foredoomed this defendant to be seriously ill.

"The actions of this young man, " Haas said, "were influenced by a certain environment and certain associations—that is, people he ran into and met and was influenced by and certain statements by governors and public officials. He became more and more involved in this social upheaval in our country, which he began to believe was his struggle to preserve his God and his country. It became an obsession—from Monday morning to Sunday night—such an obsession that it overrode every impulse, every desire of a young boy growing up.''

As Haas paced up and down in the spacious, well-lighted courtroom, Tarrants, neatly dressed in a dark blue suit, white shirt and tie, gazed at the floor or stared straight ahead. His expression was blank and emotionless, his humiliation betrayed only by the way he occasionally worked the fingers on his badly mangled right hand.

Tarrants attempted the bombing, Haas told the jury, because his mental disease took "complete control of him and made him as he sits here today. It was not a sudden thing. No disease is any sudden thing—or any simple thing. His disease is like a cancer that begins to spread from the bottom of the body to the top of the body. We expect to show that in his sick mind he became compelled to become a guerrilla fighter for God and country.''

For the prosecutors, George Warner and Joe Clay Hamilton, the case against Tarrants was cut and dried, and they believed a local jury would reject the insanity argument, especially since Tarrants had shot a Meridian policeman. Warner, in a brief opening statement, gave the jury a bare-bones outline of the case and said the state would produce witnesses to prove that Tarrants had willingly sought to dynamite Meyer Davidson's house, and that he knew right from wrong when he did it.

The prosecutors were so sure of a conviction that after submitting physical evidence of the bombing attempt, they wrapped up the state's case with testimony by only two witnesses—Detectives Hooky Willoughby and Ralph McNair. They testified they had seen Tarrants douse his car lights as he drove up to the Davidson driveway, then watched him get out of his car and walk up the driveway carrying a box containing twenty-nine sticks of dynamite.

The first defense witness was the defendant's forty-three-year-old mother, Doris Tarrants. She looked distraught and fought back tears as she testified that her son had led a "normal childhood" in Mobile until he reached his junior year at Murphy High School in 1963, when a federal court ordered it to desegregate. Just before school started in September, Tarrants telephoned Alabama governor George Wallace's office in Montgomery and, using his own name, warned there would be trouble if Murphy was compelled to integrate. FBI agents were soon knocking on his door wanting to know what he had meant. School officials took his call as a threat and Tarrants was suspended for the first two weeks of school. After his suspension, his mother said, he began withdrawing from normal teenage activities.

"My son became more and more engrossed in the Bible," she testified. "He used to read his Bible day and night. He seemed to find comfort in it. His whole personality changed in that he thought communists were taking over the country. He quit everything. He became so he didn't want to watch television because he thought it was poisoning people's minds against democracy."

The next year, Tarrants made threatening calls to a rabbi and painted a swastika on the side of a synagogue. His mother finally took him to a psychiatrist, but he refused to go back because he didn't think there was anything wrong with him. Instead, he became an avid reader of hate literature and became a regular associate of Bob Smith, who headed the Mobile unit of the National States Rights Party. Mrs. Tarrants testified that her son became completely absorbed with fighting Communism and looked up to people who, to him, were fighting for democracy. He was, she said, "something less than sane."

Next came Dr. Claude Brown, a Mobile psychiatrist, who testified that interviews he had conducted with Tarrants in his jail cell a month earlier showed that Tarrants had "a paranoid reaction, a severe form of mental disorder." He was extremely suspicious, felt harassed and abused, had delusions of grandiosity and was rebellious, Dr. Brown said. Tarrants chose to wage war on Communism because "Communism is a big thing—a thing of worldwide importance," the psychiatrist testified. "He doesn't choose some small item to combat, he needs to feel that he is somebody."

Haas asked whether Tarrants had control over his physical activities. "Yes and no," Dr. Brown replied. "He has the kind of control that will let him tie his shoes, shave or shut the door, but the kind of control he has is affected by his illness. His control over violent impulses is far, far less than a normal person's. He does not have full awareness of right and wrong."

In rebuttal, the prosecution called to the stand Dr. R. P. White, a psychiatrist and director of the East Mississippi State Hospital for the Insane. He testified that while Tarrants probably was emotionally disturbed, he "would know what he was doing" when he carried dynamite to the Davidson house.

In his closing argument to the jury, Warner said, "Eyeball witnesses have proved the commission of the crime." And, citing the Bible, he said Tarrants had sown destruction and "he should reap destruction."

In the end, Haas appealed to the jury to show mercy, declaring that he was not arguing that Tarrants should be acquitted outright, but that the jury should find him innocent by reason of insanity so that he could be sent to a state mental institution and treated. "In our enlightened society we don't put sick people in gas chambers like dogs," he said. "I'm appalled at the thought of taking an insane man and gassing him to death."

The trial had lasted only two days. Around six o'clock in the evening on November 27, 1968, jurors trooped out to the jury room to deliberate. Court officials and reporters covering the trial walked several blocks to Widemann's Restaurant to eat dinner during the deliberations. Judge Lester Williamson and Bill Minor, who was covering the trial for the New Orleans *Times-Picayune*, sat together and discussed the case. Neither had any doubt about how the jury would come down. Williamson's only concern was whether he should sentence Tarrants to death, to life imprisonment or to lesser punishment.

"What do you think I should give him?" he asked Minor.

"Thirty years," said Minor. "He'll have to serve at least ten."

The jurors had been out an hour and fifty minutes. A bailiff rushed into Widemann's and informed Judge Williamson the jury had reached a verdict. Williamson and Minor, along with several other court officials and reporters, hurried back to the courthouse. Outside, darkness was falling. Tarrants stood straight beside the defense table and stared at the jury, a picture of cold defiance. The verdict was, as he knew it would be, guilty as charged. On Haas' advice, he had not testified during the trial, and now he declined to say anything before sentencing. Judge Williamson ordered him to serve thirty years in the state penitentiary at Parchman.

BOOK TWO

15

Nineteen sixty-eight was a year of tumultuous, often catastrophic events. The Tet offensive in Vietnam shattered national confidence and redoubled antiwar protests. Martin Luther King, Jr., was assasinated in Memphis. The riots that followed in major cities across the country took forty-six lives. Robert F. Kennedy was gunned down. The Democratic convention descended into chaos, splitting the party and assuring Richard Nixon's election that November. The civil rights movement was cracking apart as well; calls for "Black Power" replaced the strains of "We Shall Overcome."

I was still based in the South, operating out of my one-man bureau in Atlanta—dashing from protest march to court case to funeral procession. I had covered King in Selma, Memphis and other civil rights battlegrounds. Along with other reporters I was transfixed the evening of April 3, 1968, listening to his "mountaintop" sermon at the Mason Temple in Memphis when he said he "would like to live a long life," but was no longer concerned about that. "I'm not worried about anything," he said. "I'm not fearing any man. Mine eyes have seen the glory of the coming of the Lord!" As we left the church we all agreed the sermon sounded like a premonition. The next night he was dead.

It was an exhausting year, but reporters are energized by momentous events. I was seldom home, and when I was, I was usually on the phone. I was used to telephone calls in the middle of the night, like the one that June when Chief Gunn promised me a "Goddamned big one." The story of the foiled Klan attempt to bomb a Jewish businessman's house was a page-one headline in the *Los Angeles Times* the next morning: "Mississippi Police

Thwart Dynamiting: One Dead, One Wounded." Aided by Roy
Moore and the FBI and Roy Gunn and the Meridian police, I
followed up with a series of long investigative profiles of Tommy
Tarrants, Kathy Ainsworth, Sam Bowers and the White Knights.

With all the momentous events of 1968 dominating the news,
the Meridian story and the White Knights soon faded from the
headlines and the evening news. But for me, it was a story that
wouldn't go away. I kept getting cryptic calls from Ken Dean,
telling me that there was "a lot more to it."

Then, one night in late November, his telephone call was much
more explicit. "You know they didn't expect to take them alive
out there that night, don't you?" he said. "They paid somebody
to get them to come out there. And they didn't expect Kathy
Ainsworth to be in the car with Tarrants. They expected Danny
Joe Hawkins. You follow me?"

I was not sure what to make of what he was saying. He had
become obsessed with the Meridian shoot-out. And even though
I had known him for several years and he was one of my best
sources, I found it hard to believe the scenario he painted. Who
could believe the police and the FBI would plan an ambush? Who
could believe the Jewish community would bankroll it? In fact, I
hoped Dean was stretching things. After all, Roy Moore also was
one of my most valuable sources. We had developed a great mutual
trust.

I could not dismiss what Dean was telling me, however. Not
only had he always been reliable, but he had unique access to
information on law enforcement, racial matters and Klan activities. He had literally risked his life fighting for racial justice, yet
unlike most religious figures involved with civil rights he had managed to maintain a relationship with many staunch segregationists,
even some Klan members, including Danny Joe Hawkins. Although he loathed the Klan and all it stood for, Dean often said
that as a minister he felt he should work for the redemption of
all souls. He nurtured his contacts with Klansmen and other white
supremacists by telling them that while he opposed their methods,
he understood some of their frustrations. He made no secret of
his disapproval of extralegal and at times illegal tactics authorities
themselves adopted in combating the Klan.

Dean loved intrigue. He seemed to enjoy moving back and
forth between the armed camps, trading bits of information with

both sides. He was considered a valuable conduit by both the FBI and the Klan. Everyone dealt with him. And while not many people trusted him completely, a few key players in the Meridian story did. Jim Ingram, Moore's assistant in charge of civil rights investigations, told me he never doubted Ken Dean at any time. And the ADL's Bee Botnick said Dean was "courageous, highly motivated and put his life on the line."

I had first met Dean in Jackson in June 1965, when he called with a tip about a savage racial attack outside town. A gang of whites had beaten a young black ROTC lieutenant after he had blundered into a whites-only night spot called the Stork Club. A few years before, when he had played trumpet in the band there, it had been called the Ebony Club. At Jackson's University Medical Center, where the youth's mother took him for treatment, a state trooper looked at his battered face and said, "He got what he deserved. He should have known it was a white club." At first the hospital refused to admit the youth. "Just some niggers fightin' again on Saturday night," a white supervisor said. At that point, Dean, a beefy six feet two inches and 235 pounds, showed up and threatened dire consequences if he wasn't admitted. The officials backed down and admitted the youth to a floor set aside for blacks.

After that encounter, Dean and I developed a close relationship. I knew other Mississippi ministers who considered it their duty to save souls, but Ken was the only one I knew who would face down the State Police and the medical establishment to obtain treatment for a black man.

For a Baptist, he had exceptionally close ties with Jewish leaders, including Rabbi Perry Nussbaum. Dean also worked closely with the ADL, especially with Botnick. In a 1968 memo, Dean noted that they had a cooperative and trusting relationship, that he and Botnick spoke often and that their contacts had increased because of "the surge of anti-semitic literature by the White Citizens' Council, National States Rights Party and the KKK."

Botnick proved to be another good source for information on the Klan and other hate groups. The ADL, founded in 1913 with the goal of "stopping the defamation" of the Jewish people and securing "justice and fair treatment to all citizens alike," had investigative resources of its own and worked closely with the FBI monitoring such organizations. The sizes, locations, backers, membership and violence potential of the Klan and other hate groups were under "constant ADL surveillance," according to an ADL pamphlet.

If Dean and the ADL shared a common antipathy for the Klan, the young minister proved to be far too liberal on civil rights for the ADL and some members of the Mississippi Jewish community. What alarmed Jews who supported the status quo was Dean's close contact with militant civil rights organizations such as the Student Nonviolent Coordinating Committee (SNCC) and the Congress of Racial Equality. Botnick suspected them of Communist influence. The ADL was relatively conservative in its approach, acutely sensitive to the widespread feeling in those days that Jews themselves were too far to the left. In combating anti-Semitism, the ADL had come to embrace some of the FBI's obsessive concern about Communist influences in the civil rights movement. And the two organizations kept some of the more militant civil rights groups under constant surveillance.

Their hunt for Communists and Communist sympathizers in the movement made for strange bedfellows. The Mississippi Sovereignty Commission and the state's two veteran senators—John Stennis and James O. Eastland, both outspoken segregationists—exchanged investigative information with the FBI and the ADL.

Botnick, named regional director of the ADL in 1964, was affable and fairly well liked by most—but by no means all—of his associates. My friend Bill Minor, Jackson correspondent for the New Orleans *Times-Picayune,* thought Botnick considered himself "a super Communist hunter" and had an exaggerated opinion of his investigative ability.

Police work fascinated Botnick, and I perceived in him the same conspiratorial outlook and sense of paranoia not infrequently found in policemen. He would sidle up to reporters, lower his voice and say, "Entre nous"—then impart his latest tidbit about purported links between militant blacks and Communists.

In fact, much of Botnick's interest in the movement focused on militants and suspicions about Communist influence. He was especially upset by a SNCC-produced film on racism that Dean allowed to be shown at a statewide meeting of the Council on Human Relations. Amateurishly made, the film portrayed the church, big business and government as enemies of the civil rights movement.

Botnick was so incensed about the affair that he wrote a confidential memorandum to the ADL in New York implying that Dean was a Communist sympathizer. "This is not to say that he follows the rigid discipline of the communist line," Botnick wrote. At the same time, he found the minster too eager to explain away the "radicalism and protest of the kids of COFO [the Council of Federated Organizations, another civil rights group] and SNCC. . . . He therefore refuses to see or admit there can be any kind of organized manipulative motive behind the actions of these 'dedicated young people.' "

The ADL set out to oust Dean as the director of the Mississippi Council on Human Relations. This put the Southern Regional Council—the Mississippi group's parent body—in a tight spot because Jews were among the major contributors to the SRC. In the end, however, Leslie Dunbar, the head of the council, stood behind Dean and refused to fire him.

The episode reflected the ADL's lingering obsession with Communist subversion, whereas Dean had a different set of priorities. For Dean, the fight for racial justice came first; everything else was secondary. For the ADL, civil rights and racial justice were important, but the protection of Jews was paramount.

A week after Tarrants' trial ended, Roy Pitts, a Meridian attorney who had assisted in his defense, filed notice that the conviction would be appealed to the Mississippi Supreme Court.

And Tarrants, in his first interview since the ambush, threw a scare into the Roberts brothers by telling a Meridian television reporter that he had been the victim of a Ku Klux Klan double cross. The Davidson bombing attempt, he said, had been "arranged by a person who was in collusion with the police and the FBI for the purpose of collecting a reward—and to protect their informer they didn't plan any survivors."

Tarrants did not name an informant, but by now Raymond and Alton Wayne Roberts felt sure Tarrants knew they were the ones who had betrayed him. Fearing Klan retaliation, the brothers took extra security precautions and asked the FBI to protect them under the Federal Witness Protection Program. Raymond began leaving the floodlights around his house turned on all night.

On December 13, one week before his twenty-second birthday, Tarrants and five other prisoners—three whites and two blacks—were transferred to Parchman state prison. Tarrants was pleased, even though Parchman had long been known as one of the nation's crudest penal institutions. He figured it would offer better opportunities to escape than the Lauderdale County jail, and he was increasingly preoccupied with the idea of escaping.

When he arrived at the sixteen-thousand-acre penal farm, Tarrants discovered that prison officials were taking extra precautions against just such possibilities. The five other prisoners from Meridian were routinely assigned to a receiving ward in the prison hospital, where they would be kept until they were assigned to one of the prison's twenty-two compounds, but Tarrants was driven directly to a maximum-security unit known as Little Alcatraz. A fortresslike building of concrete, brick and steel, it was located in a flat area and surrounded by a twelve-foot chain-link fence topped by a strand of barbed wire. Tall brick guard towers anchored every corner of the yard.

At first, Tarrants was assigned to a cell on death row, but a week later, after he refused to take part in an uprising that erupted among other death row prisoners, the authorities made him a technician in the compound's hospital. He was elated. Escaping from death row would have been next to impossible, but security was not as tight at the hospital.

Once again filled with purpose, Tarrants gave the appearance of having settled into prison life. In reality, he was casting about for a partner in his budding escape plan. And after a few weeks, he persuaded Louis Shadoan, a forty-six-year-old clerk in the hospital identification office, to join in the scheme. Shadoan, a man of medium height and build and exceptional intelligence (prison officials said he had an IQ of 160), had once worked as a journalist, but bank robbery had been his most recent occupation. Together they studied the hospital's daily routine and found a weak spot: if they could bribe one of the outside tower guards and overpower an inside night watchman they might be able to escape. To assist them they recruited a third prisoner, Malcolm Houston, a twenty-nine-year-old hospital orderly who had failed in a previous escape attempt and was eager to try again. Shadoan began cultivating a trusty who served as a guard on one of the towers and Tarrants studied the night watchmen to see which one might be overpowered most easily. He soon settled on George Miller, a short, plump, slow-moving middle-aged man.

From another inmate, Tarrants secured a map of the terrain

and roads of the prison farm. He also worked out a scheme to communicate with Danny Joe Hawkins through letters smuggled in and out of prison. In one of the letters, Hawkins assured Tarrants that on the day of the escape attempt he would be waiting with a car in a wooded area near the prison to whisk them away to a hideout near Jackson, some 140 miles away.

"I had no intention of remaining in prison because America was being undermined by the Communist-Jewish conspiracy," Tarrants later observed. "I needed to be free and in the thick of the battle against it."

In April 1969, about four months after Tarrants was transferred to Parchman, I got yet another telephone call from Ken Dean, this one more insistent than the last. As usual, his tone was cryptic, but this time there was also a note of anxiety, even fear. He told me he was certain that agents provocateurs and money from the Jewish community had been used to lure Tarrants and Kathy Ainsworth into a death trap. He feared that if he was identified as a source in a story, he would be branded an anti-Semite. And he sounded concerned about his own physical safety. He suggested I call Botnick, who, he said, had been extremely upset about the killing of Ainsworth and had asked him if he knew of a psychiatrist he could consult. I was not to let Botnick know that he was my source of information, Dean said.

The whole thing still sounded almost unbelievable. Maybe Dean had seen too many miscarriages of justice, too many blacks beaten and murdered, too many churches and synagogues bombed or burned. A number of people were wary of Dean. Maybe I had been too trusting. Besides, I was painfully aware that Dean's accusations were aimed at some of my best sources in both the FBI and the ADL, and I was not eager to alienate them.

I must have sounded less than enthusiastic about pursuing the matter because Dean launched into a long lecture about justice. If the federal government could use the local police to operate outside the law, he said, then that was a major miscarriage of justice. And if justice was to be served in the Meridian case, he argued, all the facts would have to come out. I agreed it was a matter of public interest and all the facts needed to come out. I said I would call Botnick.

•   •   •

While Tarrants was plotting an escape, his father was making periodic trips to Meridian, still complaining that his son had been set up and still trying to find witnesses to prove it. And the police were still trying to discourage him.

In mid-July, the elder Tarrants was confronted at Meridian's Downtowner Motel by Mike Hatcher, backed by several other Meridian police officers. Hatcher's wounds had healed. A student of karate, he was once again hard as nails. An altercation ensued and Tarrants was badly beaten. Chief Gunn told me that Tarrants had been "mouthing off" about the police and Hatcher "beat the hell out of him."

Treated at a Meridian hospital, Tarrants was then jailed on charges of disorderly conduct, disturbing the peace and resisting arrest. After he was released on bond, he spent a week at a hospital back home in Mobile recovering from his injuries.

As I had promised Dean, I telephoned Botnick at his office in New Orleans.

Botnick was a Mississippian by birth. The son of Russian immigrants, he had been born in Hattiesburg, but he had grown up in New Orleans. His father made eyeglasses in a district where most of the shop owners were Jewish and most of the customers were black. Young Botnick entered the army in World War II and was sent to Officer Candidate School at Fort Benning, Georgia. Energetic but not very athletic, he failed to meet the physical standards necessary to graduate. Later he joked that "I was known as the fat little Jew who couldn't make it through the obstacle course."

After the war, he graduated from Louisiana State University and went to work for his father-in-law in the retail clothing business in Baton Rouge. He later said that he could have made much more money and provided a better material life for his wife and three children if he had remained in the clothing business. He was proud of his part in fighting anti-Semitism, however, and said he and his family had gladly sacrificed financial reward for a life dedicated to social justice.

I told Botnick that I had heard rumors that he was upset about what happened that night in Meridian. I also said I had information that a group of Jewish businessmen had furnished money to the FBI and Meridian police—money that was to be used for paying Klan informants to set up an ambush. Although no other reporters were working on the story, I used a typical reporter's trick and told him that two or three other reporters were poking around on it.

For a long moment, there was silence. Then Botnick acknowledged that Tarrants and Ainsworth had been lured into an ambush, and he said he had helped plan it. He could not "morally blow the whistle" on the FBI and the Meridian police, he said, because they had stopped the Klan's attacks on Jews. I agreed they had stopped the violence—there had been none since the ambush—and said I could understand his point.

Cradling the telephone receiver on my shoulder, I typed notes as Botnick resumed talking: "It was logical someone had paid to set up the Klan members . . . he had helped raise funds for the purpose . . . wouldn't say how much was paid . . . wouldn't want to see the ADL involved in a story about the Meridian incident . . . four guys know I was in on the original planning . . . it was a trap—you know that."

Before Botnick agreed to participate in the planning, he said, the FBI played the tape recording of a Klan threat to blow up a synagogue full of people, including women and children, on which one Klansman could be heard to say, "Little Jew bastards grow up to be big Jew devils. Kill 'em while they're young."

Trying to draw Botnick out, I assured him again that I could understand why the police would resort to extreme measures with Klan violence running unchecked. In fact, I did understand how Botnick felt. If I had been a Jew in Meridian and knew that Klansmen were threatening to blow up synagogues with people inside, I probably would have contributed to the fund too and probably would have muttered, "Never again."

At the same time, I was a reporter, and if what I was hearing could be substantiated, what happened at Meridian was one hell of a story that raised serious questions about law enforcement methods used in this case. Discussing his own role, Botnick said, "We were dealing with animals and I would do it again."

But he acknowledged that he was profoundly upset when he learned a woman had been shot to death. "I threw up when I heard what happened that night."

For all his candor, Botnick said he did not want anything written about the events leading up to the Meridian trap and certainly did not want to see the ADL portrayed as being involved. None of the participants would talk to me anyway, he said, and I did not have enough facts to write a story.

Afterward, Botnick telephoned Dean to tell him of our conversation, and Dean, ever the faithful memo writer, described the call:

> In a telephone conversation on April 30, "B" Botnick told me that Jack Nelson had called him with a lot of questions concerning the Meridian situation. Botnick said that he and Nelson talked frequently and that Nelson's questions probably arise out of logical curiosity. He said that Nelson tried to scare him into talking by saying that two or three reporters were digging into the story. He said that Nelson told him that he had learned that a group of Jewish businessmen purchased the setup in which Ainsworth was killed and Tarrants was shot. Botnick said that fortunately Nelson didn't have any facts and that he couldn't write on the basis of his curiosity.

As of then, Botnick was right. And I was so busy covering other stories in the South that I did not immediately have time to devote to a project that might be an exercise in futility.

At Parchman, only one detail remained to be taken care of in the escape plan. In a letter smuggled to Tarrants, Danny Joe Hawkins had said he would be waiting to whisk him and the others out of the area as soon as they broke free of Little Alcatraz. The rendezvous point had been established with the aid of the Parchman map that Tarrants had gotten from another prisoner. But how could they set a specific date and be certain Hawkins was ready? Telephone calls were out of the question and smuggling letters was too slow.

Tarrants finally worked out an answer: Hawkins would place a classified ad in the *Jackson Daily News* letting him know the day he would be at the rendezvous point. The ad was to read: "Lost: German Shepherd. Name Sam. Black and Silver in Color. Large Size." (Sam was the name of Hawkins' dog, apparently named after Sam Bowers.) The ad would mean nothing to anyone else, but when Tarrants read it, he would know Hawkins would be standing by that evening.

Late in the afternoon of July 23, almost thirteen months after the Meridian ambush, Tarrants, Shadoan and Houston waited anxiously for the arrival of the *Jackson Daily News*. It arrived shortly after five o'clock. The ad was there.

Shadoan, using keys obtained from a cook he had befriended, secured three butcher knives from the hospital kitchen. When George Miller, the hapless guard they had picked as their target, appeared on his rounds, he and a trusty accompanying him were quickly subdued and tied up. Tarrants pocketed the keys to Miller's car, a Ford Falcon parked just outside the fence surrounding the compound.

Quickly now, the prisoners rushed down the front hall of the hospital to the now-empty night guard's desk. Shadoan used the intercom to call the trusty on the watchtower who had been bribed to cooperate. Tower guards were routinely summoned to the hospital for a variety of reasons, so the trusty would have aroused no concern if anyone had seen him sauntering into the hosptial. A few minutes later, he too was tied up. Now came the critical moment: Shadoan called the other guard in the front area of the compound and instructed him to come to the hospital. If he was suspicious and sounded the alarm, there would be no way out. But luck was with the prisoners. The guard came at once and was trussed up with the rest. Soon Tarrants and his two companions were walking calmly out of the hospital, passing through the unguarded front gate and driving away in Miller's car.

They drove slowly down the road, then veered off on a dirt road that ran through a cotton field. About a mile down the dirt track, they came to an irrigation creek. The bridge over the creek had been washed out by a storm. Tarrants knew that from the prison grapevine. He was counting on it. Once prison authorities found the abandoned car, he had reasoned, they would assume the prisoners were on foot and would concentrate their search on the vast prison grounds, rather than on the highways Hawkins would use to carry them to freedom.

Still a mile from the rendezvous point and already wet from the heat, the prisoners sloshed waist deep across the muddy creek, then ran through another cotton field to a wooded area on the edge of the prison property, where Hawkins was to be waiting with the car. The area was deserted. Exhausted by the run, they searched about frantically in the gathering darkness.

"Danny Joe, where are you?" Tarrants cried out several times. Minutes passed. They were sitting ducks for the guards and dogs that would soon be on their trail.

Suddenly, lurching out of the woods came a car. It was a Buick convertible, gray, with its lights out. Hawkins was driving and another Klansman sat beside him. The three prisoners piled into the backseat. As the car roared off, the Klansman handed Tarrants an AR-15 automatic rifle and gave pistols to Shadoan and Houston. There were two more automatic rifles on the front seat, and a sack of grenades on the front floorboard. They reached U.S. Highway 49 without meeting anyone and Hawkins sped off toward the hideaway. Tarrants' plan had worked. While they drove, prison guards, preceded by yelping dogs, combed the prison grounds expecting to catch the escapees fleeing on foot.

The hideout was an abandoned farm in rural Rankin County about two miles from the Jackson Municipal Airport. The farmhouse was empty but they chose the barn because it sat farther back from the road. Hawkins had brought plain brown pants to replace their blue-and-white-striped prison jeans and promised to return the next day with food and other supplies. The three spent a restless night, taking turns standing guard. The area was deserted, but Tarrants felt exposed in the barn; they could easily be surrounded there. His nervousness increased the next day when Hawkins returned, accompanied not by the original Klansman but by a young woman Tarrants did not know. It was an inexcusable breach of security, he protested, but Hawkins vouched for the woman. Nonetheless, the next morning Tarrants took the additional precaution of moving their camp from the barn to a nearby patch of underbrush, in the middle of which the prisoners set up a pup tent. Hawkins had brought more guns too, as well as a grenade launcher.

That evening, Tarrants was on guard behind a clump of bushes near the highway. They were dividing the job into three-hour shifts, but Shadoan was apparently restless in the tent and came to relieve Tarrants a half hour early. Tarrants went back to the camp and was so exhausted by now that he dropped off to sleep almost immediately. About five minutes later, squads of state and county police, armed with shotguns, rifles, machine guns and grenade launchers and accompanied by FBI agents, slipped up on Shadoan. Officers later said Shadoan fired at them with a .357 Magnum and had a grenade in his hand when they cut him down.

Jarred awake by the gunfire, Tarrants and Houston scrambled out of the tent and sought cover behind a tree. Suddenly a police helicopter whirred in overhead, and over the roar of the helicopter they heard Roy Moore shouting on a bullhorn that Shadoan had been killed and that they were surrounded and had better surrender. The two escapees emerged, holding their hands up high and shouting, "We're coming out, we're coming out, don't shoot!" Almost two dozen grim-faced officers were waiting, guns leveled. They ordered Tarrants and Houston to strip naked and lie on the ground. Satisfied they were unarmed, the officers allowed them to dress, then tied their hands tightly with nylon cord. Escorting them past the body of Shadoan, his head half blown away, one of the officers declared, "Here is what you did."

The FBI had acted on information from an informant, but never disclosed the informant's name. Tarrants always suspected it was the woman who had accompanied Hawkins to their hideout, but Hawkins insisted she was trustworthy.

Back at Parchman, Tarrants, still true to the Klan's code of silence, refused to talk to the FBI agents waiting to interrogate him. He was put into a six-by-nine-foot cell in a maximum-security unit.

Convicted of escape and armed robbery—stealing the night guard's car at knifepoint—Tarrants was sentenced to an additional five years, bringing his total sentence to thirty-five years. Even with time off for good behavior, that would mean he could not even be considered for parole for at least another eleven years.

In periodic telephone calls, Dean was still insisting that something should be written about Meridian. But I had seen little in the way of hard evidence to support what he and Botnick had said and could not write the story without heavy documentation and eyewitness accounts.

Dean remained obsessed with the Meridian story. Hearing of Tommy Tarrants' father's experience with the police, he contacted him and began exchanging information with him. Dean agonized over how to expose what had happened. He began consulting friends, including Hodding Carter III, editor and publisher of the

Greenville *Delta Democrat-Times,* and Leslie Dunbar, the former
Southern Regional Council director who now was head of the
Field Foundation. On October 29, 1969, Dean wrote a letter to
Dunbar asking him to "help set up a course of action."

In the letter, Dean told of his meetings with Tarrants' father
and of the father being "beaten almost to death" by the Meridian
police for trying to investigate what had happened to his son.
Tarrants' father's life has been threatened a number of times and
there had even been a plot to kill him, according to Dean, who
wrote that "this man's information concerning his son matches
my information almost point for point."

The elder Tarrants did not approve of his son's activity, Dean
said, but felt so strongly that society and the government had not
dealt fairly or honestly with his son that he had spent forty thousand dollars in legal fees trying to prove he had been entrapped.

"You know that I have been living with and considering this
matter for almost a year and a half," Dean wrote. "Only recently
have I come to a position on this matter which is satisfactory in
my mind and heart. I am convinced that we who care for the
South and its problems, and this as it relates to the country as a
whole, must accept the responsibility for making right this situation. I know that this is complex and that it may be painful, but
as I have attempted to deal with the matter I can come to no
other conclusion."

Dunbar advised Dean to tell what he knew about the Meridian
incident to a journalist he trusted. Dean had come to the same
conclusion himself. He came to my Atlanta office and gave me a
copy of a memorandum he had written for his files entitled
"Memo on Reported Activities of the ADL, FBI, and the Meridian Police Department Concerning the White Knights of the
Ku Klux Klan and Anti-Semitism in Meridian."

Typewritten and single-spaced, it ran to eleven pages. It was a
hair-raising document. In sum, it said the FBI and the Meridian
police had used money supplied by the Anti-Defamation League
and the Mississippi Jewish community to pay the Roberts brothers
to arrange for two Klan hit men to attempt a bombing so that
the police could execute them in the commission of a crime. The
memo quoted Botnick as saying Chief Gunn and Mayor Key had
asked him if he "would make a contact somewhere in the North,
such as Chicago, to have two klansmen liquidated."

The memo was based largely on what Dean said Botnick had told him in a series of face-to-face conversations. Even though it was mostly hearsay, much of the information dovetailed with things Dean knew from other sources and with things I knew about the Meridian case, including what Botnick had told me. The memo was precise, detailed and generally persuasive. Still, part of me did not want to believe it because I had worked so closely with the FBI, the Meridian police and the ADL. Not only were these people trusted sources, I had grown genuinely fond of some of them. On the other hand, the memo could be the starting point for an important story, one that needed to be told. Regardless of whether the allegations were true in every detail, the police and FBI obviously had used extraordinary means, and people were entitled to know and decide for themselves whether those means were appropriate.

I telephoned Chief Gunn and told him I wanted to do another story about how the police and FBI had broken the back of the White Knights. He was glad to hear that I planned another story because he felt the police had never gotten full credit for what they had done. I assured him that if I got the right kind of co-operation he could expect that a lot more attention would be paid to what the police had done. I did not exactly promise they would get more credit, but neither did I give him any reason to believe that I thought there might be a darker side to the events of that night.

"You need to talk to Luke Scarbrough," Gunn said. "He's the one who dealt with the informants. I'll tell him to talk with you."

16

"Hell, this is a story Hollywood couldn't make up," Scarbrough said as we began a tape-recorded interview in my room at the Downtowner Motel.

He was eager to cooperate. Like Gunn, Scarbrough believed the police had never gotten proper credit for stopping the Klan violence. In fact, he felt personally slighted; he had been the key player among Meridian officers, but had hardly been mentioned in the subsequent press coverage. Most of the credit had gone to Hatcher, who had been wounded, and to Gunn's favorite, Sergeant "Gigolo" Joyner of "Joyner's guerrillas," who was given community awards and honored by the International Association of Chiefs of Police.

After the tension and danger of the endless meetings in the trailer, Scarbrough resented the fuss over Joyner, but acknowledged that the press could not be faulted for overlooking him. Of necessity, he had operated in utmost secrecy. No one had even considered disclosing details of the meetings with informants and other clandestine operations that had led up to that night in Meridian. That is, no one had until Gunn told Scarbrough to cooperate with me.

"If you really want to know what happened," Scarbrough said, "I've got a whole stack of reports of meetings with informants that will tell you. I can get them for you. But I think I should be paid something."

In two decades as a reporter I had never paid for information. Like most journalists, I had always felt that paying for an interview would raise questions about the credibility of the information being provided. This case seemed different, however. Any payment would be for access to copies of documents, not for an interview. And documents were the highest form of evidence. I told Scarbrough I was sure a payment could be arranged, but it would require approval from a senior editor in Los Angeles. Scarbrough said he had to run an errand anyway, and would return shortly to see what had been arranged.

I telephoned Edwin Guthman, the *Times'* national editor and a longtime friend. Earlier I had briefed him on the Meridian story and we had flown together to Jackson to confer with Ken Dean. Guthman recognized it as an explosive story, one that required thorough documentation. When I relayed Scarbrough's request for money and told Guthman the detective had not put a price on the documents, he suggested offering him five hundred dollars.

If the story was as great as Scarbrough promised, it surely was worth more than that, I replied. If it was worth five hundred dollars, it was worth a thousand—probably a lot more, based on what Scarbrough had said—and I did not want to be in a position of haggling over price.

"Offer him a thousand," Guthman said.

When Scarbrough returned, I told him that the *Times* would send him a certified check for one thousand dollars for providing the documents—big money for a man whose salary was still less than four hundred dollars a month. He left immediately for the police department and returned in about thirty minutes carrying a stack of records in a manila folder.

"Here they are," Scarbrough said, handing me the folder. "The Roberts brothers would go apeshit if they knew I was doing this. But that's their problem. Everybody knows they were the informants anyway."

Trying to conceal my excitement, I opened the folder. It was a mother lode of official documents with everything Scarbrough had promised and more. The records were all dated and neatly typed with only an occasional typo. They began with a May 29, 1968, report on the bombing of Temple Beth Israel and the Meridian police plans to call on the Mississippi State Highway Patrol to send in its "goon squad."

I hurriedly thumbed through the records, looking for something that named the Roberts brothers and for evidence that Tarrants and Ainsworth had been lured into an ambush. I had Scarbrough's word on the Roberts brothers' involvement and on how the trap had been set up. Now I needed documentary evidence to buttress his statement.

Suddenly, the words *set up* jumped out at me. The June 17, 1968, document began, "Tonight informant and his brother will meet with Hawkins or the night of June 18, 1968 and they will attempt to set up a job on Al Rose's house."

Moments later, I came upon a memo in which Scarbrough reported that he had told George Warner, the district attorney, that "the two Roberts boys were the keys to the case and they would talk for $85,000" and could clear up the synagogue bombings in Meridian and Jackson and nine church bombings.

Scarbrough let me borrow the papers long enough to have them copied. I casually walked out of the Downtowner Motel, trying not to betray my excitement. Once across the street, I literally ran the four blocks to Joe Clay Hamilton's law office in the Citizens Bank Building, where I used a copying machine to duplicate the entire file.

In making the copies, I noticed that while Marie Knowles had typed Scarbrough's name at the bottom of each of his reports, the detective had not signed the reports. So after returning to my motel room, I asked Scarbrough to initial each page of my copies. "Where you want me to do it?" he asked in his thick Southern drawl.

"The right-hand corner at the top."

I handed him my fountain pen and he inked "L.S." on each page. I figured this would verify the authenticity of the documents. Scarbrough was a man of infinite patience, and from the beginning we had established an easy rapport. I did not think he made the records available mainly for the money. To him the money represented long overdue recognition for his courage and the weeks of hard work he had endured to end Klan violence.

For the interview, we sat facing each other in two easy chairs, a tape recorder on a small coffee table between us. To make it clear that the thousand-dollar check was for the records, not for the interview, I began by asking if he was cooperating "for the purpose of making the truth known in a case of public interest" and he replied, "Yes." Then, for more than an hour, he poured out details of the story. There were elements of it that lay elsewhere—in Jackson, for example, and in Laurel—but he had been directly involved in the most crucial part. While he said he did not want to identify the informants' intermediary by name, he slipped several times and referred to him as Hendricks. The former FBI agent also was mentioned by name several times in copies of the detective's reports Scarbrough had given me.

The police had expected a shoot-out, Scarbrough said, and had not expected to take either member of the Klan alive because they thought that Tarrants would be accompanied by Hawkins and that the two men would be heavily armed. When the two Klansmen bombed the Meridian synagogue the previous month, he said, they both were armed with machine guns, and Danny Joe remarked, "Well, brother, from here on in we ain't got nothing to lose."

Scarbrough said Raymond Roberts telephoned police forty-five minutes before the bombing attempt at the Davidson house and told them a woman, not Danny Joe Hawkins, was with Tarrants. "When I got the word Danny Joe was a woman," Scarbrough said, "I like to shit."

Finally, turning to the details of the setup itself, Scarbrough said that when he was dispensing money to the informants at his trailer, they were supposed to divide it evenly, but "they'd damn near fight over it."

"Alton Wayne and Raymond?" I asked.

"Yeah, they'd count that damn money and say, 'wait a minute, son of a bitch, you got twenty dollars more 'n me' and shit like that."

"Really?"

"They didn't trust anybody."

"Well, why did Raymond let Alton Wayne split it down the middle when Raymond was doing most of the negotiating with Danny Joe and them, wasn't he?"

"Well, one reason, Alton Wayne is stronger with the Klan than Raymond. They believe in him. And that's one more reason it went over as well as it did, on account of Alton Wayne cooperating."

Scarbrough said Al Binder and George Mitchell, who brought money to his trailer to pay to the Roberts brothers after the shoot-out, were prepared to pay the brothers even more money if they would testify against Klan leaders.

"But who would they have had to implicate then? Because, you know, Tarrants was all shot up."

"They was wanting to expose Bowers and Matthews."

"Bowers and Matthews? Well, what did the Roberts brothers say about that? They just wouldn't do it?"

"They just wouldn't do it—hell, we tried to get 'em to do it for months."

"Did they acknowledge that Bowers and Matthews had anything to do with it?"

"Yeah."

"They'd tell you, but they wouldn't testify?"

"That's right."

"Did Botnick at any time have the money? He never held the money, all he ever did was negotiate?"

"Right."

"And help raise it?"

"Right."

Scarbrough said Raymond had bought himself a Thunderbird with some of the money he was paid and Alton Wayne had bought himself a Cadillac.

"Had anybody warned them it would create suspicions that they were informants if they immediately spent much of the money?"

"You damn right. Hell, we preached to 'em day and night not to do it."

"Everybody did? You did and Rucker and Watts did?"

"Yeah, you damn right. They were just ignorant."

"And told 'em not to be spending any money?"

"Right."

"And they went right out and did it anyway."

"Just nuts."

"What else did they do? I heard Raymond paid off his mortgage, too, forty-five hundred dollars or whatever it was."

"Aw, hell, I don't remember. He probably did. He's just an idiot. First night we met him he had on this motorcycle helmet and dark glasses, you know, he went in for all shit like that."

I read aloud several of Scarbrough's more crucial reports and then had him state for the record that they were part of the official Meridian police files. Again, I wanted there to be no question about the authenticity of the records.

Near the end of the interview that day, I asked Scarbrough whether the police had shot a dog during the shoot-out with Tarrants, a rumor I had picked up from somewhere.

"If you call Tarrants a dog."

Scarbrough had to leave before I had finished questioning him, but he offered to return the next morning to complete the interview. Deciding the Meridian story was so sensitive and potentially explosive that another reporter needed to be present to witness the rest of my research, I telephoned Guthman in Los Angeles. He said he would have Nick Chriss of our Houston bureau fly to Meridian the next day.

At my request, Chief Gunn also asked Sergeant Joyner and Officer Hatcher to drop by my motel to be interviewed. Joyner told me how he and three other officers fired shotguns at Tarrants from about fifteen feet away as Tarrants lay on the ground. Joyner said, "We had in mind killing him, I don't mind telling you," and stated that they thought Tarrants still was armed with a machine gun and a hand grenade. But given the circumstances of the chase and the fact that Tarrants had fallen to the ground after touching an electrically charged wire, that would have been highly unlikely, if not impossible.

Concerning the policy of harassing the Klan, Joyner said, "We harass 'em all. That's our job. They're in constant fear we got somebody set up now. We keep 'em scared to death."

Joyner and Hatcher said fear of the police was the major factor in the Roberts brothers' decision to cooperate in arranging the ambush. "That's what broke the case—fear, not the money," Hatcher said.

"He [Raymond Roberts] believed we were going to kill him," Joyner said. "We helped him believe it. We acted like we were going to do it."

Nick Chriss flew in the next morning. Later that day the two of us sat down in my motel room with Scarbrough and a tape recorder and I finished questioning the detective. We went over some of the same subjects covered the day before, again discussing several crucial Scarbrough reports so their authenticity would be verified in Chriss' presence. I wanted there to be no question about the thoroughness of the story I would write or about what Scarbrough said or the records revealed.

"One of the things I wanted to ask you, Detective Scarbrough," I began, "was—and you probably told me this in the tape-recorded interview from yesterday—that on every step of the way on this, you were working with FBI agents Rucker and Watts."

"Right."

"You never acted alone on any of it."

"Right."

Reading from a Scarbrough report that "informants wanted a written commitment concerning immunity which was given to them and signed by myself," I asked, "The FBI agents didn't sign that too, did they?"

"Uh-uh."

"You're the only one who signed that?"

"Right."

"But they were there? I mean, they knew that, they were in on all of that too?"

"Right."

Once again I asked about the fact that Raymond Roberts had let the police know only about forty-five minutes before the shoot-out that a woman instead of Hawkins was accompanying Tarrants. Scarbrough frowned and looked pained.

"I'd rather you wouldn't play that up too damn big, 'cause a couple of the boys feel pretty bad about that."

"About it being a woman."

"Yeah."

Citing a Scarbrough memo saying "We have received authority to spend a thousand dollars tonight," I asked him the source of the authority.

"Botnick," he said.

"Who first suggested the Meyer Davidson house?" I asked. "Did one of the Robertses just say, 'Well, there's a guy we can set up'?"

"Yeah."

" 'We can get 'em to come down and do a job on Davidson'?"

"Because they were mad at him."

"Because they were mad at Meyer Davidson?"

"Because he was instrumental in raising the reward money."

As we wound up the interview, Scarbrough said, "I don't know of anything you overlooked."

"God, we've been over it and over it and over it and the tape's been on for an hour and a half."

Thanking Scarbrough for all his help, I told him that Ed Guthman had said a certified check for a thousand dollars was in the mail for his having provided the documents. Chriss and I shook hands with him and we all agreed he was right, it was a story Hollywood couldn't make up.

"I'll be interested in reading your story," he said as he walked from the room.

As I closed the door behind Scarbrough, Chriss rolled his eyes to the ceiling and said, "I'll betcha he'll be interested in reading your story—more than he even knows."

The next stop was New Orleans and a visit with Botnick at the ADL regional office. We arrived unannounced, but Botnick smiled broadly and welcomed us. I told him we wanted to talk with him for a few minutes. After exchanging how-you-doing pleasantries, I reminded Botnick of our discussion about the Meridian case the previous April. Suddenly, he was frowning. He simply could not recall much about our conversation at that time, he said.

"Remember, you said you couldn't 'morally blow the whistle' on the FBI and the Meridian police for setting up a trap in Meridian because they had stopped the Klan violence?"

"I don't remember that."

Reading slowly from my typewritten notes of the interview with him, I said, "Here's what you said: 'Four guys know I was in on the original planning. It was a trap—you know that.' You remember that, don't you?"

"I don't remember that," he said, shaking his head sideways.

"Remember, you said the FBI played a tape recording for you of a Klansman talking about blowing up synagogues full of people, including women and children, and one Klansman said, 'Little Jews grow up to be big Jews,' and 'Kill them while they are young.' Remember, you talked about raising funds and you said, 'We were dealing with animals and I would do it again'? But you said when you learned a woman had been killed it made you sick and you said you went in and threw up when you heard about it?"

Botnick said he could not remember details of the interview, but the comments I cited to him were "incorrect."

I began to tell him some of the things I had learned from Scarbrough and from the detective's records.

"It's fantastic—like something out of Orwell's *Nineteen Eighty-four,*" he said. He also denied that Gunn and Key had asked him to arrange to have the Roberts brothers liquidated.

Leaving Botnick's office, I felt certain I had just lost a source.

Chriss and I talked about that as we walked back to our car for a trip to Jackson to see Roy Moore for the final interview before I would begin writing my story.

"You do what you gotta do, but you'll never get anything out of ole Bee Botnick again," Chriss said.

There was no question that he was right and I regretted it. Binder and Harris and other Jews in Jackson who had dealt with Botnick did not think much of him, but I had gotten along well with him and genuinely liked him. He had been a valuable news source, often telephoning me with tips about the Klan. He had also granted me access to the ADL's files on the Klan and other hate groups, which sometimes contained information from the ADL's own informants and from its close contact with the FBI.

Chriss and I arrived in Jackson early in the afternoon and checked into the Admiral Ben Bow Motel on the outskirts of downtown. I had put off interviewing Roy Moore until last; when talking to him I wanted to have as much information as possible. I telephoned the FBI office and asked to speak to him.

Moore came on the line quickly. Without giving me a chance to say anything, he said, "God, Jack, where have you been? I've had telephone calls from all over—from New Orleans, Atlanta, Washington, New York. People have said, 'What's Jack Nelson up to, what's he trying to do? Is he going after the FBI? Is he going after the ADL?' I told 'em, 'Don't worry about it, Jack's our friend.' Come on down here now and let's straighten this thing out."

I told Moore that Nick Chriss was with me and we would be right down.

Moore greeted us with a smile and a handshake, and so did Jim Ingram, his trusted colleague, who had been a key figure in breaking the back of the White Knights. It was clear that Moore and I would be doing the talking and that Ingram and Chriss were there as witnesses and to take notes.

We sat down and chatted about the weather and about how long it had been since Roy and I had seen each other—a few months—and then he said, "Well, let's hear about it. What's this all about? Whatever it is, I know we can straighten it out. We've worked together too long not to be able to do that."

I felt uncomfortable raising the issue of an ambush with a man who not only was one of my best sources and a friend, but also had a sterling reputation as a law enforcement official. He was right, we had been through a lot together. But I told Moore that a police source had related the whole story behind the shoot-out and had given me records to document it, and that what happened at Meridian raised serious questions about abuse of police powers. At best, the tactics had the earmarks of entrapping the Klan members, a legal defense in a criminal case. I did not raise the worst-case interpretation of the evidence: that the plan involved a death trap.

Even so, Moore was visibly shocked that I would even consider writing a story that raised a question of entrapment. "You have to understand," he said, "there is a fine line betwen entrapment and good law enforcement, and what happened at Meridian was good law enforcement."

If that was the case, I said, then all the facts should come out and people could judge for themselves.

He rushed on, speaking forcefully, as though I had said nothing: "If the agreement the Meridian police had with the Roberts brothers was that the money should be paid to them even if the perpetrators were killed in the act, I see nothing wrong with that—nothing unethical or illegal. Tried, true and accepted police practices were used at Meridian."

Although an abundance of documentary and eyewitness testimony clearly marked it as a joint FBI–Meridian police operation, Moore insisted that it was strictly a local show with the FBI merely providing guidance.

"Our investigation developed that Klansmen in Jackson were going to the Meridian area and we disseminated that information to local officers," he said. "We gave counsel and guidance to police as to how to deal with informants. They had no experience dealing with informants like that."

"If you knew everything that occurred leading up to the Meridian shoot-out," he said, "you would feel that the Jewish community should be commended for the part it played in raising funds for the informants because they supplied the wherewithal for it and it saved their people's lives."

I told Moore I was not questioning the Jewish community's

role in raising funds for the informants, but the information I had developed did raise serious questions about abuse of police powers.

"If the kind of story you're talking about is published, it will be a disservice to law enforcement and to the Jewish community," he said. "I feel very strongly about that and the fact that there was nothing wrong about paying the informants the way the Roberts brothers were paid. I can't believe you'll write a story in that vein, the kind of story you're talking about. We've gone through too much together, cooperated on too many stories, for you to write something like that."

If his aim was to make me squirm, he had succeeded. But I told him that, based on everything I had learned, it was a legitimate news story that needed to be told and I was going to write it, and I figured that the publisher and editor of the *Los Angeles Times* would decide to publish it.

He took one more shot at trying to convince me that a story should not be written. "If you write the story, the blood of innocent people will be on your hands," he warned. "It will yank the rug out from under our law enforcement program in Mississippi."

The phrases were ominous, but I did not believe the story I was working on would ever have such dire consequences. To me, Moore's warnings mainly reflected his frustrations at not being able to get me to drop the story. I told him that I would carefully consider everything he had told me but I still expected to write it, and that it would be up to the editor whether to run it.

My stomach was churning when I left Moore's office. With a single story that I had not even yet started writing, I had already managed to alienate both the ADL and the FBI. And losing the FBI as a source was a major blow for any investigative reporter. For years I had been one of the favored few reporters who got leaks from the FBI on major stories because the bureau liked what I wrote. Ever since the Ku Klux Klan murder of Lemuel Penn in July 1964 in Madison County, Georgia, the FBI had been my most important source when covering the Klan.

After we left his office, Moore sat down and dictated a "cover your ass" memo for the files that said Chriss and I, after exchanging pleasantries, indicated we were working on a story on the Tarrants case and had a Meridian police source who had "told them the whole story. I explained to them that this was strictly a local case and that I would have to give them a 'no comment' in that I was unaware of the full details."

Moore wrote that certain things Nick and I had said led him and Ingram to believe that "someone in the department" also had talked with me. "Without exhibiting any undue curiosity, we listened to what they had to say and their facts generally were accurate, although we did not acknowledge this. But the one factor that bothered us was that Jack Nelson indicated he thought he was going to write a story slanted along the lines that Tarrants had been 'set up' by informers so he could be shot by the police. Of course, this is not true and it appears as though Mr. Nelson was trying to resurrect an old case through some different slant to give it a current news value."

After explaining in the memo that he had praised the Meridian police for "excellent work," Moore wrote, "As the files will reflect, this is not entrapment in that no one was caused to do anything that had not been already planned by the Klan, rather, officers were successful in convincing one of the participants that he should cooperate and furnish them with the time and place of the next planned act of violence."

Moore noted that he had told me if I planned to write the story I should report only the facts, and if I did, "this would be a commendable article concerning the PD and other city officials in Meridian."

The next morning Chriss returned to Houston. I took a plane to Washington, having been transferred there from Atlanta. I began trying to write a story, but it wasn't easy because it involved a complicated series of events and a large cast of characters. Worse, my stomach was tied in knots and I had trouble sleeping. I would go to bed at night thinking about what Moore had said about the blood of innocent people being on my hands and yanking the rug out from under law enforcement. I still thought he had been talking for effect, trying to dissuade me from writing the story, but the words rang in my ears. As I was struggling with the story, I received a registered letter from Detective Luke Scarbrough that was even more disturbing. He had enclosed in the envelope the thousand-dollar check the *Los Angeles Times* had sent him. The letter read:

Dear Jack:

Enclosed you will find your check in the amount of $1,000. I would not feel honorable if I accepted it. The only reason I discussed the case with you was due to your high calibre reputation and trustworthiness. I was also led to believe that you were a close friend of Roy K. Moore's in whom he confided. I feel that any release on this case should have come from Mr. Moore, or the Chief of Police, Mr. Gunn. Jack, I told you at the start that I would never name any informers or other people who were involved. You are writing about vicious, blood-thirsty Klansmen who are waiting for certain names to be made public and there will be a retaliation by them. This blood will be on your hands and your conscience. You told me that you knew who the informers were, but in case of a libel case there are only three people who actually know and we would have to testify that we never received any information from them. There is never a good way to handle a case of this type, but this one was handled in the only way possible and just as a matter of record I want you to know that I never wanted or expected a personal gain from my share of duty performed in this case. I sincerely hope you will see and understand my position. You are a high-classed writer with a good reputation and I hope you won't let one story ruin your future. You know, being transferred to Washington, D. C., a good reputation will mean a lot to you.

Yours truly,
L. L. Scarbrough

The letter was unsettling, to say the least. Obviously, Roy Moore had talked to Gunn and Scarbrough. Once again I had been warned about the harm that could come to innocent people, but there were other warnings, too, including the possibility of a libel suit for naming the informants.

I thought the talk about Klan retaliation and the blood of innocent people was overstated. Tarrants, Bowers, Hawkins, Matthews and others within the Klan already knew that Raymond and Alton Wayne Roberts, hardly innocent people, were the FBI's informants, and no retaliatory action had been taken against them. As for libel, by this time my story was so thoroughly documented that I was convinced a libel suit would be an exercise in futility. Moreover, I did not believe that, if it came right down to it, Scarbrough or Watts and Rucker would be willing to perjure themselves.

The one threat that caused me real concern—and would later turn out to be anything but empty—was the suggestion that my reputation and future might be damaged if the story ran. I knew J. Edgar Hoover already had me on his "enemies list" because of a book I was working on about the circumstances under which state police officers killed three students and wounded twenty-seven others at South Carolina State College during a civil rights demonstration on February 8, 1968. Later published as *The Orangeburg Massacre,* with Jack Bass as coauthor, the book documented the fact that many of the student protesters had been shot in the back and that FBI agents had lied in denying their presence at the scene of the shootings in order to avoid having to discuss what the state police had done. Hoover was furious. If the FBI set out to ruin a reputation, it obviously could do some damage, so I anguished over the Meridian story as I wrote it.

Yet there was never any real question in my mind about whether I would write the story. I've always been a near absolutist on the First Amendment. And when it comes to one of the government's most awesome powers—police enforcement of the law—I believe the press has a special obligation to lay out all the facts.

After two weeks of work, I handed in a six-thousand-word story that was scrutinized by editors and lawyers in Los Angeles. The *Times* published the story at the top of page one:

POLICE ARRANGE TRAP:
KLAN TERROR IS TARGET

The article, which detailed how the Roberts brothers had helped arrange the trap, moved over the Los Angeles Times/ Washington Post News Service wire, and *The Washington Post* published it in a series of three page-one articles. With the three-hour time difference between Washington and Los Angeles, Hoover read his initial account in the first *Post* article and it infuriated him. He issued written instructions that the FBI should have no further contacts with me. When he was upset, Hoover had a habit of scrawling terse messages on FBI memoranda and signing them simply "H.," and he scribbled several of them on records dealing with the Meridian case. Even before the first article appeared,

Hoover had scrawled on the memo from Roy Moore: "Our Jackson Office should be more circumspect with Nelson as any representative of L. A. Times can't be trusted. H."

The Meridian story touched off a flurry of memoranda: FBI officials flatly denied the FBI's involvement in arranging the trap even though facts in the story were demonstrably true and had been heavily documented by Meridian police records and interviews.

On one memo, which quoted Moore as saying the FBI's Jackson office had had "excellent working relations with Jack Nelson," Hoover wrote, "It is obvious now that Nelson played Moore for a sucker." On another memo denying any FBI role, he wrote, "I hope SAC [Special Agent in Charge] Moore now realizes Nelson doesn't have a halo over his head."

In another memo, Deputy Director Cartha (Deke) DeLoach declared: "This is a typical Jack Nelson article filled with lies and vicious innuendo."

Twice before, in early 1968, Hoover and other FBI officials had castigated me for my reporting, the first time for disclosing that FBI agents had lied about the Orangeburg incident, and again when Nick Chriss and I managed to interview some witnesses in the Martin Luther King assassination case before FBI agents had contacted them. Once you were on Hoover's "enemies list," almost anything you did was subject to the most scathing criticism from the director and his sycophants.

One memo denied the FBI had any role even in investigating the Meyer Davidson bombing attempt and declared, "Nelson's allegation that the FBI played recordings of a klansman talking about blowing up synagogues is absolutely false. Nelson quotes SAC Moore as saying that a story disclosing the tactics used by the FBI and police would jeopardize their system of informants and hurt the cause of law enforcement. What Moore actually told Nelson was that if his story was slanted in any way it could hurt the cause of law enforcement."

Another memo said, "In this article, Nelson continues his fantastic account of the alleged role that the FBI played in a 1968 incident at Meridian."

Despite all the misstatements and outright falsehoods about the Meridian story in the FBI memoranda, one memo contained a conclusion that was demonstrably true: The Meridian ambush "broke the back of the klan in Mississippi, and klan violence, which up to this time had been a common occurrence, has for all practical purposes ceased to exist."

However, the FBI now wanted no credit for that.

The ADL wanted no credit either. In a brief statement by Arnold Forster, its general counsel, the ADL contradicted its own representative, A. I. Botnick, by denying that the ADL had participated in police activity or had any part in disbursement of money for informants:

> In an effort at the time to stem planned murders and the tide of actual bombings of Jewish houses of worship and other communal establishments, the Jewish community of Mississippi raised funds to obtain information leading to the apprehension of the perpetrators of these acts of violence. Because human lives were in jeopardy, ADL's representative in the area recommended to Jewish leaders that they assist in this fund-raising effort as a matter of civic responsibility. This was the extent of ADL's involvement in the situation. We had no part in the disbursement of funds nor any contact with informants nor any participation in the police activity. So far as we know, there is no basis for criticism of the law enforcement authorities.

The *Los Angeles Times,* in a lead editorial, characterized the events in Meridian as "most painful and disturbing" and said the authorities had stretched the law beyond acceptable limits. "No matter how great the provocation, the police can never take it on themselves to decide who is guilty, who is innocent; who is to live, and who is to die." In one note to me about the story, Nick Williams, the editor of the *Times* declared, "rough, rough, rough," and in another he said, "I know that was a tough one for you. We also did a lot of agonizing here about the editorial on it as to what to say. The last time I heard, our legal counsel had fainted for the third time and I'm not sure whether he's gotten up again."

In the crush of news during that period, the Meridian story did not penetrate the national consciousness. But it did provoke reaction in certain circles. Several other newspapers and two liberal organizations despised by the Klan—the American Civil Lib-

erties Union and the American Friends Service Committee—
called for an official investigation.

In Meridian, Roy Gunn said: "I owe no apologies to anyone
and should the same thing occur again it is possible the same
method would be used. This is a police matter in which my department learned in advance of the plans of the Ku Klux Klan to
commit murder. There is a great difference between legal and
illegal entrapment. We constantly consulted with legal authorities.
There was nothing illegal or unethical about the method that my
department used to prevent these murders."

Gunn also told reporters that Klan informants had advised him
that in covering the Meridian story I had told people that I was
part of a group "which had as its purpose writing a story to
discredit my police department and the FBI, and actually remove
Mr. Hoover, who they believed had set himself up as a czar. This
apparently is a left-winged group that does not want law enforcement."

I had no idea what an informant might have told Gunn, but
one thing I knew for sure: the smear campaign had started. Gunn's
statement smacked of something drafted by Hoover's men at the
seat of government.

When the 1970 story was published, there were still many more
layers to peel away before all the facts could emerge. At that time
I was unaware of the existence of some key witnesses to the
planning and execution of the trap. I knew nothing about the
roles played by Al Binder and other embattled members of
the Jewish community in Jackson and Meridian—nothing of their
isolation, their fear or the desperate resolve described to me by
Joe Harris in 1991: "What we were doing was for ourselves and
nobody else. We had no help from the local community—not
from the Chamber of Commerce or businesses. Nobody. Our only
friend was the FBI. We didn't look for any more help."

And I had no inkling back in 1970 that the Meridian story
would continue to haunt me over the next two decades, nor that
a strange and totally different new life would unfold for Tommy
Tarrants after his unsuccessful prison break. What would soon
happen in the life of the "mad-dog killer" was as incredible as all
that had gone before.

17

At first, Tarrants viewed his unsuccessful escape attempt as no more than a setback. With his boundless self-confidence, he thought freedom was only a matter of devising another plan. As before, he began to study the security system, looking for weak spots to exploit and people to use or manipulate. He soon discovered, however, that prison authorities were not so easily gulled a second time. He was locked alone in a narrow maximum-security cell and allowed out only twice a week for a trip to the showers. His contact with other prisoners was reduced to a minimum. Escape was virtually impossible.

The reality crashed down on him, and with it bitter frustration. He plunged even more deeply into the realms of hate, devouring Klan literature sent by friends. He pored over the latest diatribes from the John Birch Society and the National States Rights Party. He ordered Adolf Hitler's *Mein Kampf* and similar books through the mail. Reading this type of material only reinforced his racism and anti-Semitism.

Almost a year after his escape, sometime in the spring or early summer of 1970, Frank Watts, still intent on building cases against Sam Bowers and L. E. Matthews, visited Tarrants at Parchman. Watts tried once again to persuade Tarrants to testify against the Klan leaders. If he would tell what he knew about Bowers, Matthews and Danny Joe Hawkins, Watts told him, a way might be found to shorten his stay in prison. Unless he cooperated, he would have to serve one third of his thirty-five-year sentence before he could even be considered for parole. If he helped, he might get out sooner.

Tarrants responded with a bitter taunt: "Tell you what you do:

you help me get out of here and I'll kill your enemies for you. I know that as a law enforcement officer you've got to have enemies. I'll kill 'em for you if you'll just help me get out." He would never testify against fellow Klansmen, he vowed.

Watts told him to quit talking like that or he might never get out of prison. Despite Tarrants' belligerence, there was something about him that gave Watts hope that he might yet obtain his testimony. Watts could not put his finger on exactly what it was, but as he left the prison he knew that he would stay in contact with Tarrants.

Eventually, as the months dragged on, Tarrants began to tire of the hate literature. Somehow, the old religion was losing its capacity to give meaning and purpose to his life. He begin to search for something else.

At first, he went back to the Bible, the book he had read so compulsively as a young teenager. In those fevered years, it had seemed a logical step to go from being a serious Christian to being a radical conservative—a militant defender of Christian civilization, as Tarrants had seen it. This time, the Bible led him to the world of philosophy. He began by reading Hegel's *Philosophy of History,* then plunged into Plato, Aristotle, Socrates and the Stoics, a course of reading he found had "a profound effect" upon his life.

On July 8, 1970, Ken Dean drove to Parchman to visit Tarrants. In Dean's earlier visit with Tarrants' father, the elder Tarrants had expressed increasing concern about his son's mental health. Though the trial judge had found him competent to stand trial and the jury had rejected the insanity defense, the father was beset by fears that his son was mentally ill. Now the Baptist minister had decided to see for himself.

Dean had never met Tarrants. Peering through the bars of the tiny cell, Dean saw "a tall, thin man standing in his shorts and undershirt" talking loudly to other inmates in nearby cells. He appeared "nervous, hostile, not well composed and rude." Tarrants greeted Dean with a cold, appraising look. "I've heard good things about you from my parents," he said, his words dripping with sarcasm. "You must be quite some person!"

Dean first thought Tarrants appeared to be mentally ill. He

drew him into conversation, however, and as they talked the prisoner seemed to change. He grew calmer, and he talked more seriously, with less posturing. Dean had noticed thirty or forty books neatly arranged on a shelf over the cell's bunk. Tarrants said he was taking a correspondence course in theology and suggested they discuss some questions that had been on his mind. What, he asked, did Dean think about Saint Paul's concept of salvation? Did he believe in the idea of once saved, always saved?

A serious discussion of theology was right up Dean's alley. "Saint Paul was a man who grew," he said. "The Book of Hebrews represented some of his thinking regarding salvation, and it suggested that one could actually taste of salvation and yet later reject it."

For a time Tarrants, tight-lipped, eyed him suspiciously. Finally he said, "Well, let's get on with the real purpose of your visit. What do you think about what happened to me in Meridian? Don't you think the police and the feds are guilty of acts of injustice?"

The question was uncomfortably direct. And with the guard and the assistant chaplain standing close enough to overhear, Dean worried that they might take a dim view of a visiting minister encouraging a prisoner in a complaint about police misconduct. Dean simply said he was sorry the incident had ever taken place.

"I am, too," Tarrants said. "However, that doesn't answer my question. What I want to know is whether or not you think the police in Meridian and the FBI are guilty of committing a crime and with carrying out an act of injustice against me."

Realizing Tarrants would persist until he received a satisfactory answer, Dean leaned close and, in a voice so low the chaplain and the guard could not hear him, whispered, "I am here."

"Oh, I understand," Tarrants replied, taking Dean's words as a signal that he shared Tarrants' view but was not free to discuss it. "Then your concern about me is spiritual," Tarrants said, lowering his own voice, "and if your concern is spiritual it is individual and that means if they could do what they did to me, they could do it to somebody else, and if they could do it to somebody else, they could do it to you, and if they could do it to you, they could do it to anybody. And if that is the situation, then it is both a matter of a spiritual problem and a problem of justice, and while you would say that you are concerned about the spiritual aspects, you too are actually concerned about the criminal act of injustice."

Dean decided he would stay in contact with Tarrants, a man he now believed to be emotionally disturbed but not insane, and whose soul the young minister felt might yet be saved.

Both Watts and Dean began to make increasingly frequent visits to Tarrants at Parchman. As they did, each began to notice what appeared to be a growing absorption with religion on Tarrants' part. It was a process that would go on over many, many months, and in the end it would produce what may have been a most unexpected turn in Tarrants' life.

His journey through philosophy eventually led him back to the Bible, and he began to examine not only his beliefs but his life. His obsession with radical right-wing ideology, he later wrote, had sprung not from considered judgment but from a desire to cast himself in a dramatic role that would give meaning and importance to his life. For the first time, he said, he saw "the evil I had done all my life." As he pondered the question posed in the New Testament, "For what is a man profited, if he should gain the whole world and lose his own soul?," Tarrants said, it "just exploded in my mind and my heart and I realized that I had been doing precisely that, selling my soul for the thrill and excitement and adventure of this cause that I was married to."

The result, Tarrants said, was a profound religious conversion. "I got on my knees in that cell and just gave my life completely to Christ and asked him to come in—I didn't even know that he wanted it—but I said, 'Lord, I've ruined my life, but if you want it, I'll just give it to you completely. Here it is.' And something changed inside of me when I did that, I could even feel it. Something happened and I became different."

Officially, Watts' mission in visiting Tarrants was to obtain his testimony against other high-level members of the White Knights. And when J. Edgar Hoover learned of Tarrants' claim that he had found religion, he dispatched Watts and Rucker to interview the prisoner again to see if he was using it as a cover to plan another escape. "I went back and there was no question he was a different individual from before," Watts recalled. "His countenance had changed. He put his arm around me, hugged me. I realized he was a changed individual, bearing in mind that I had referred to him as an animal in Meridian and I called him a mad-dog killer."

Watts, who also had become a born-again Christian in the aftermath of the ambush, responded to the change he saw in Tarrants with more personal contact. He went to see him on weekends at least once a month, often accompanied by Meridian businessmen who were religious activists. Watts' wife, Joyce, a born-again Christian active in prayer groups and Bible studies, also began visiting Tarrants and sending him religious material. The FBI agent got permission for his wife's prayer group to visit Parchman to pray with Tarrants on the prison grounds. After that, Mrs. Watts and other members of the group periodically fixed picnic lunches and, accompanied by their husbands, drove the 150 miles from Meridian to Parchman to spend Sunday afternoons with Tarrants at the prison.

One Sunday afternoon, the picnic marked a special occasion. Three carloads of Meridian couples, including Watts and his wife, gathered around a small, tree-shaded pond just outside Camp 19, a minimum security center, to attend a special baptismal cere-mony. While a young guitarist played religious music, Tarrants, shoeless but clad in a sport shirt and trousers, waded into the water and was baptized by the prison chaplain. Among those looking on were several Meridian businessmen and a junior-col-lege president, along with a number of prison staff members.

Watts called the change in Tarrants "a real religious experi-ence" and said, "I've seen some that were completely fake, just wanted to get out of the pen. But he had a real born-again ex-perience."

By some measures, the change in Watts was a least as remark-able as the transformation of Tarrants. The FBI agent who had used informants to set up the ambush now decided he must work to set his prey free.

Watts was joined in this effort by prison authorities and Parch-man's chaplain, and by Dean, whose clout in the state had in-creased considerably, although not as a result of his work with the Council on Human Relations. Dean had been named presi-dent of Jackson's WLBT television station after it was awarded to a local group that had successfully challenged the previous owner's license for failing to provide minority programming. Dean had led the drive to revoke the license.

The efforts of Watts and Dean and prison authorities who supported Tarrants began to focus on a study program that offered prisoners opportunities for early release if they qualified.

While Watts and Dean were trying to help Tarrants get out of prison, Meridian police officials were following up on the promise to help Alton Wayne Roberts win an early release from his ten-year sentence in the Goodman-Schwerner-Chaney case. Roberts was serving his time at the Leavenworth federal prison.

In Roberts' case, there was no religious conversion, but Gunn and Scarbrough jointly wrote a letter to the federal parole board recommending early release. They wrote that from the time of his conviction and while his case had been on appeal, he had "made every effort to make a good citizen; worked hard, looked after his wife and children and gave every evidence of having been fully rehabilitated. It is our belief that in the event he is given favorable consideration, he will continue to be a good citizen, a productive citizen and a good father and husband and will be a credit to any community where he may live."

True to his role as an FBI agent, Watts also continued to hammer at Tarrants to help in the prosecution of Bowers and Matthews. Now that he really knew Christ, Watts told him, he had a duty to testify against dangerous lawbreakers and help put them in prison. Tarrants replied that it would be contemptible for someone to betray friends for personal advantage. The crimes he committed with other people, he said, were done with mutual trust and out of a common commitment and it would be wrong to testify against those people, especially because they were no longer engaged in violence.

"If the violence resumes," he said, "if Danny, L.E. and Sam begin to do the same sort of things again, I will write them a letter warning them to stop it and specifying that if they don't I'll testify to everything I know."

Watts became so dedicated to obtaining Tarrants' early release that he decided to take the extraordinary—some said foolhardy—step of seeking Al Binder's support. Binder could be crucial to the cause not only because he had been a key figure in raising funds for the informants and working with the FBI on the bombing cases, but because he had important political contacts and was the attorney for Governor William Waller. Visiting Binder in his Jackson law office, Watts told him he was preparing to retire from the FBI and wanted to give him a report on Tarrants.

"Tommy's been in this terrorist stuff since he was fourteen and he had older people who taught him all this hate crap," Watts said. "But Al, he's truly repentant and has accepted the Lord."

"Why are you telling me all this?" Binder asked.

"I want to help him get out of prison," Watts said.

"Let him rot in hell," Binder retorted. "If you want me to tell the Jews it's okay for him to get out of prison, I can tell you I'll never do that."

Watts left Binder's office dejected, but determined not to give up.

Although there had been no Klan violence since Meridian, the idea that some of the terrorists still walked the streets as free men still preyed on Binder's mind. How could he be an advocate of clemency for the man who had bombed his synagogue and his rabbi's house, who may have threatened to blow up synagogues with women and children inside, and whom the FBI and Watts himself had called a "mad-dog killer"? In fact, Binder was so concerned that Klan violence might erupt again that he paid his own personal informant to report on the Klan's anti-Semitic activities. Racism still ran deep in Mississippi and Klan literature still included vicious anti-Semitic material.

One day in September 1973, Binder's worst fears were confirmed. His informant came to his law office and told him Bee Botnick, the ADL director from New Orleans, was in danger.

"They plan to kill him," he said.

"Who is 'they'?" Binder asked.

"The Klan."

"How?"

"With a bomb."

"Who's going to do it?"

"Byron de la Beckwith."

"Oh, my God, when was the decision made?"

"Yesterday."

"When will this happen?"

"In a few days."

"Who's going to make the bomb?"

"The same guy that makes all the bombs, a guy from right below Jackson."

"Where's he going to deliver the bomb?"

"Downtown."

The informant spelled out the details. The bomb had a timing device and the bomb maker would deliver the device to Beckwith at the Mayflower Café in downtown Jackson. Beckwith had been tried twice for murder in the 1963 ambush slaying of Medgar Evers, the NAACP field secretary, but both times all-male, all-white juries reported that they could not agree on verdicts and mistrials were declared.

Binder immediately took his information to the Jackson FBI office. Agents told him they had received the same report from one of their informants. They made plans to observe the meeting and have Beckwith intercepted afterward. At the appointed hour on September 26, Binder and an FBI agent sat down at a table in the Mayflower Café next to one occupied by the man the FBI called the Klan's chief bomb maker, L. E. Matthews. Beckwith soon joined Matthews at his table.

"There I was sitting next to them trying to eat," Binder said. "It was a very horrible day for me. It was a very hot day and I remember sweating and it dripping on my salad and I couldn't eat. And then Beckwith took the bomb and they walked out and Beckwith got in his car and started driving to New Orleans."

About one o'clock the next morning, New Orleans Police Department intelligence agents arrested Beckwith at a roadblock on Interstate 10 at the twin bridges where the city limits begin. In Beckwith's car they found a bomb with its timing device ticking, as well as three rifles, a machine gun and a map with a route to Botnick's house clearly marked. Police disarmed the bomb and seized a .45-caliber automatic stuck in Beckwith's belt.

Beckwith was later convicted in a New Orleans state court of transporting a bomb into the state without a license. He would serve five years in Angola state prison. Whether for fear of blowing an informant's cover or for some other reason, Matthews was never arrested in the case.

After that incident with Beckwith, Al Binder was even less inclined to help a Klan terrorist get out of prison.

• • •

The day after Beckwith's arrest, Tarrants telephoned Dean from Parchman and said that the news had ruined his day, that the bombing attempt probably would kill any chance of early release. He asked Dean whether it would help if he made a statement to the press denouncing the attempted bombing. Dean advised him to remain silent. Beckwith's action would indeed be a setback for Tarrants' chances, but any public comment might be counterproductive.

By now, because of his religious activities and his record of good behavior since his escape, Tarrants was assigned to do clerical work at the prison. Characteristically, he ingratiated himself with the people who counted at the prison. Soon he was clerking for the chaplain and given new housing—in a garage apartment behind the home of the new prison superintendent.

A voracious reader, Tarrants was articulate and highly intelligent, so much so that prison officials came to view him as one of the brightest prisoners ever confined there. They counted on him to research penal reform programs in other states and to draw up proposed legislation they planned to present to Mississippi legislators. He became friends with several of the officials and their families, including the superintendent and his wife and children.

In the beginning there was skepticism among prison staffers who saw his newly acquired religion, his "jailhouse conversion," as a con game—part of a ploy to escape or win early release. But Tarrants continued to win over the skeptics.

He eventually was moved to the prison's prerelease center and he talked often by telephone and in person with Ken Dean, who believed in reconciling people with their enemies and wanted to arrange for Tarrants to meet with a member of the Jewish community. Frank Watts kept working on the same thing. Upon returning from a visit to Israel, he went to see Binder again.

"He brings me a bread knife from Israel," Binder recalled, "and he says, 'Oh, what a wonderful people in Israel, what a wonderful way of life, what a great democracy.' And he says, 'I'm truly a better man now.' Then he says, 'Have you heard from Tommy Tarrants?' And I said I was the last one he'd ever write to."

Once more Watts urged Binder to visit Tarrants, but the lawyer was adamant. "I don't want to talk about it anymore, I'm trying to forget the past," he said.

Neither Watts nor Dean would let him forget. They continued to press him to visit. So did an increasing number of other influential people. Through Mrs. Watts' Baptist prayer group and religious activitists in the Meridian business community, Tarrants had tapped into one of the largest and most important networks in all of Mississippi. Binder recalls being practically besieged. "Many preachers and FBI people came forth and tried to get Tarrants out of prison because they said he was truly repentant and a Christian now. And they begged me to go down and talk to him."

Finally, reluctantly, Binder agreed. Just before his visit, on October 24, 1973, Dean alerted Tarrants that he was going to be visited by an "important Jewish man." Right away Tarrants asked if the man was Binder. Dean told him it was and asked how he had guessed. Tarrants, as Dean noted in a memo, answered that in the latter part of 1967 Sam Bowers ordered him to "investigate Al Binder for a possible No. 4 and he said this meant liquidation or extermination and not just a bombing."

Accompanied by Dean, Binder drove to Parchman, skeptical but prepared to listen. He stiffened as he shook hands with the man who had bombed his synagogue and his rabbi's house.

The session got off to a tense start. Tarrants explained that prison authorities, convinced he had been rehabilitated, had recommended that he be allowed to participate in a study-release program. Binder, in trial-lawyer style, peppered Tarrants with questions about why he had gone after the Jews and why he was not willing to testify against Bowers and Matthews.

Binder wanted to bring a civil damages suit against the White Knights; Tarrants' testimony would be invaluable. Tarrants once more insisted he did not think it would be right for him to testify against his former Klan colleagues. Nor would it be "the right thing to gain my freedom by being part of a legal action against others." Tarrants' explanation left Binder cold, but there was one thing that did impress him: Tarrants' candor in discussing his own violent Klan missions.

"We had you on the list, too, Mr. Binder," Tarrants said. "Let me draw you a picture of your house."

"This bastard," Binder recalled, "proceeds to draw me a map

of my house—the bedrooms, the bathrooms, everything! That's what frightened me."

The meeting lasted three hours. Dean was present during all but thirty minutes of the session and later typed an eight-page, single-spaced memo for his files.

Tarrants insisted he no longer held the racist and anti-Semitic views that had made him a Klan hit man and said he realized the fallacy of the conspiratorial theories propounded by extremist organizations. He repudiated his earlier view that the participation of Jews in the Bolshevik Revolution of 1917 made Communism a Jewish plot. He said he now realized that Jews had been in the forefront of the civil rights movement not because of a conspiracy, but because historically they had been an oppressed minority.

Binder poked and probed. If Tarrants had not in fact undergone an almost miraculous transformation, he must be one of the biggest liars and con men in the state. And question Tarrants as he might, Binder could find no basis for refusing to believe he was sincere. In the end, the lawyer told Tarrants he too would try to help him, though Binder attached a condition: Tarrants would have to help in combating anti-Semitism in Mississippi.

The day after the visit, Tarrants wrote Binder a letter. "It gives me a very warm feeling inside to know that in spite of everything, you are willing to forgive me," Tarrants wrote. "I think it's a beautiful thing for enemies to be reconciled and become friends." On the subject of combating anti-Semitism, he wrote: "My attitude toward Jewish people, is not one of tolerance, but rather of love and acceptance, as, indeed, it is toward all peoples. And it is the nature of love—true Christian love—to genuinely care as much about others as about one's own self. Translating this into concrete action with regard to Jews means working to eradicate the problem of anti-semitism."

In reply, Binder wrote Tarrants that he appreciated the fact that Tarrants felt the need to do something to combat anti-Semitism, but if he was truly rehabilitated, he was in a position to testify and "bring to justice certain people that have broken the law." That the victims of the violence were Jews was not the most important point, Binder wrote, because "they also are good Americans and a wrong perpetrated against them is as harmful to the Christian community as it is to the Jewish community."

Despite being disappointed that Tarrants had not mentioned testifying against his Klan colleagues, Binder wrote, "I plan to see you in the near future and we will talk again."

Four and a half years had passed since my second Meridian story, but it still rankled Roy Moore. He was only six months away from retirement and he told other agents he would be leaving the FBI "with Nelson being the only fly in the ointment," my story the only blemish on an otherwise spotless record. The bureau as a whole was also sensitive to the suggestion that the ambush had gone beyond the law. FBI agents visited Tarrants at Parchman seeking a signed statement denying that he and Kathy Ainsworth had been entrapped at Meridian. The FBI wanted what amounted to legal absolution.

Finally, after repeated requests, Tarrants gave them a statement, which was leaked to the New Orleans *Times-Picayune.* The story was carried under the headline "Tarrants Absolves FBI of Entrapment."

The statement did not change the facts. The evidence was abundant that the Roberts brothers, in concert with the FBI and Meridian police, had played a pivotal role in the planning of a second bombing in Meridian and in selecting Davidson's home as the target. Moreover, Scarbrough's reports amounted to overwhelming evidence that the brothers set up Tarrants and that Raymond, acting for the FBI and police, pressed for the bombing attempt to be carried out on their timetable.

Not long afterward, at Dean's urging, Binder returned to Parchman. This second visit persuaded him that Tarrants indeed was a changed man.

"When I went down a second time to talk to him, I thought I got a better idea, a better understanding of why some people do these things," Binder later said. "And I finally became convinced that Tommy Tarrants had accepted Christ. I'm sort of a street-smart person myself and he just sold me. I told him I would work to get him out."

Tarrants applied for early release and Binder recommended that the application be approved. In late summer of 1974, Bill Hollowell, Parchman's superintendent, gave his approval. Tarrants had been accepted by Duke University, Rutgers College, and

Earlham College in Indiana. Eventually, he also applied to the University of Mississippi and was accepted there. Governor Bill Waller found the issue of early release a "sticky" political problem, however, and ruled that if Tarrants wanted to attend college it would "have to be at Parchman," where he already was taking some college correspondence courses from the University of Alabama.

In early 1976, Governor Cliff Finch, who had succeeded Waller, did grant Tarrants' request to go to Washington, D.C., to attend a two-week prison discipleship program directed by Chuck Colson, the former Nixon White House official and Watergate scandal figure. Colson had turned to religion after pleading guilty to a felony charge of obstructing justice and serving seven months of a three-year prison sentence.

During the discipleship program, Tarrants became friends with both Colson, a conservative Republican, and former Senator Harold Hughes, a liberal Democrat and reformed alcoholic. Colson also introduced the former Klansman to Eldridge Cleaver, one-time minister of information of the militant Black Panther Party. "Are you sure this guy's saved?" Tarrants jokingly asked.

In December 1976, Parchman warden John Watkins interviewed Tarrants for possible early release. As Tarrants later wrote, Watkins was far from convinced of the prisoner's conversion. "I'm not going to release you because of your religion, because I don't think it's worth five cents," Watkins said. "But I do believe you have changed and deserve a chance to make something of yourself. That's why I'm going to release you."

On December 13, 1976, Governor Cliff Finch approved Tarrants' release from prison to attend the University of Mississippi. Tarrants had served eight years at Parchman, less than one third of the thirty-five years he had been sentenced to spend behind bars, and four years less than he would have been required to serve under normal parole procedure.

Binder, convinced that Tarrants had changed but afraid he might slip, paid an informant to keep tabs on him at the university. "I spent over ten thousand dollars that year having him watched at various and sundry times," Binder said. "I kept him under surveillance. I got his grades. He made straight A's. He made A in Greek. And then—and he doesn't know I'm having him watched—he writes a book condemning what he did to the Jews. He went straight and he tried to do something about anti-Semitism."

Tarrants would spend two years at Ole Miss studying the classics and focusing heavily on Greek and the New Testament, continuing to get straight A's. He became a popular speaker on religion and was tapped to address the annual governor's prayer breakfast in Jackson. At a dinner the night before the breakfast, Binder was surprised when Tarrants appeared. "He came in the room and saw me—of course, everybody knew who he was—and he ran over to me and threw his arms around me," Binder recalled. "I felt so self-conscious. But I have never really regretted that decision of forgiveness."

In 1978, his final year at Ole Miss, Tarrants, with the assistance of Will Norton, a journalism professor at the university, wrote a small book, *The Conversion of a Klansman.* It was published by Doubleday in 1979. Not surprisingly, perhaps, the book was highly selective in the subjects it dealt with and those it did not. Except for an account of what had happened in Meridian on the night of June 29, 1968, Tarrants wrote little about his Klan activities or the issue of justice raised by the ambush. Instead, he concentrated on his earlier background, his prison life and his Christian conversion. He did not go into detail about the issue of justice in his case, he explained in the book's afterword, because that "would have distracted from the book's theme and purpose, the love and mercy of the Lord for a wretched sinner."

He did declare once more, however, that he had considered Meyer Davidson a high-priority target before the Roberts brothers mentioned him as a target. He repeated his contention that entrapment was not involved because "the FBI did not lure us into doing something we had no intention of doing." Had it not been for the FBI's intelligence program, Tarrants wrote,

> there would have been ten times as much violence by right-wing radicals. Fear of informers, sophisticated listening devices, telephone taps, and other surveillance procedures promoted disunity, dissension, distrust, suspicion, and paranoia that prevented us from planning and executing many acts of violence. Those who have reservations about the use of an FBI intelligence program directed toward radical groups might do well to put

themselves in the place of the potential victim. Liberals and conservatives alike should realize that their lives may one day depend on such a program—just as Meyer Davidson's did.

In an epilogue, Harold Hughes wrote, "Tommy is now an intelligent, quiet, shy, and loving servant of the Lord."

About the time his book was published, Tarrants left Mississippi, saying he thought the book could provoke some of his old Klan buddies and it might not be prudent for him to remain in the state. He moved to another state, where he became involved in religious teaching and Bible training.

His conversion, Tarrants told me in 1991, "initiated a process of change that's still going. The hatred for blacks and for Jews, I began to recognize that. I stopped cursing overnight. I used to curse every other breath, I mean the worst case you've ever seen. I used to say the most outrageous things. And that went away overnight. And these attitudes, I began to get light as I began to read the Bible and I began to understand how the Bible and the teachings of Christ applied to me and what I was doing. . . . I'm still changing. But the racism, the anti-Semitism, those things went away early on. And a tremendous love has come into my life for people, it doesn't matter what color they are. And it's just an ongoing process, purifying, changing me, delivering me from what I used to be."

EPILOGUE

The Meridian ambush left a mark on nearly everyone associated with it. In my own case, my coverage touched off an FBI vendetta against me. Although the campaign inflicted no long-term damage, it offered a glimpse of what could happen to people who crossed J. Edgar Hoover.

In those days most Americans thought of Hoover and the FBI as heroic and almost invincible. The public was largely unaware of a sinister side to Hoover and the FBI, that in addition to investigating crime they collected vast files of unverified gossip, rumor, innuendo and personal data on thousands of politicians and others—files used to discredit or intimidate bureau critics. As Bill Moyers, a close aide to President Lyndon Johnson, said in a *Parade* interview: "Were we frightened of J. Edgar Hoover like Kennedy was? Like Nixon was? Absolutely. We were scared to death of him. Just like Nixon said in those tapes: 'Hoover could bring us all down.'"

The FBI director certainly scared off much of the press. During the late 1960s and early 1970s, not many journalists, aside from columnist Jack Anderson, my colleague Ron Ostrow and myself, were tackling FBI abuses. If presidents had reason to fear him, what could he do to a reporter who angered him? In my case, he branded me a drunk, tried to get me fired and ridiculed me in public. As Curt Gentry wrote in *J. Edgar Hoover: The Man and the Secrets,* Hoover moved me to the top of his enemies list, "the FBI director ordering him smeared as an irresponsible drunk." Speaking to reporters at the American Newspaper Women's Club in Washington, Hoover denounced me as a skunk, a disparagement he used more than once. He spurned a request by David

Kraslow, the *Times* Washington bureau chief, to meet with me to discuss his criticism, and said he could only lose "in a pissing contest with a skunk."

Hoover's campaign did not stop with me; he ordered all FBI offices to stop having contact with *Times* reporters. Two weeks after my stories on the ambush appeared, the FBI captured black militant professor Angela Davis, who was wanted in connection with the murder of a judge. Every other major publication was notified of her arrest, but not the *Los Angeles Times,* even though Davis taught at UCLA and the search for her was a major running story in Los Angeles. When Kraslow complained that the *Times* had not been alerted, FBI spokesman Tom Bishop told him, "When you get rid of that son of a bitch that has a vendetta against Hoover and the FBI, we'll cooperate with you. He's gone around town drunk telling people he was going to get Hoover and the FBI."

It was simply untrue that I was out to get Hoover or that I had a drinking problem. In the early 1970s I did do my share of drinking. Since my wife and three teenage children remained in Atlanta after I moved to Washington in 1970, I spent a lot of evenings at the Class Reunion, a bar and restaurant three blocks from the White House, a hangout for journalists and political figures. It was my home away from home where I got calls from White House sources and even from the CIA, so whatever drinking I did did not interfere with my work.

At first I was not too concerned when the FBI began circulating the drinking stories among my colleagues. After all, you could hardly ruin a newspaperman—at least in those days—by calling him a drunk. But then Hoover and his underlings told the same thing to my editors in Los Angeles. Hoover accused me of having "a Jekyll-Hyde personality" and a "deep-seated hatred of the bureau," and said I went around telling people he was a homosexual. All the charges were baseless. I never discussed Hoover's sexual preferences, if any, and did not care about them one way or the other.

In meetings with my superiors, Hoover often brought up Meridian. When the *Times'* general manager, Robert Nelson (no relation), traveled to Washington to meet with him in an attempt to patch up the deteriorating relations between the FBI and the *Times,* Hoover was ready with an eight-page memo summarizing the FBI's complaints about me. It included a diatribe about what he claimed were inaccuracies in stories I had written, including "lies and vicious innuendoes" in my Meridian stories. He said the FBI "did not investigate the attempted bombing, did not participate in the stakeout, shootout, or arrest" and that the agents were "present in the neighborhood only because Tarrants was a Bureau fugitive charged with interstate transportation of a stolen motor vehicle."

Soon I began getting signals from my editors that they would prefer that I concentrate on something other than the FBI. At the time Ron Ostrow and I were working on several stories involving financial irregularities at the bureau. One would have shown that Hoover pocketed seventy thousand dollars from his book *Masters of Deceit,* which was written by bureau ghostwriters on government time, but our findings were never published. We were also looking into incidents involving Cartha (Deke) De-Loach, the number-three man in the bureau, but were called off the story after DeLoach conferred with our superiors. It was the first and only time in my career that I was reined in on a story, and it so upset me I was on the verge of resigning. Eventually, realizing that quitting would only hurt me and please Hoover, I stayed.

It's true that I had investigated several cases that brought out the darker side of Hoover and the FBI, especially the "Orangeburg Massacre." In many ways, Orangeburg was worse than Kent State, but it did not get one tenth of the media attention. After managing to examine hospital records, I reported that most of the killed and injured students had been shot in the back or soles of their feet as they were running away. Later, with Jack Bass I coauthored *The Orangeburg Massacre.* The book came out within months of the Meridian story and further infuriated Hoover. He wrote letters to top *Times* executives denouncing it and put pressure on World Publishing which then cut its promised first printing by two thirds despite widespread favorable reviews and many news stories based on its disclosures.

FBI pressure—through letters, telephone calls and personal visits—finally became so intense that even my boss, national editor Edwin Guthman, began to feel the heat. Guthman himself was in a delicate position because he had once worked for Robert Kennedy in the Justice Department and had his own history of rocky relationships with FBI officials. He started to worry that the perception of anti-FBI bias was taking hold.

Later, Ron Ostrow and I disclosed that the key witness against Father Philip Berrigan and other Catholic antiwar activists in the alleged conspiracy to kidnap Henry Kissinger was an FBI agent provocateur. Word then came from Los Angeles that we were spending too much time looking into FBI activities. I complained bitterly to Guthman that the paper seemed to have lost interest in follow-up stories. He then wrote me a letter expressing concern that we not "muckrake" or appear to be carping in dealing with such "sensitive and emotional subjects" as the FBI and the Berrigans. "A paper can be made to appear to be harassing a public official," he said.

I found it distressing to receive such a cautionary message from Guthman, a good friend and a tough, hard-driving former investigative reporter. After reading his letter, I banged out an emotional response on my typewriter, saying that while we were dealing with sensitive subjects and I sometimes got "rather heated up," I "did my damndest to be fair and balanced" and disagreed with him on muckraking. "Lincoln Steffens and many others were honorable muckrakers. Ralph Nader is a muckraker and probably the best one in Washington if you judge by results. Hell, didn't you used to be one? In any event I plead guilty to being a passionate muckraker."

While these incidents still rankle an old investigative reporter, they pale in comparison to the strong support Guthman and other Los Angeles Times editors gave me for years of investigative stories, including subsequent stories I wrote about Hoover and the FBI.

By early 1972, Hoover's status as an icon had begun to slip. On Capitol Hill there were calls for his ouster, and other publications were taking a critical look at Hoover and the FBI.

Hoover died on May 2, 1972, and the Los Angeles Times' relations with the FBI improved dramatically under his successors. The FBI continued to keep a list of the bureau's "friends and enemies," but I was no longer singled out as a foe. After the Times named me its Washington bureau chief in November 1974, FBI director Clarence Kelley, in a letter of congratulations, said, "My associates and I wish you continued success in your future endeavors." Typed at the bottom of the FBI's file copy of the letter was:

"NOTE: Bufiles [bureau files] reflect Nelson was a critic of the Bureau and former Director Hoover. Mr. Kelley met with Nelson on 8/14/73 and Nelson recounted several incidents which strained his relationship with the Bureau. Mr. Kelley pointed out his open-policy stance toward the press to Nelson. Since that time, our relations with him have been cordial."

The FBI's practice of keeping such lists finally faded and William H. Webster, who was the FBI director in the 1980s and became my friend, told me, "We're out of that business forever. Along with the rest of the country, we are keeping pace with what the First Amendment is all about."

Detective Luke Scarbrough retired from the Meridian Police Department two years after the ambush, but what happened that June night in 1968 continued to trouble him. "It was the only thing that could be done," he would tell his wife, Vic.

"He hated it mightily that that girl got killed," said Mrs. Scarbrough, who in 1992 was working in the county tax collector's office in Meridian. "She wasn't even supposed to be there, you know. But he always said they did what they had to do. He felt bad about Tarrants, too, being shot up and almost killed. Luke always marveled that he lived."

After retiring as assistant chief in charge of the detective bureau, Scarbrough worked as a special agent for a railroad, then as a deputy sheriff and finally as a state investigator. He died in Meridian on April 2, 1986.

Less than a year after the shoot-out, Chief Roy Gunn fired his old rival, Sam Keller, the assistant chief. Gunn accused Keller of knowing about the Klan plot to harass him and his family and failing to report it.

Gunn touted the Tarrants case as the Meridian Police Department's finest hour, and he continued to run the department in his own crusty way. In March of 1970, alerted that anti–Vietnam War protesters would demonstrate against the Meridian draft board, he wrote the board chairman that he had "no patience with these bastards" and that "we do not intend for our selective service board or our citizens to be upset by a bunch of communists. . . ."

Before retiring in June 1971, he wrote the city manager a letter saying, "My epitaph, I hope, will be as the great Apostle Paul wrote the day before his execution, 'I have fought the good fight and I have kept the faith.' " He died on July 21, 1976. The epitaph is engraved on his tombstone.

Marie Knowles, the secretary who typed up Scarbrough's reports of meetings with the informants and worried that she had participated in a murder plot, lives in Meridian, where she serves as secretary of the Seventh-Day Adventist church and as a teachers' assistant at the church's school.

She has never gotten over the role she played and still talks of how Officer Bo Partridge was never the same after firing loads of buckshot at Tarrants at close range. "Partridge was a zombie after that," she said. "He shouldn't have been asked to take part. He was scared to death. If you went by and visited him after that, he would be staring off into space."

But her eyes light up when she talks about the excitement of those days. "Nothing much interesting happens in Meridian anymore," she said.

Agents Frank Watts and Jack Rucker retired from the FBI about ten years after Meridian, a case they considered the highlight of their careers. They continue to maintain that the police were justified in taking extraordinary measures to stop the Klan violence.

Rucker works for a security firm in Mobile, Alabama, and resides in nearby Daphne.

Watts, now retired and living in Gulf Breeze, Florida, remains friends with Tarrants and stays in close contact with him.

After being released from prison, Tarrants told Watts he would like to return to Meridian and apologize to the Jewish community. "I tried to get them to let him make an appearance and apologize for his acts against them, but they refused," Watts said. "I went to Al Rosenbaum and his wife, Lucille, and even to Meyer Davidson, who became my closest friend after all this happened, but none of them would hear of it."

Tom Hendricks, the ex–FBI agent who acted as the intermediary between the lawmen and the Roberts brothers, retired from his law practice in 1980 and lives in Meridian. He still fumes over what he considered unfair treatment by the FBI. "Scarbrough brought a briefcase full of money to the trailer and told the Robertses it was a hundred thousand dollars and that was what they were supposed to get. But they double-crossed them. The FBI didn't live up to their word. When I was in the FBI, we kept our word."

When Roy Moore retired from the FBI at age sixty in 1974, he was honored by local and state leaders and the Anti-Defamation League for directing the FBI's Klan-busting activities.

He later served as director of security for the state's largest bank, Jackson's Deposit Guaranty National Bank. He retired from there in 1982 and lives in Jackson.

Moore still insists that there was no entrapment and that police used no illegal or unacceptable practices at Meridian.

Jim Ingram retired from the FBI at age fifty in 1982 and succeeded Moore at the Deposit Guaranty National Bank. He lives in Jackson. In 1992 he was appointed Mississippi's commissioner of public safety, the state's top law enforcement post.

Ingram disagrees with his close friend Moore about what happened at Meridian. "It was an ambush, that's what they meant to do," Ingram told me. "No question about that. They meant to kill them out there that night."

A. I. (Bee) Botnick still runs the ADL office in New Orleans, but goes to extraordinary lengths to keep a low profile. Neither Botnick nor the ADL is listed in the directory of the building that houses his unmarked office on the fifth floor. A woman in a first-floor office said, "He doesn't want anybody to know he's in the building."

The Meridian incident and the episode in which Byron de la Beckwith attempted to bomb his house had a traumatic impact on him. When I went to see him, he told me he just could not talk anymore about the Meridian case.

Al Binder has a flourishing law practice in Jackson. He has remained friends with Tarrants. "I hear from him every Christmas. And I send him a card. I think he's cured."

Binder still worries, though, about racists and anti-Semites in Mississippi and their potential for violence. When he goes to sleep at night he keeps a pistol at his bedside.

Rabbi Perry Nussbaum, never the same after his house was bombed, was "shattered and went into a shell," said Jim Ingram. "He told the FBI he wanted to know about it if there was a threat on his life, but 'otherwise I don't want to be involved with you guys anymore.' "

Nussbaum retired in 1973 and moved to San Diego. Bitter that Ken Dean had accused the FBI and police of entrapping Tarrants, he accused him of "playing footsie with the Klan with evangelical zeal." In a letter, he told Dean: "If the FBI hadn't been on top of a scheme to murder a Meridian Jew by using informers, another klan killing would have ended as just another statistic in Mississippi's terrorism."

At a program in Jackson's Galloway Methodist Church in 1984 honoring him for contributions to civil rights, Nussbaum recalled the days of terrorism and remembered "meeting here and someone in the congregation objecting to having a Jew in this building."

Nussbaum died on March 30, 1987.

Ken Dean is still obsessed by the Meridian case, its place in the civil rights movement's history and its implications for equal justice under the law.

The role he played in dealing with lawbreakers while dealing with law enforcers caused some to doubt his veracity and question his motives. I never did. Neither did Jim Ingram, who worked closely with him on civil rights investigations. "I never doubted Ken Dean at any time," he told me. "Others did. Ken was always very straight with me. We have to remember that Ken was a minister, a man of the cloth, and I think that he practiced that. There is no doubt in my mind, Ken at all times wanted to prevent violence."

Dean lives in Rochester, New York, where he is a pastor of the First Baptist Church.

The Roberts brothers keep a lower profile these days. For years, say acquaintances, they lived in fear of retribution for their roles as informants. Spotlights on Raymond's house were kept lighted at night and a watchdog roamed inside the fence.

Despite the letter from Chief Gunn and Detective Scarbrough recommending parole for Alton Wayne, he served six years of his ten-year sentence—almost two years beyond the date he was first eligible for parole consideration. For a while, he seemed changed; he took up painting in prison. After his release, he even presented one of his paintings and a string of fish to the Reverend Charles Johnson, the black minister his brother Lee had threatened to shoot after he made a U-turn in downtown Meridian. With tears streaming down his face, Roberts asked Johnson to forgive him.

Not long after that, however, Roberts was back in trouble. He and a confederate were hanging around a small rural airstrip in Stewart County, Georgia, waiting for a plane loaded with marijuana, when the sheriff surprised them. Roberts and the other man overpowered the sheriff and tied him up. Later, police arrested them, and Alton Wayne eventually pleaded guilty to kidnapping and aggravated assault. In 1982 he was ordered to serve four more years in prison.

In 1989 Alton Wayne underwent open-heart surgery, but by his fifty-third birthday in 1991 he appeared to have recovered and was back operating a Meridian nightclub, the Other Place.

Raymond Roberts, who turned fifty in 1991, developed diabetes and other serious health problems. His hair turned almost white and he had to walk with the aid of a cane. People who have known him for years said he lived reclusively and was seldom seen around town.

Sam Bowers served more than six years at McNeil Island federal prison in Steilacoom, Washington, for his role in the Goodman-Chaney-Schwerner killings. Released in 1976, he returned to Laurel to resume operating the Sambo Amusement Company. He walks the streets a free man, never convicted in the Dahmer case and never prosecuted for any of the other murders, bombings and beatings the FBI attributed to him and the White Knights.

In May of 1991 while my wife, Barbara, and I were in Meridian, I telephoned his office and asked for an interview. Devours Nix, Bowers' chief aide, returned the call. He said Bowers had written his own book and would give me 10 percent of the royalties if I could get it published. After I explained I could not do that, Nix said that he would try to arrange an interview with Bowers, but that for twenty-five years he had been unsuccessful in trying to get the imperial wizard to agree to be interviewed.

My wife and I then drove the fifty miles from Meridian to Laurel on the chance Bowers might talk if we showed up unannounced. Driving down Laurel's Fourth Avenue was like being in a time warp. Everything looked as it had twenty-three years earlier when I had tried to interview him. The Sambo Amusement Company was still housed in an old dilapidated frame structure that needed paint, and across the street smoke was belching from the sprawling old Masonite plant.

As we drove past the firm, an old gray Lincoln Continental pulled slowly into the street. I had not seen Bowers in twenty-three years, but I immediately recognized him, did a quick U-turn and followed him several blocks before he got out at the Jones County library. Clad in an old dark blue summer suit, a starched white shirt and a blue-and-red-striped tie, he carried a manila folder of papers under his arm.

I jumped out of my car and introduced myself.

"I *know* who you are," Bowers said, spurning my hand. "I'm not talking to you." He turned and hurried into the library, half smiling, half smirking. Except for looking older, he had scarcely changed since his trial in Meridian: the same sandy hair neatly combed to the side and graying only slightly—and the same mad gleam in his eye.

He never agreed to an interview. But in a rambling, almost incoherent three-page letter neatly printed in ink on notebook paper, he wrote that he could not talk with me until his own book was published even though he considered me "the cleanest whore of the hierarchial prostitution system of the captive press."

"Still," he added, "with the long-term prevalence of the media aids virus, and the vulnerability of patriots to that aids virus, extreme caution, on a continuing basis, is properly indicated in all situations of liasons and adventures into that dangerous situation."

L. E. Matthews still boasts that despite all the efforts of the FBI, he never spent a day in jail for making any of the bombs used in

Klan violence. "They did everything they could to charge me with something. They intercepted my mail and harassed me and everything else," he said.

When I telephoned his rural residence south of Jackson, he said he had diabetes and liver problems and did not go out much anymore. But he invited me to his house for an interview and offered to have Danny Joe Hawkins present, too.

He sent Danny Joe's mother, Johnnie Mae Hawkins, to meet me at a Texaco gas station just off I-55 to lead the way. Mrs. Hawkins, the Klanswoman who had been a close friend of Kathy Ainsworth, was waiting at the station as I pulled up. A matronly-looking woman, she wore glasses and a flowered dress and was driving a late-model Audi station wagon. Upon seeing me, she rolled down her window, smiled and said, "Follow me."

We drove down winding roads for several miles until we came upon a modern split-level frame house in the country. Danny Joe, dressed in shorts, sandals and a sport shirt, met me at the front door. His brown hair was long—almost to his shoulders—but neatly combed, and he had a mustache. We shook hands and he asked, "You remember me, don't you? I haven't gotten that old, have I?"

"Sure, I remember you well," I said. "You haven't changed at all except for the mustache."

My Southern friends would say I was talkin' the talk and walkin' the walk to win his cooperation. And, of course, they would be right. But it was true that the intervening twenty-three years had been kind to Danny Joe. He was forty-seven but still trim, and he could have passed for ten years younger.

Although Hawkins was indicted in the Meyer Davisdon bombing attempt, he was never brought to trial; his case was put on the court's dead docket. But unlike Matthews, he could not boast that he had never served any time. Arrested thirteen times by Jackson police between 1963 and 1980, mostly for firearms violations, he finally served thirty months of a three-year federal prison sentence that was handed down in 1974 for giving false information in the purchase of a gun in violation of the 1968 Gun Control Act.

In the living room, lounging on an easy chair with his feet propped up and gazing at me impassively, was Matthews. He looked every bit his sixty-eight years. He was wearing dark trousers and a white sport shirt, and was puffing on a cigar. He shook hands with me perfunctorily, but said nothing. As I sat down and turned to question Hawkins, Matthews never took his eyes off me.

"Nothing's changed," Hawkins said, "except maybe I'm a little more radical."

"How could you be more radical?" I asked.

"Well, we were just Baptist patriots doing what we were doing for God and country before," he said, smiling. "And now I'm a radical for Mother Nature—an environmentalist. Of course, I don't belong to any environmental organizations."

Hawkins had not reformed; he now espoused the radical environmental line of a new White Knights of the Ku Klux Klan, a supermilitant racist and anti-Semitic group organized in 1987 and headquartered in Kansas City, Missouri. This White Knights, according to a 1991 Anti-Defamation League report, was armed, boasted about two hundred members and had "a potential for serious troublemaking." The April–May 1991 issue of *White Beret,* the group's publication, declared: "We of the White Knights are proud to say that we are fanatical ecologists. We want to give our Aryan children a future with a land with fresh air, unpolluted water and soil."

Hawkins said the Roberts brothers had been able to dupe Tarrants and himself because Alton Wayne, having been convicted in the Philadelphia killings, had credibility with other Klan members and it never occurred to them that he would be an FBI informant. "I considered myself extra careful," he said, "but being that Raymond was Alton Wayne's brother, I just became too trusting. I took the Klan oath seriously and I thought I was helping a brother Klan member."

I asked Hawkins about an FBI memorandum suggesting that he had had an affair with Kathy Ainsworth. He vehemently denied it and said he was never alone with her.

His mother, Johnnie Mae, who had been sitting quietly on a sofa, stiffened and said, "I loved her like she was my own daughter or my sister. I hope the Roberts brothers will be looking over their shoulders as long as they live. They'd better be."

I mentioned that Alton Wayne Roberts had suffered from a serious heart ailment and had undergone open-heart surgery.

"Good," she said. "Good."

"I don't want him to die like that," Danny Joe said. "I want him to die a violent death. It's a wonder that the Roberts brothers have managed to live as long as they have."

Danny Joe said his father, Joe Denver, who had helped train Kathy Ainsworth to fire a machine gun, was killed in "a nigger robbery" in 1974 at the age of fifty. An alcoholic, Joe Denver was drinking late one night in his small construction shack in Jackson when he was beaten to death by a robber.

Suddenly, Matthews spoke up, boasting that he had never spent a day in jail, but complaining that the FBI had harassed him continually during the 1960s. "They kept me under surveillance," he said, "and if I happened to be going out with a lady, they would try to get her fired from her job."

Matthews said agents told him, "We're planning on killing you," and one of them showed him a picture of a bomb and said, "That's a bomb you made."

I told Matthews that FBI agents and bureau documents identified him as the major bomb maker for Klan violence in Mississippi during 1967 and 1968.

"You could do a lot of things with the things I made," he said. Hawkins smiled knowingly and rolled his eyes to the ceiling.

Hawkins said that the nation can expect an upsurge in violence by right-wing extremists during the nineties and that "what happened in the sixties is nothing to what's going to happen in the nineties. There's no doubt in my mind that it will make the sixties in Mississippi look like a Sunday-school picnic. We were just good ole Southern Baptist patriots, but there are much more violent people just waiting to take action when the time is ripe, a lot of them out in California."

After the interviews, as I started to drive away, Danny Joe came up close to me and said, "One last thing. Remember: the future belongs to us."

By the spring of 1992, more than fifteen years after his release from Parchman state prison, Tarrants was teaching at a college-level school for missionaries preparing to work in urban areas around the world. Twelve years earlier he had married a member of a wealthy and prominent North Carolina family. He and his wife now have two daughters, who in 1992 were eight and ten years old.

As a result of Meridian, the man once known as a "mad-dog killer" finds scenes of violence and bloodshed so disturbing that he disconnected the antenna on the family television set to shield his daughters from violent programs; the girls watch carefully screened movies on the VCR instead.

In March of 1992, Reverend Ken Dean visited Washington to meet with Tarrants and accompany him to a biracial prayer breakfast conducted every Wednesday at the Martin Luther King Library by Democratic congressman Tony Hall of Dayton, Ohio. During the services, both men offered prayers and Reverend Richard Halverson, chaplain of the United States Senate, told the audience that the FBI had once known Tarrants as "the most dangerous man in Mississippi," but that he had known him for fifteen years as "a gentle man and a servant of the Lord." Congressman Hall said, "He's an amazing example of how God can shape and turn around a person. He was once known as a killer and now he's deeply spiritual and would give you the shirt off his back. Every time I see him I shake my head in amazement."

Tarrants agreed to numerous interviews for this book, asking in return only that I not mention where he lives because "Sam Bowers is dangerous and he's got a long memory."

I first met Tarrants on April 22, 1990, in a restaurant near Washington. I had arranged the meeting by telephone after learning where he lived. I was sitting down waiting for him when he walked in, immaculately dressed in a blue blazer and gray trousers, and wearing dark-rimmed glasses. His thick, dark hair, parted on the side, was combed straight back. He was leaner and much younger looking than I had expected, but I recognized him immediately from his pictures of twenty-two years earlier. He was now forty-three, shy and soft-spoken, a stark contrast to the profane, tough-talking Klansman who had terrorized Mississippi's Jewish community.

At first he was guarded about discussing his Klan activities, but then he talked in detail about the Klan, his role as a hit man and his relationship with Sam Bowers, Danny Joe Hawkins, Frank Watts, Ken Dean and Al Binder. He discussed his Klan work with Kathy Ainsworth, too, but drew the line at their personal relationship.

He laments the fact that virulent racist organizations such as Tom Metzger's White Aryan Resistance have turned Ainsworth into "a martyr figure, a rallying point." At rallies in Meridian and at her grave in Magee in April 1991, Metzger and other Aryan Resistance members and a band of Klansmen and neo-Nazis invoked her as "someone who fought for her race."

Looking back on his own life as a terrorist, Tarrants said, "The scary truth is that I would not have gotten caught if I had continued the way I originally started off operating, which was to never tell anybody about anything, to operate only by myself and to strike with an element of surprise. Terrorists who operate that way—if they don't have a previous record where they are under some kind of surveillance or suspicion—are virtually impossible to find."

He admits his involvement in terrorism did not stem solely from ideological conviction. "I was selling my soul for the thrill and excitement and adventure of this cause I was married to. It was a big ego trip at the very heart of it. I'm glad it's all over now. It would be terrible to be locked into that darkness and deception."

Part of his mission now, he says, is to fight extremism, especially the kind that makes Jews scapegoats for society's problems by portraying them as members of a powerful worldwide conspiracy. "We need to educate people more about the fallacy of this conspiratorial theory of history. This virus has been going around a long time. Hitler had it, and there are still a lot of people in these circles today."

ACKNOWLEDGMENTS
AND SOURCES

Many people helped me, and some were crucial to the writing of this book. My friend Richard T. Cooper, deputy chief of the *Los Angeles Times* Washington Bureau, and my wife and best friend, Barbara Matusow, senior writer for *Washingtonian* magazine, worked closely with me every step of the way. I am deeply indebted to them.

Several people agreed to numerous interviews and in some cases helped with other research. Foremost among them was Ken Dean, my original source for the ambush story, who gave me access to his voluminous memoranda and correspondence. Others included Jim Ingram, the ex–FBI agent, who also helped arrange interviews with other former agents; Bill Minor, the Jackson journalist, my long-time friend, who lent me files of his excellent coverage of the Klan and civil rights in Mississippi; Marie Knowles, the former secretary of the Meridian Detectives Bureau, and Joe Clay Hamilton, a Meridian attorney and former prosecutor, both of whom aided in arranging other interviews. I am also deeply indebted to ex–FBI agents Roy Moore, Frank Watts and Jack Rucker; attorneys Al Binder of Jackson and Bill Ready of Meridian, and Thomas Albert Tarrants III, whom I interviewed more than a dozen times and who permitted me to quote his book, *Conversion of a Klansman*.

I was inspired by Ronald Goldfarb, my agent, who prodded me to undertake this book even while I was continuing my duties with the *Los Angeles Times*. Alice Mayhew's editing was superb, her advice invaluable, and she and other Simon & Schuster editors helped turn an unwieldy manuscript into a book.

Many others, including the following, were interviewed or assisted in various other ways: In Washington—Terry Adamson, Mary Pat Clark, Steve Clark, Katrina Clifton, Aleta Embrey, Lester G. Fant III, Barbara Fitzpatrick, Ed Friedman, Caleb Gessesse, Nick Kotz and Mary Lynn Kotz, Marlene Marmo, Ronald J. Ostrow, Gene Roberts, Jr., Phil Ruiz, Pat Welch and John White.

In Mississippi and other places—Ann Abadie, Dr. William Ackerman, Rev. William Apperson, Omeara Austin, Robert Berman, Nancy Binder, Tom and Norma Bourdeaux, A. L. and Joan Cahn, Lee Cahn, Hodding

Carter III and Patricia Darien, Lynn Clark, Obie Clark, Emanuel and Elaine Crystal, Sammie Davidson, Luther Dunbar, Billy Entrekin, Ken Fairley, Sid Geiger, Bishop Duncan Gray, Lloyd Gray, Winifred Green, Edwin Guthman, Joe and Maxine Harris, Mike Hatcher, Danny Joe Hawkins, Johnnie Mae Hawkins, and Ernestine Kornegay, William Kunstler, John Hart Lewis, Elsie Logan, L. E. Matthews, Gloria Minor, George and Thelma Mitchell, Jerry Mitchell, O. M. Moore, Charles Morgan, Jr., Gail Nardi, Billy Neville, Devours Nix, Will Norton, Arene Nussbaum, C. E. Oatis, Charles Overby, A. C. Owen, John Proctor, Lawrence and Clo Ann Rabb, Amelia Gunn Rawson, Roy Reed, Dan Selph, I. A. and Lucille Rosenbaum, Calvin Scarbrough, Victoria Scarbrough, Milton and Bette Schlager, Jack Shanks, Kathy Spray, Tom and Sandy Taylor, Rev. Thomas Tiller, Dexter Torrance, George Warner, Tom Webb and Charles Young.

I used numerous written sources, including FBI files secured under the Freedom of Information Act and records of the Meridian Police Department as well as magazine articles by Jon Nordheimer in *The Miami Herald,* by Gail Nardi in the *Richmond Times-Dispatch,* and by Jerry DeLaughter in the *Memphis Commercial-Appeal;* and records of the Mississippi Department of Archives and articles in the *Los Angeles Times, Jackson Daily News, Jackson Clarion-Ledger,* Meridian *Star,* and *Mobile Register.*

Jack Shanks's three history volumes—*Meridian: The Queen with a Past*—and the following books were sources:

Abernathy, Ralph David. *And The Walls Came Tumbling Down.* New York: Harper & Row, 1989.

Ayers, Brandt, and Thomas H. Naylor, editors. *You Can't Eat Magnolias.* New York: McGraw-Hill Book Co., 1972.

Cagin, Seth, and Philip Dray. *We Are Not Afraid: The Story of Goodman, Schwerner and Chaney and the Civil Rights Campaign for Mississippi.* New York: Macmillan Publishing Company, 1988.

Clendenen, Dudley, editor. *The Prevailing South: Life and Politics in a Changing Culture.* Marietta, Ga.: Longstreet Press, Inc., 1988.

Dees, Morris, with Steve Fiffer. *A Season for Justice.* New York: Charles Scribner's Sons, 1991.

Evans, Eli N. *The Provincials: A Personal History of Jews in the South.* New York: Atheneum, 1973.

Garrow, David J. *The FBI and Martin Luther King, Jr.* New York: W. W. Norton & Co., Inc., 1981.

Gentry, Curt. *J. Edgar Hoover: The Man and the Secrets.* New York: W. W. Norton & Co., 1991.

Huie, William Bradford. *Three Lives for Mississippi.* New York: Signet Books, 1968.

Isaacs, Stephen D. *Jews and American Politics.* Garden City, N. Y.: Doubleday and Co., Inc., 1974.

Johnston, Erle. *I Rolled with the Boss.* Baton, Rouge, La.: Moran Publishing Corp., 1981.

———. *Mississippi's Defiant Years: 1953–1973.* Forest, Miss.: Lake Harbor Publishers, 1990.

Kunstler, William M. *Deep in My Heart.* New York: William Morrow and Co., 1966.

Loewen, James W., and Charles Sallis, editors. *Mississippi: Conflict and Change.* New York: Pantheon Books, 1974.

Mars, Florence. *Witness in Philadelphia.* Baton Rouge, La.: Louisiana State University Press, 1977.

McMillen, Ed R. *Dark Journey: Black Mississippians in the Age of Jim Crow.* Urbana, Ill.: University of Illinois Press, 1989.

Meier, August, and Elliott Rudwick. *CORE: A Study in the Civil Rights Movement, 1942–1968.* New York: Oxford University Press, 1973.

Morris, Willie, editor. *The South Today.* New York: Harper & Row, 1965.

Perkins, Cathy, editor. *COINTELPRO.* New York: Monrad Press, 1975.

Polner, Murray. *Rabbi: The American Experience.* New York: Holt, Rinehart and Winston, 1977.

Powledge, Fred. *Free at Last?: The Civil Rights Movement and the People Who Made It.* Boston: Little Brown and Co., 1991.

Roche, John P. *The Quest for the Dream: The 50th Anniversary Book of the Anti-Defamation League.* New York: The Macmillan Co., 1963.

Salter, Jr., John R. *Jackson, Mississippi.* Malabar, Fl.: Robert E. Krieger Publishing Co., 1987.

Silver, James W. *Mississippi: The Closed Society.* New York: Harcourt, Brace & World, 1963.

Sims, Patsy. *The Klan.* Briarcliff Manor, N.Y.: Stein and Day, 1978.

Stanton, Bill. *Klanwatch: Bringing the Ku Klux Klan to Justice.* New York: Grove Weidenfeld, 1991.

Tarrants, Thomas Albert III. *Conversion of a Klansman.* New York: Doubleday and Co., 1979.

Theoharis, Athan. *From the Secret Files of J. Edgar Hoover.* Chicago: Ivan R. Dee, 1991.

Wade, Wyn Craig. *The Fiery Cross: The Ku Klux Klan in America.* New York: Simon & Schuster, 1987.

Watters, Pat, and Stephen Gillers, editors. *Investigating the FBI.* Garden City, N.Y.: Doubleday and Co., 1973.

Whitehead, Don. *Attack on Terror: The FBI Against the Ku Klux Klan in Mississippi.* New York: Funk and Wagnalls, 1970.

INDEX

ABOUT THE AUTHOR

Jack Nelson, Washington Bureau Chief of the *Los Angeles Times*, is a Pulitzer Prize–winning reporter who covered the South for the *Times* from 1965 to 1970. Born and raised in the South, he previously worked for *The Atlanta Constitution* and the *Biloxi Daily Herald*. As an investigative reporter in the *Times* Washington Bureau during 1970–75, he wrote extensively about J. Edgar Hoover's FBI, the Watergate scandal, the Richard Nixon impeachment proceedings, and other major events. As bureau chief he covers politics and the White House, and oversees a staff of forty-six reporters and editors. A regular panelist on PBS's "Washington Week in Review" since Watergate days, he also appears frequently on other network television programs.

Nelson studied economics and journalism at Georgia State College and during 1961–62 was a Nieman Fellow at Harvard University. A visiting committee member at the journalism schools of Miami University and Maryland University, he is the author of *Captive Voices* and co-author of *The Censors and the Schools, The Orangeburg Massacre, The FBI and the Berrigans,* and *Beyond Reagan/The Politics of Upheaval*. He lives in Bethesda, Maryland, with his wife, Barbara Matusow.